# THE ESSENTIAL GUIDE TO
# WOODWORK

# THE ESSENTIAL GUIDE TO
# WOODWORK

Chris Simpson

MURDOCH
B O O K S

# CONTENTS

# Introduction

*Working with a natural material such as timber is both a rewarding and satisfying pastime. Timber has a special quality that is like no other material – it is a pleasure to touch and a delight to look at.*

Every piece of timber is unique, with a diversity of colour, texture and strength. Its versatility and unique qualities are a source of constant inspiration to the creative woodworker. It is an appreciation of these qualities, combined with good function and design, that will give you many years of enjoyment in fine furniture making.

*Above: Much of the joy of working with wood is derived from the fact that timber is a natural living product.*

*Opposite: Sori Yanagi's 'Butterfly' stools (1956) show how timber can be converted into fine pieces.*

To gain the most pleasure from your woodworking experience, it is important to give yourself a firm skill base that will allow your interest and enthusiasm to develop fully. To help you achieve this, this book has been divided into four sections.

The opening chapter 'Wood and Other Materials' gives general information on the foundations of woodworking, including an introduction to the natural resource of timber and its unique qualities and challenges. This will help you to make the right choices when you come to choose, buy and store wood for yourself.

The second chapter, 'Design and Construction' concentrates on the importance of design and shows how every piece that you make needs to be both functional and aesthetically pleasing. There are useful tips that will help you to achieve a harmonious balance between the two.

The third chapter 'Tools and Techniques' moves onto the practicalities of woodworking. It opens with advice about workshop design, and the accessories and tools that you will need to begin your woodworking experience. All the basic skills needed to produce fine woodwork are clearly and succinctly explained with illustrations and photographs to help wherever relevant. From straightforward common processes, such as sawing and planing, and to more specialized aspects of woodworking, such as carving and turning, this section will enable you to master and develop your skills.

**Project rating**

*Basic*

Simple woodworking exercises that are suitable for beginners.

*Intermediate*

Moderately difficult projects for those woodworkers who have some previous experience.

*Advanced*

Complex challenging projects for more advanced woodworkers.

The fourth chapter features stylish projects, which will enable you to put your skills into practice. Divided into basic, intermediate and advanced, you will be able to go straight to a project that is suitable for your level of expertise. From a simple letter rack, to a challenging workbench, to a complex linen cupboard, these pieces will make stunning additions to your home.

Each project contains a materials list, a tools list and step-by-step instructions. Illustrations and photographs are included to help you make each project, and drawings show the sizes of components and how they fit together. Measurements are given both in metric – metres and millimetres – and imperial – feet, inches and fractions of an inch. It is important to choose one method or the other as the measurements are not direct conversions. Do not use a mixture

of the two as this may not work out exactly. When making the projects, never cut all the timber pieces to the size given in the materials list. Work through the steps and always check measurements as you progress.

This book provides a sound foundation for the acquisition and development of your woodworking knowledge and skills. It also provides you with the opportunity to develop your skills through a wide range of interesting, creative and useful projects. The importance of precision and accuracy are emphasized, as is the need to develop a sense of, and an ability to, appreciate and produce quality work. Producing quality work requires much effort and skill, but the sense of achievement and the pleasure of working with the unique natural resource of timber are what makes woodworking such a popular and rewarding experience.

*Right: Getting to grips with basic woodworking skills is a fundamental part of your woodworking adventure.*

*Far right: Make sure that you have all the necessary tools that you need for each project before you start.*

# WOOD AND OTHER MATERIALS

# A NATURAL RESOURCE

*Timber is a natural product, unlike so many of the materials we use for everyday living. So the woodworker could be said to renew the essential bond between man and nature that has, to some extent, been lost in our modern world.*

The range of different timber species – both hardwoods and softwoods – offers an extremely wide choice of materials. Each species has its own properties and characteristics. Even when using the same species of timber, each piece will present different challenges. They will also differ in appearance, giving variations in colour, pattern, texture and finish.

*The beauty of a growing tree contributes to the pleasure of woodwork.*

In order to gain the best results from working with timber, it is important to be aware of some basic facts about the material – for example, how trees grow, how they are converted for use and how we can utilize these characteristics.

## Ecological concerns

The issue of ecological matters is an important concern, and it has rightly become difficult to source endangered species. It is now recognized that forests must be maintained to ensure a continuous supply of quality trees. In a well-run forest, mature timber is extracted with care and new planting is constantly taking place.

The science of forestry has greatly improved in the developed world and pressure is also being put on developing countries to ensure forests are carefully managed so that the disastrous effects of deforestation are avoided in future. Many nations are also seeking to help sustain their economies by not exporting the logs they produce, but carrying out conversion nearer the source.

## How a tree grows

To appreciate the various properties of timber, it is useful to understand how a tree grows

and to learn about its structure. A tree is an extremely efficient organism. The trunk is the main conduit for transferring water and minerals, which are absorbed from the soil through the roots. The leaves of the tree take in carbon dioxide, give off oxygen and harness the energy of light, which, through the process of photosynthesis, produces all the nutrients that the tree requires to thrive.

### Tree structure

The trunk's structure consists of tubular cells, which are held together with a chemical known as lignin. The direction of these cells determines the nature of the timber's grain. The cells tend to be long and thin, running lengthwise along the trunk and branches.

Food storage and the sap circulation take place through the cells of a tree. In a softwood tree the cells have a simple structure of hollow, spindle-like cells, while hardwood trees have long and needle-like cells. This difference in cell structure is what distinguishes a softwood from a hardwood.

A section through the tree's trunk shows the pith at the centre. This is formed from the original sapling, is often weak and can suffer from

*A cross-section of a tree trunk shows the various layers of growth.*

This annual growth can be seen in concentric rings, or growth rings, through the timber and can be used to determine a tree's age. Each growth ring contains large earlywood and smaller latewood cells. Earlywood is the part of the annual growth rings that grows at the beginning of the season. Latewood is produced towards the end of the season, and has a different texture. It is usually denser and darker than the earlywood is.

The growth rings in hardwood timber can be categorized as either ring porous or diffuse porous. Ring-porous timber shows a difference in cellular structure between timber laid down in the different growth periods of the tree – open cells when the tree is growing in spring and summer, and tighter grouped cells when growth slows in autumn and winter. Diffuse-porous timber is found in trees where there are no marked seasonal changes and the cells are much more regular in size. This relatively even distribution and regularity of fibres make diffuse-porous hardwoods, such as beech, easier to plane and sand to a finish than ring-porous hardwoods, such as ash or oak.

fungal attack. The heartwood, which surrounds the pith, is the mature timber that forms the structure of the tree as well as providing some food transference. Sapwood surrounds the heartwood, and is where most of the transference and storage of nutrients takes place. Sapwood from most timbers is not used for furniture making since it offers little resistance to fungal and insect attack.

A tree trunk has medullary rays, or ray cells, which conduct nutrients through the sapwood. These medullary rays are usually quite visible in hardwoods, but can be difficult to see in softwoods.

### Growth rings

Each year, the tree grows because the living cells in the cambium layer, which lies immediately behind the bark, sub-divide. As the tree grows, the cells in the cambium layer develop into specialized sapwood cells, and a new sapwood ring is formed around the growth from the previous year. At the same time, the oldest sapwood converts into heartwood. This means that, with each period of annual growth, the heartwood becomes larger, while the size of the sapwood does not vary much during the lifecycle of a tree.

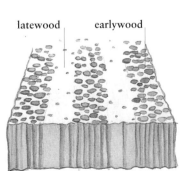

Earlywood and latewood

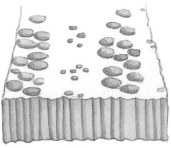

Ring-porous timber

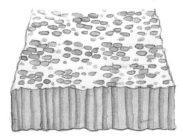

Diffuse-porous timber

13

# HARDWOODS AND SOFTWOODS

*The terms 'hardwood' and 'softwood' do not refer to the hardness or softness of a specific timber species. They are biological divisions and not a description of the timber's durability.*

Even though most hardwoods are hard and most softwoods are soft, hardness cannot be used to classify different woods. Balsa is a hardwood and some softwoods can be very hard.

Hardwoods grow in most parts of the world, and are generally preferred by furniture makers. Although they are often more expensive than softwoods, they are usually more durable and come in a larger range of colours with widely varying figure.

They can, however, be difficult to obtain and a few of the more expensive exotic hardwoods are cut into veneer leaves to make better use of the timber. Most countries have indigenous species, even though fashion has, in the past, led to the importation of particular timbers for specific uses, such as teak for outdoor furniture and boats and mahogany for fine furniture.

Softwoods are usually light in colour, ranging from an off-white to a mid-brown. They can be easily identified by looking at the growth rings where the contrasting grain pattern of the earlywood and latewood is found – these two differ in colour and density. Softwoods often have a more open grain, are easier to work and are generally used for building and joinery work. Fashion has intervened however and there is a strong market sector in many countries for pine furniture.

*Hardwood trees growing in their natural habitat.*

*Softwood trees growing in their natural habitat.*

# Species of hardwood

*The term 'hardwood' generally refers to trees that have broad leaves. Hardwoods are found in both temperate and tropical climates and can be either deciduous or evergreen. They are generally preferred by furniture makers because there is a wider range of colours and textures. Below and overleaf are some examples of the most commonly used hardwoods.*

*Pericopsis elata*
AFRORMOSIA

**Origin:** West Africa
**Characteristics:** Durable type of timber, with a grain that varies from straight to interlocked. Yellow-brown in colour, which darkens over time when exposed to light. It is similar to teak, but less oily and often used as a teak substitute in furniture making (as is Iroko, see page 16).

*Fraxinus spp.*
ASH

**Origin:** Europe (right), North America (left)
**Characteristics:** Heartwood and sapwood of similar colour in pink, grey and cream. Prominent growth rings best highlighted using back-cut of live-sawn board with a tangential cut. Quarter-sawn boards produce straight grain. Suitable for laminating and steam-bending. Sands and finishes well.

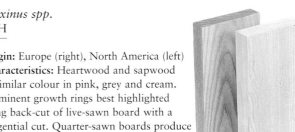

*Fagus spp.*
BEECH

**Origin:** All over Europe, best from Baltic regions
**Characteristics:** This type of timber is whitish in colour with little variation between sapwood and heartwood. Growth rings visible with distinctive fleck produced by medullary rays. Easily worked and commonly used in furniture for bent timber pieces. Cracking and warping can occur if seasoning is not carefully controlled.

*Buxus sempervirens*
BOXWOOD

**Origin:** Southern Europe and parts of West Asia
**Characteristics:** Boxwood is a fine and even-textured timber; straight grain and dense. Often found as a hedgerow tree and therefore seldom available to buy in plank form. It is most commonly used for making small items of furniture, such as those produced by turnery or carving.

*Liriodendron tulipifera*
AMERICAN TULIPWOOD

**Origin:** Central and South America
**Characteristics:** Dense and fairly hard, texture can vary but it usually has irregular grain. The wood has very attractive colour in the grain ranging from pink to red stripes over a yellow base. Difficult to work and, due to limited availability, it is usually just used for smaller items or veneering.

*Toona Australis*
AUSTRALIAN CEDAR

**Origin:** East coast of Australia
**Characteristics:** Rich red colour in heartwood; sapwood pale cream to pink. Medium-density with tendency to be a little soft – requires careful handling. Good grain pattern in back-cut boards; quarter-sawn boards produce straight, even grain. Scarce and expensive in large section sizes. Sands well and can be polished to mirror finish.

*Acacia melanoxylon*
BLACKWOOD

**Origin:** Tasmania and east coast of Australia
**Characteristics:** Medium-weight hardwood. Sometimes called Tasmanian blackwood, the resins can stain your hands black. Fairly straight grain, some interlocking can give fiddleback appearance. Pinkish-yellow to mud-brown tones with dark-brown growth rings. Works well with sharp tools. Sands well, finishing to a high polish.

*Guilbourtia demensei*
BUBINGA
Also known as African rosewood

**Origin:** West Africa
**Characteristics:** Coarse but even-textured timber; grain varies from straight to interlocked and irregular; relatively durable. Bubinga is red-brown in colour with a purple hue. It can be used in fine furniture making when crafted and finished.

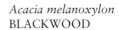

## *Cedrela*
## CEDRELA

**Origin:** Brazil and Mexico
**Characteristics:** Cedrela is a prized timber from Brazil that is used extensively in furniture manufacturing throughout Europe. White-coloured sapwood, tending to pink; heartwood pinkish brown with purplish highlights. Works particularly well and has a fine texture, allowing you to achieve a high-quality finish with minimal effort. Sands, glues and polishes well.

## *Ceratopetalum apetalem*
## COACHWOOD
Also known as satinwood

**Origin:** Australian east-coast rainforests
**Characteristics:** Pink to light brown colour with good grain pattern when tangentially cut and straight grain when quarter-sawn. Easily machined with distinctive odour when cut or sanded. Finishes well with hand tools, sands well and accepts most polishes. Becoming hard to source and relatively expensive.

## *Ulmus spp.*
## ELM
Also known as nave or red elm

**Origin:** Central and Southern Europe, Scandinavia and North America
**Characteristics:** Sapwood yellow to white, contrasting with brownish red heartwood. Medullary rays are not prominent and pores are fine, giving a fine texture. Used in joinery and cabinet making. Difficult to achieve fine finish.

## *Milicia spp.*
## IROKO

**Origin:** West Africa
**Characteristics:** Medium yellow-brown in colour and can be difficult to work because of occasional stone deposits. It has an interlocked grain and is strong and durable. Like Afrormosia (see page 15) it is used as a teak substitute because it is very durable but less oily. It is good for external use as well as for internal furniture.

## *Dyera costulata*
## JELUTONG

**Origin:** Malaysia and Indonesia
**Characteristics:** Classified as hardwood though soft in texture. Exercise care in handling. Close, even grain in a pale colour range. Grain has tendency to crush when chiselling, so sharp tools are important. Easily workable by machine and used extensively for pattern making. Sands and polishes well.

## *Prunus spp.*
## CHERRY

**Origin:** Europe (left), Asia Minor and the United States (right)
**Characteristics:** Open grain with dark, open pores and pink-to-brown heartwood; often used as decorative veneer. Susceptible to insect attack and shrinkage. Can be machined easily, but warps badly if not seasoned properly. Sands well and holds a finish very well – it is particularly good to use for cabinet making.

## *Diospyros spp.*
## EBONY

**Origin:** Parts of Africa and India
**Characteristics:** Very dark to black heartwood with black grain structure. Sapwood lightish pink. Extremely hard but works well with sharp tools. Available in very small sizes and quantities, hence restricted for use as inlays and on musical instruments. Density means it can be difficult to polish. Sanding dust can stain pale timber.

## *Astronium fraxinifolium*
## GONÇALO ALVES
Also known as zebrawood (UK) or tiger wood (USA)

**Origin:** South America
**Characteristics:** Difficult to work because of its irregular grain that varies in hardness; medium-textured and durable. Its character is given by its dark streaks and it can be very attractive when used in furniture either as solid or veneer.

## *Eucalyptus marginata*
## JARRAH

**Origin:** South-western Australia
**Characteristics:** Hard, heavy timber. Heartwood varies from pink to dark red. Fairly coarse texture and generally straight grain. Back-cut boards can show pleasant grain pattern, but gum veins and pockets sometimes spoil finish. Can be difficult to work owing to hardness. Sands well and finishes to a high polish.

## *Dalbergia cearensis*
## KINGWOOD
Also known as violet wood and violetta (USA)

**Origin:** South America
**Characteristics:** Lustrous and even-textured timber, which has very attractive colouring and is fairly good to work. Kingwood is usually straight-grained and durable. Due to its limited availability, it is often used as veneer, inlay or in marquetry. Also used in turning.

*Guaiacum officinale*
## LIGNUM VITAE

**Origin:** West Indies
**Characteristics:** Known as the heaviest of all hardwoods. Even grain and texture, with greasy feel. Brown colouring with a green tinge. Density and oil content makes it very durable. Mainly used as decorative trim piece in fine furniture. Density makes it hard to work and gluing is difficult owing to high oil content.

*Swietenia spp.*
## MAHOGANY

**Origin:** Honduras, the Caribbean islands and Mexico
**Characteristics:** Medium-weight of varying density. Yellow sapwood and pink to reddish brown heartwood. Revered cabinet timber for several centuries now. Grain pattern can range from plain to magnificent. Works very easily and stain highlights the grain patterns tremendously.

*Quercus spp.*
## OAK

**Origin:** Europe (right), North Africa, North America (left) and Asia
**Characteristics:** This type of timber is strong and durable with pronounced pores. Can be extremely heavy. European variety generally yellow and North American pink to reddish. Commonly used in furniture, boat building and kitchen cabinet work.

*Platanus spp.*
## PLANE
Also known as lacewood

**Origin:** Europe, except far north, and Asia Minor
**Characteristics:** Yellowish sapwood and copper-coloured heartwood. Strong, close-linked medullary rays. Used in woodturning, fine cabinet making and inlay work. Sands well but can be difficult to finish.

*Gonystylus spp.*
## RAMIN

**Origin:** Borneo, Indonesia and the Philippines
**Characteristics:** Medium-density tropical rainforest timber prone to infestation of insects and fungi. Pale yellow to white in both sapwood and heartwood. Straight, even grain, making it easy to work in all directions. Glues well and can be easily polished.

*Tilia vulgaris*
## LIME

**Origin:** Europe
**Characteristics:** Straight-grained timber with uniform texture. Fairly soft and light in colour, which darkens to light brown with exposure – it is best to treat it with a preservative. Lime is good to work and is often used in carving, turning and for making some musical instruments.

*Shorea spp.*
## MERANTI
Also known as Pacific maple and lauan

**Origin:** Malaysia, Indonesia and the Philippines
**Characteristics:** Colour ranges from pale brown to pink and dark red. Susceptible to insect attack. Weight and density varies greatly. Plain grain pattern with occasional interlocking grain. Not ideal for external work. Best used as base product for veneering over, or it can be easily stained.

*Pterocarpus spp.*
## PADAUK
Also known as African coralwood and Andaman redwood

**Origin:** Africa and South-East Asia
**Characteristics:** Medium density with striking red colour – ideal highlight or contrast timber in marquetry or inlay work. Straight grain and even texture; can have fiddleback feature. Unfortunately the very strong colour on recently worked timber darkens with time.

*Peltogyne spp.*
## PURPLEHEART
Also known as amaranth (USA)

**Origin:** Central and South America
**Characteristics:** Fine- to medium-textured timber, which is strong and durable. Generally straight-grained and attractive purple colour when freshly worked but darkens over time. Purpleheart is commonly used for furniture making, veneer work and turnery.

*Dalbergia spp.*
## ROSEWOOD

**Origin:** Brazil, India, Honduras
**Characteristics:** These tress are short so sawn timber is often not of great length or width. Very dense and hard to work. Sapwood off-white and heartwood yellow to pale pink, with dark brown to purplish veins. Best suited for small decorative projects such as jewellery boxes and inlays.

*Castanea sativa*
### SWEET CHESTNUT

also known as European Chestnut and
Spanish Chestnut

**Origin:** Mediterranean, Switzerland and Germany
**Characteristics:** Similar appearance to oak.
Sapwood is much whiter than heartwood.
Used for handles, shutters, in woodturning
and for kitchen-cupboard door making,
rather than actual cabinet making. Sands
and polishes well. Slight acidity can corrode
metals and stain timber.

*Tectonais grandis*
### TEAK

**Origin:** India, Burma and South-East Asia
**Characteristics:** Whitish sapwood and heartwood
brown to ochre with dark growth rings. Oily
and waxy to the touch. Natural oils make it
very durable, and water and fungus resistant.
Sands well; gluing may cause problems. Ideal for
outdoor furniture. Machines well. Recommended
finish of teak oil. Expensive and hard to acquire.

*Millettia laurentii*
### WENGE

**Origin:** Central and East Africa
**Characteristics:** Very hard and heavy timber.
Difficult to work and be aware of painful
splinters when working. However, wenge has
a superb black colour with either fine grain
or an elaborate figure. It can be used to
make interesting furniture and is also used
in turnery. When finishing, use black wax.

*Acer pseudoplatnus*
### SYCAMORE

**Origin:** Europe and West Europe
**Characteristics:** Sycamore has a fine
texture, often straight-grained but
boards with quarter-sawn fiddleback
grain are very sought after for some
musical instruments. Sycamore is
one of the whitest types of woods
but its grain darkens over time.
Good to work and makes attractive,
light-coloured furniture.

*Juglans spp.*
### WALNUT

**Origin:** Eastern United States (right) and
Canada, and mild regions of Europe (left)
**Characteristics:** Dark brown with
occasional purplish tinge. Used for high-
quality cabinet making. Mostly straight
grained but can exhibit fiddleback grain.
Walnut is a generic term often applied
to many species of dark brown timber.

*Microberlinia brazzavillensis*
### ZEBRANO

Also known as Zingana and sometimes zebrawood
(not to be confused with Gonçalo Alves, see page 16)

**Origin:** West Africa
**Characteristics:** Coarse and open-textured
timber, which is light in colour with interlocking
grain. Expensive to buy and so generally used
as veneer or inlay, though it is sometimes used
in fine furniture or cabinet making.

# Species of softwoods

*Softwood refers to types of trees that grow in colder regions, primarily in the northern*

*hemisphere. Softwoods tend to have needles instead of leaves and are usually evergreen.*

*Pseudotsuga menziesii*
### DOUGLAS FIR

**Origin:** North America, Canada and Europe
**Characteristics:** Straight, pronounced grain; clear
definition between earlywood and latewood.
Yellow with prominent orange growth rings.
Tough and water resistant. Used as building
timber, but prone to splitting so should be
coated with preservative to improve external
durability. Nails tend to follow grain direction.

*Tsuga spp.*
### HEMLOCK

**Origin:** North America, Himalayas to North
Burma, West Vietnam, China and Japan.
**Characteristics:** Pale yellow with distinctive
growth rings. Even textured with good, straight
grain. Easy to work, but predrill for nailing near
end sections. Poor seasoning can cause surface
checking. Not very durable for exposed work
and does not accept preservative treatment well.

## *Larix spp.*
## LARCH

**Origin:** All over Europe and North America
**Characteristics:** Straight-grained, uniform texture tougher than many other softwoods. Heartwood pale to rich red. Dries fairly rapidly, which can result in shrinkage and distortion and cause knots to fall out. Not particularly durable and resists preserving treatments. Slightly difficult to work and should be predrilled for nailing and screwing.

## *Araucaria angustifolia*
## PINE, PARANA

**Origin:** South America
**Characteristics:** Mid-weight and straight-grained with an even texture, its growth rings are not very conspicuous. Heartwood light brown with occasional red streaks. Can distort during the seasoning process and end splits are conspicuous. Treat with preservative when using externally. Tendency to twist and jam on blade when sawn.

## *Pinus strobus*
## PINE, YELLOW

**Origin:** North America and Canada
**Characteristics:** Quite soft, but with straight grain and mild texture. Pale yellow to brown; can show resin-duct marks. Easily dented so protect when being worked. External use not recommended; treat with preservative. Works easily but cutters must be sharp to avoid furry finish. Nails well; screws can strip thread if inserted by a screw gun.

## *Picea abies*
## SPRUCE, EUROPEAN

**Origin:** All over Europe
**Characteristics:** The 'Christmas tree'. Pale with little colour difference between sapwood and heartwood. Straight-grained, even-textured and visible growth rings. Can be very knotty. Not a durable timber so treatment with preservatives is recommended for external use. Easily worked and glues quite well, but staining can be patchy.

## *Thuja plicata*
## WESTERN RED CEDAR

**Origin:** North America
**Characteristics:** This type of wood is used externally as it is very durable. Light pink to reddish-brown, changing on external exposure to silver/grey. Extremely light and not particularly strong; avoid structural use. Larger sections suffer from collapse during seasoning, but can be reconditioned. Works well, glues easily and accepts all finishes.

## *Pinus sylvestris*
## PINE, HARD

Also known as Scots Pine

**Origin:** Western Europe and Great Britain
**Characteristics:** Tall tree of up to 40m (130ft); plantation planted in many countries. Light yellow to reddish-brown colour and can have much resin present, particularly in sapwood. Distinct figure and matures to beautiful colour over time. Can suffer distortion and resins may bleed through a finish.

## *Pinus Ponderosa*
## PINE, PONDEROSA

Also known as British Columbian soft pine (Canada), Western yellow pine and Californian white pine (USA)

**Origin:** Western USA and Canada
**Characteristics:** The sapwood is soft and even-textured, while the heartwood is darker, striped and resinous. It is used widely in furniture making and joinery.

## *Sequoia sempervirens*
## SEQUOIA

**Origin:** North America
**Characteristics:** Texture can vary but generally straight-grained, coloured reddish-brown with a contrast between earlywood and latewood. Generally non-resinous. Owing to its properties, it can be used for exterior work such as shingles, exterior claddings and posts, but it can also be used effectively for interior joinery.

## *Picea sitchensis*
## SPRUCE, SITKA

Also known as Menzies Spruce and Western Spruce

**Origin:** North-western United States
**Characteristics:** Tree grows up to 75m (245ft). Straight-grained with even texture, non-resinous and creamy white with occasional pink tone. Treat with preservative for external use. Works well with sharp tools, but knots can bleed resin. Relatively high strength-to-weight property.

## *Taxus baccata*
## YEW

Also known as Common, Irish or European Yew

**Origin:** Europe, North Africa, Middle East, India
**Characteristics:** Tough and very hard. Heartwood orange-red to purple-brown; sapwood light. Decorative interlocked grain patterns. Durable but can be difficult to work. Gluing difficult due to oily nature. Stains well and finishes to a high-quality polish. Burr pieces often used in veneers.

# TIMBER CONVERSION AND SEASONING

*Once the tree has been felled the wood is converted into workable pieces of timber, which are then dried out or 'seasoned' in the open air or in kilns.*

## Converting the logs

Felled trees are cut into logs, which are then sent to sawmills to be converted into planks or boards on large bandsaws or circular-saw machines.

Usually only the trunks or very major limbs are converted. Branches help to support the foliage, hence wood from branches has a high degree of movement and contains reaction timber that is prone to splitting, making it economically unviable for use in a piece. Instead it is used for chipping in certain manufactured boards.

*Through and through sawn timber at the sawmill.*

## Methods of conversion

When timber dries it shrinks and, because this shrinkage can cause distortion, the annual growth rings always try to straighten out. Therefore, timber cut from different parts of the trunk will move in different ways – for example, planks cut horizontally across the top of the trunk will be more prone to distortion than those cut across the centre.

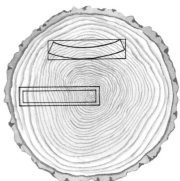

*The orientation of growth rings determines the degree of distortion.*

### Through and through sawing

Timber is very often converted 'through and through', which means the log is sawn into planks in a series of slices. As a result, planks cut from the edge have different properties to those cut across the centre. This is also known as plain-sawing, and although it produces timber at its widest, it is prone to uneven shrinkage and distortion. These boards can show a

highly figured grain pattern because they are cut across the growth rings.

*Through and through sawn timber.*

### Quarter-sawing

Where minimum timber movement is required, the log can be quarter-sawn. True quarter-sawing would mean boards being tapered, but this is uneconomic and less wasteful methods of sawing are used. Quarter-sawn timber shrinks more evenly and produces a more stable plank because a smaller amount of growth ring is available to shrink. Quarter-sawn boards have much straighter grain patterns.

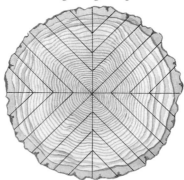

*Quarter-sawn timber.*

## Methods of seasoning

All newly cut timber contains a high percentage of water, which must be removed by a process of drying out called 'seasoning'. This water is present either as free water or as moisture, the latter being present in the cell walls. The first stage of seasoning is to remove the free water and then, as seasoning continues and moisture is lost from the cell walls, movement and shrinkage will start to occur within the timber. If, however seasoning takes place too quickly then stresses are created within the timber. The whole process therefore needs to be very carefully controlled.

There are two main methods of seasoning timber – air drying and kiln drying.

### Air drying timber

Planks that are seasoned by the air drying method are stacked on spacer battens at least 450mm (18in) apart – the air spaces between each plank are essential to avoid mould and fungal attack. The stack is built in a dry sheltered spot and protected from rain and direct sunlight. It takes approximately one year to dry every 25mm (1in) of board thickness for hardwoods and slightly less for drying softwoods. With this method, timber can only dry to the ambient humidity – the humidity of the atmosphere it is drying in – which is generally about 15 per cent. If the timber is meant for interior use, the humidity needs to be reduced in a kiln where the extraction of moisture is carefully controlled.

### Kiln drying timber

A kiln for drying timber is like a large oven in which temperature and humidity can be carefully controlled, so that moisture content is reduced to about 8 per cent or less. Planks are fed into the kiln on trolleys, a mixture of hot air and steam is introduced, then the humidity is slowly reduced to the required moisture content. Kiln-dried timber needs to be stored in a controlled environment. If it is dried to below air level and then placed outside, it will take up moisture again.

*Timber drying naturally in the open air, with spacer battens in between the planks.*

*An industrial kiln for drying large quantities of timber.*

21

# BUYING AND STORING TIMBER

*When buying wood, it is best to visit a timber yard personally in order to*

*examine the timber for defects and to select the best pieces to suit your needs.*

## Buying hardwoods

Hardwoods are cut from the tree into planks and the stated thickness of the board is the sawn size. However, the maximum dimensions you have to work with need to allow for planing the plank all round so it is flat and square. For example, a sawn plank purchased at 25mm (1in) will finish between 21 and 23mm ($^{13}/_{16}$ and $^7/_8$in)

depending on how much needs to be removed in order to make it flat, straight and square. In order to arrive at a specific dimension of 25mm (1in), a thicker board would have to be purchased, thus giving more waste. You also need to consider how much width you will get out of a plank.

When buying hardwoods in planks, there may be some resistance to you turning

over too many boards in a stack to find the best grain characteristics or colour, especially if you require only a small amount. However, if you are reasonable enough then generally timber dealers will be happy to oblige.

## Buying softwoods

You will encounter a similar situation regarding measurements of sawn softwoods, but the dealer will normally allow you to pick the pieces out for yourself. Sometimes softwoods can be purchased 'planed all round' (PAR) or 'dressed all round' (DAR) – that is, planed or dressed on all four sides. However the size given would be expressed in the original sawn size – for example, a timber labelled 50 x 25mm (2 x 1in) will actually be about 46 x 23mm ($1^{13}/_{16}$ x $^7/_8$in), but will not be to an exact measurement. It will be to the nearest size that the timber yard can plane in order to achieve a reasonable finish on all faces. As a result, a purchase made on one occasion may differ on another.

## General pointers

Finished sizes also vary according to the country of origin and the milling standards in that country. Some countries have standard

*When buying timber, examine any defects that are marked out on the wood.*

thicknesses and widths, allowing for a consistency of product from one yard to another. This tends to be the case particularly with common building and joinery grade timbers and milled sections such as architraves and skirtings.

The more exotic timbers for fine cabinet work are generally supplied rough sawn. If they need to be planed, then the maximum thickness and width will be provided.

When purchasing timber in large quantities the cost is often calculated by its metric or imperial cubic content, although in smaller volumes it may be sold by the length or piece. Be aware of how the dealer makes the calculations. Some dealers may want to charge you by the cubic foot, which can become quite confusing, particularly if you are used to dealing in cubic metres. Remember there are 424 cubic feet in a cubic metre. So ask the dealer for the cubic metre rate in addition to the cubic foot rate and then make sure they both add up correctly.

If you live a long way from a dealer there are mail-order companies that will supply a large range of timber of varying sizes. The product is obviously more expensive but often there is no alternative, especially if you need a specific species. Generally, however, suppliers have a reputation to maintain and give a good service.

## Storage in the workshop

Once you have obtained your timber, you must ensure that it is stored in a suitable condition. Hardwood planks are best stored in a similar way to that found in a good timber yard – horizontally with sticks in between each board and away from sunlight and direct heat sources. It is sometimes the case that softwoods are stored vertically at the suppliers, but this is best avoided unless it is absolutely necessary as a result of space constraints. In general, make sure that the workshop is dry and well ventilated.

You will find that as you undertake more projects there will be material left over. Not all of this will be waste and you should store any 'offcuts' that may be useful to use in later projects. Ensure, however, that this is undertaken methodically so that you know where to find different types.

*Timber is best stored horizontally.*

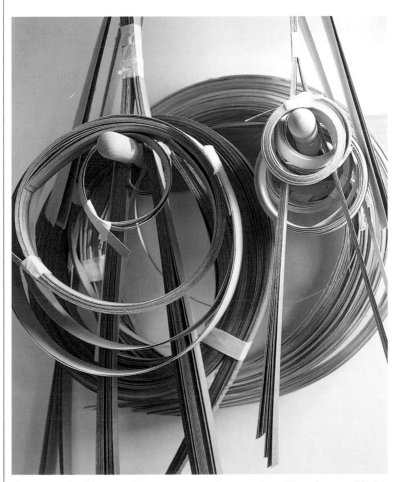

*Store wood safely out of the way on a wall, away from direct heat and light.*

# MANUFACTURED BOARDS

*Even though the natural characteristics of timber are a major part of its attraction, they also tend to cause problems including timber shrinkage in mass manufacture. Therefore the industry has developed a number of ways of using timber to make board materials that are much more dimensionally stable than natural timber and are readily available to the home woodworker.*

## Board sizes

Manufactured boards are usually produced to standard thicknesses, which are precise and expressed either in metric or imperial sizes. The sheet size is generally made to a standard 2400 x 1200mm (8 x 4ft). Larger sheets can be made available to special order – that is, approximately 3000 x 1500mm (10 x 5ft) – and some of the thinner thicknesses may be sold at a different size – for example, 2mm ($^1/_{16}$in) aeroply may be found 1500mm (5ft) square. Many outlets, however, will cut standard sheets into smaller sizes, normally increments of the standard sheets – for example, 1200 x 1200mm (4 x 4ft) or 1200 x 600mm (4 x 2ft). When tackling the projects in this book, you may decide to amend the sizes that are given in the accompanying drawings (see pages 52–3). If you do so, it is always important to consider how easily the required size can be cut from the standard sheet with the minimum of waste.

## Types of manufactured board

There are various types of manufactured board available on the market today. These include plywood boards, particle boards or chipboard, fibreboards and blockboards. Manufactured board can be used on its own, but also often forms a base for timber veneers (see pages 30–3).

*Modular storage cubes made of pre-veneered MDF (see pages 228–33).*

## Plywood boards

Plywood boards are made from constructional veneers, which are laminated and glued together, with the grain alternating along and across the board. Usually there is an uneven number of layers so that the outside grain directions on the faces of the finished boards are the same. Plywood boards are available in a range of different thicknesses – from a flexible 3mm (⅛in) sheet to a hefty 30mm (1³⁄₁₆in) board.

Plywood can have various numbers of layers – the thinnest, three-ply, has three layers. As its name suggests, three-ply is made from just three laminates – two face veneers, and a core that is sometimes the same thickness. When the centre layer is thicker it is often known as 'stout heart'.

Thicker boards, or multi-plies, are made of more sheets of laminates – always an odd number finished to the standard board thicknesses.

The performance of plywood is determined by the quality of the laminates and the type of adhesive used in the manufacturing process. Interior grade plywoods are normally bonded with an urea-formaldehyde adhesive. These are suitable for most interior work, but other types should be chosen if they are to be used for kitchens or bathrooms. Exterior grade plywoods – termed weather and boil proof or WBP – are bonded with phenolic adhesives, which are highly resistant to weather, wet and dry heat, insects and fungi. Marine plywood has laminates that are selected so that they are fault-free. For very special applications resorcinol adhesive can be used.

## Particle boards or chipboard

Particle boards, also known as chipboard, are made from small timber chips, which are glued together under pressure. They are stable but can be affected by moisture if a waterproof adhesive has not been used. Some boards are made from similar-sized particles, but often you will find boards with outside layers of high-density particles sandwiching a coarser core, such as in graded-density chipboard. Decorative chipboards are also available with faces of timber veneer or plastic laminates.

Other boards with greater tensile strength are available, but more for building work than furniture making. Orientated-strand board is made from long strands of timber. Flakeboard or waferboard is made from big chips of wood, bonded in layers with random grain direction.

Three-ply plywood

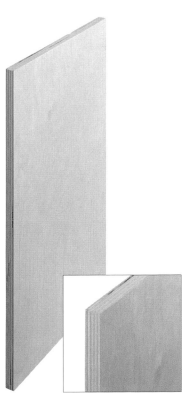

Nine-ply multi-ply

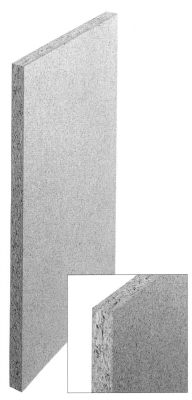

Particle board

## Fibreboards

Fibreboards are made out of tiny particles of wood (finer than sawdust) which are fixed together with a tough resin. For many years, the best-known material was standard hardboard, which normally has one smooth and one textured face. Standard hardboard is available in a large variety of thicknesses – from 1.5–12mm ($^1/_{16}$–$^1/_2$in). Fibreboard is often used for making cabinet backs and childrens' toys.

One problem with hardboard, as well as chipboard and other particle boards, is that lippings, either solid or veneer, have to be applied to the edges. To overcome this problem, medium density fibreboard (MDF) was developed. MDF has a dense smooth surface texture that is ideal for routing or painting. The edges can be polished so

**Hardboard**

**MDF**

that there is no need to use lippings. It has now become a standard material for much furniture making and also has certain applications for some interior fittings. MDF comes in thicknesses ranging from 6–32mm ($^1/_4$–1$^1/_4$in).

## Blockboards

Blockboards are constructed of solid timber strips between laminates. They are particularly suited to worktops and shelves. Boards are normally sold in full 1400 x 1200mm (4$^1/_2$ x 4ft) boards, with thicknesses ranging from 12–25mm ($^1/_2$–1in).

Laminboard is a top quality block construction board. The core strips of solid timber are quite narrow – approximately 5mm ($^3/_{16}$in) wide. It is usually edge-glued with two laminates on either side of the core, commonly with the grain of the outside in line with the direction of

the core strips. This is probably the most stable manufactured board available.

Standard blockboard has core strips that are wider than laminboard – approximately 20mm ($^3/_4$in). The core strips are not necessarily glued, and are sandwiched between outside laminate faces in one or two layers each side. A problem with this board is that the strips can show through the outside veneers, particularly if there is only one on each face.

Battenboard is a cheaper blockboard where the interior strips are much wider – from 30–40mm (1$^1/_4$–1$^1/_2$in). Obviously show-through is much more likely.

In addition to these boards, solid boards made from timber strips, jointed end to end and glued together to make a wide board, have

**Blockboard**

been used in the furniture industry and are available in many do-it-yourself outlets. If you can visually accept the pattern of the board's strips, they are stable and are a useful alternative to other boards and solid timber.

## Buying and storing manufactured boards

When you wish to depart from the sizes of the projects as given, or are happy to develop your own designs, always remember at the planning stage to reduce wastage as much as possible by checking that the components needed can be economically cut from the standard-sized sheets.

Unless you are purchasing from a company that carries a large range, the selection available from local outlets may be limited. When buying plywood, birch ply is best for making furniture because of its quality and birch veneer faces. Often the plywood available locally uses lower-quality veneers. With blockboards and particle boards, the local quality can also be variable. There are several levels of specialized boards that use different adhesives or resins as bonding agents. The best can be entirely waterproof if required, and so if you need any of the higher performance varieties it will need to be ordered from a specialist company.

Manufactured boards can be stored vertically as long as they are well supported to ensure that they do not bend or warp. Support the boards in a strong ledge fixed along one side of the workshop. They must also be stored in dry conditions because otherwise they take in moisture.

*Dining chair back made of plywood (see pages 276–81).*

*Birdhouse made of exterior-grade plywood (see pages 246–9).*

# VENEERS

*Veneers are thin sheets of timber that are used for either structural or decorative purposes. With many timbers now difficult to obtain in solid form, the use of veneers for decorative purposes is becoming more common.*

Many types of timbers have such interesting and unique characteristics that, in order to conserve and extend their use, they are made into veneers.

There is a vast range of different veneers available to the woodworker today. This is the case with timbers that exhibit highly decorative grain patterns, such as curl mahogany.

For structural use they tend to be known as constructional veneers and they are usually cut to thicknesses of between 1 and 3mm ($^1/_{32}$ and $^1/_8$in).

## How veneers are produced

In early times, veneers were produced by sawing resulting in thicker veneers – as much as 3mm ($^1/_8$in) – and a very high waste element from the sawdust. Veneer-slicing machines were developed in the eighteenth century to produce thinner veneers.

### Sliced veneers

Flat slicing is where the log is supported on a carrier and a series of slices is produced. This can be standard flat slicing, quarter-cut slicing or flat-sliced quartered. Quarter-cut slicing is used to produce veneers with a more varied grain pattern than flat slicing. Flat-sliced quartered

veneers are produced when quartered logs are cut across the log. Sometimes when slicing, fine cracks known as knife checks can occur on the back face of the veneer. This is called the open or loose face. If possible lay this face down, although when using book-matched veneers this will not be possible.

### Rotary cut veneers

The rotary cut is used for constructional veneers and some decorative veneers. The trunk of the tree, after the bark has been removed and softened by steaming, is set on a machine similar to a huge lathe. As the machine revolves, a continuous sheet is cut from the log. The cutting knife reduces in radius to give a sheet of even thickness.

*Veneers range in thickness from 1–3mm ($^1/_{32}$–$^1/_8$in).*

**SLICED VENEERS**

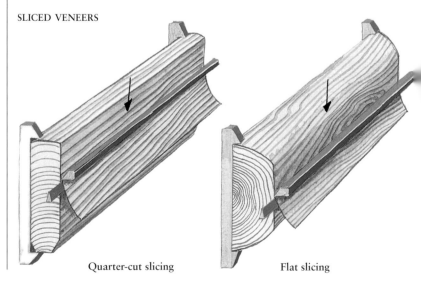

Quarter-cut slicing          Flat slicing

ROTARY CUT
VENEERS

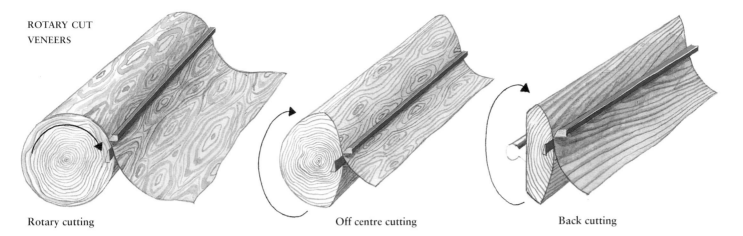

Rotary cutting                    Off centre cutting                    Back cutting

For decorative veneers, the log can be positioned in different ways so that various grains and figures are emphasized. Rotary cutting can be off centre, half-round or back cutting. Both off centre cutting and half round cutting produce a figure similar to flat-slicing. The back-cutting method is often used to make the most of curl and butt veneers.

*The surface of this tray is made with oak veneer on manufactured board – the handle and lippings are solid oak.*

## Veneer types

Many types of veneer are available today and have been made from a wide range of hardwoods, with varying colours, grains, figures and textures. The specific type of veneer is obtained by slicing the log in various ways, as described on pages 30–1. The part of the tree that the veneer comes from – for example, the main trunk, burrs or the fork – will also determine the type of veneer that is produced.

Some of the most common types of veneer that you will come across are described below.

Crown-cut veneers are the most common veneers used to decorate tables and other traditional furniture. They are produced using the flat-sliced quartered method of veneer slicing.

Curl veneers are produced from the fork of a tree where the trunk divides. They are produced using the back-cutting rotary method. The figure that is found on curl veneers is called a feather figure. Striped veneers are produced using the quarter-cut flat slicing method. This results in a radial cut being made across the width of the tree's growth rings.

Burr or burl veneers are often used for smaller pieces such as jewellery boxes or as a decorative focal point on larger pieces.

Some types of burr veneers are highly figured. They are produced using the back-cutting rotary method.

Some interesting veneers are created from hardwood timbers with irregular grain. These are called freak-figured veneers and are rotary cut.

Artificial dyes are also used to make veneers in various different colours.

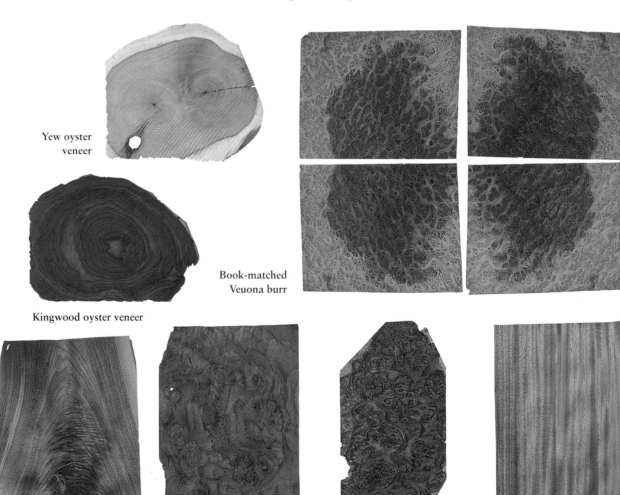

Yew oyster veneer

Kingwood oyster veneer

Book-matched Veuona burr

African walnut curl

American walnut burr

American walnut burr

Mahogany African striped

# Buying and storing veneers

Veneers are available from specialist suppliers who normally carry large stocks of many species. The most common types are normally to be found in fairly long lengths – 3.5m (12ft) or more – and between 250 and 350mm (10 and 14in) wide. Thicknesses vary, depending on the intended use. Where special and exotic veneers are needed, the size will be much smaller and will depend on the log or flitch from which they are cut. Calculate how much veneer you require and allow around 15 per cent for wastage. Every veneer is different so finding a matching veneer may be tricky.

Veneers are fairly brittle so take care when opening your rolled up sheet or it may crack. If the veneer has end splits, then mend it immediately with paper veneer tape, which is available from veneer suppliers.

Veneers should be stored flat, in a cool and dry environment. They should be stored away from strong light as the colours can deteriorate. If using matched veneers, the leaves should be numbered.

*A veneer hammer and animal glue are used in traditional veneering. Modern adhesives can also be used.*

*Store veneers in a cool, dry place, away from direct light.*

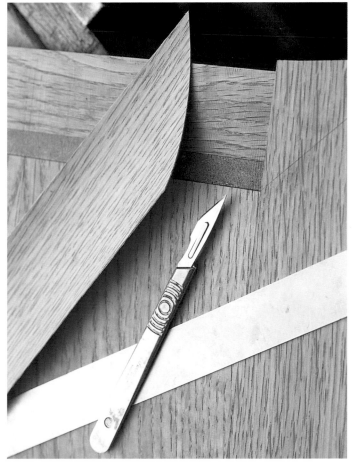

*A scalpel and straightedge can be used to cut veneers to size.*

33

# NON-TIMBER MATERIALS

*Even though most of the materials used by furniture makers are timber-based,*

*there are other furniture materials that you will sometimes wish to use. Most of*

*these are listed below and are included in some of the projects in this book.*

## Glass

If you want to use transparent panels in your furniture, then you have the choice between glass and plastic (see opposite). Glass has been used by man for many centuries, is readily available in sheet form and adds an interesting quality to many furniture pieces. It is not only available flat and clear, but interesting effects can be achieved by using frosted and other patterned varieties of glass.

Even though it is possible to learn how to cut glass in your own workshop, unless you plan to use it frequently it is easier to have it cut by a professional. Glass is generally available in most localities by suppliers of windows and glazing materials. When ordering glass, especially if it has to fit into a frame, cut a sheet of board material to the exact size needed, try it in place and then give that pattern to the glazier asking for it to be cut to that precise size. Whenever glass is to be used without a frame, as in the feature table project (see below and pages 196–9), it is essential to have the edges either linished or polished, and to have the sheet hardened so that it will not harm anyone if an unfortunate mishap does occur. These processes can normally be carried out by your glass supplier.

Store glass upright on edge, ensuring that the sheets cannot fall or be knocked over.

## Metal

You will often use different types of metal in furniture making, particularly when using screws or other fittings. The projects in this book make frequent use of bolts, machine screws and threaded studding. Metals include iron and steel, brass, aluminium and other alloys, and precious metals. While there is a large range of different metals, the most usual type in the workshop will be brass, aluminium or mild steel.

Brass and aluminium are fairly easy to work and a small metal vice with some basic metalworking tools will suffice for most purposes – the most common are hacksaws, drills and files (see pages 146–7). Mild steel requires more effort, but since the work is largely simple fabrication it is easily achievable. Even though adhesives can be used to join metals, it is easier to undertake the fabrication yourself and to take these components to a local metalworker to have them soldered, brazed or welded.

Metals are normally available in do-it-yourself stores or from local blacksmiths, engineering firms and metal stockists. Metals can be purchased in many sections or in lengths of rod, bar or tube.

It is best to store metals in a rack or vertically in cardboard tubes.

*Fittings, such as this unusual lock, are commonly made from metals.*

*Where glass is used without a frame the sharp edges must be polished.*

*Aluminium offers a lightweight and sturdy option for chair legs.*

## Fabric

Fabric can be derived from chemicals, plants such as cotton or animals. In woodworking, fabric is normally used as upholstery or as a decorative feature on a piece of furniture.

## Ceramics

Ceramics can provide additional interest to furniture. A large range of tiles are readily available from local suppliers and can add interest, colour and a very hardwearing surface to horizontal work areas.

## Leather

Leather works well in furniture making. It is not only used as an upholstery material, but also as straps for chair arms, such as on the easy chair project (see pages 250–6), and on the tops of desks. Leather is available from saddlers and leather merchants. To store leather, roll the hides.

## Plastics

Plastics, which are manufactured from chemicals, are generally used and fabricated in factory conditions. A vast range of plastics is available in many forms: sheet, powder/granules, liquids and both flexible and rigid foams. There is a huge variety of plastics and many are chemically formulated for specific uses. They are very useful in the workshop since many of the modern plastic-based adhesives and finishes can be applied to them.

As a material, however, plastics are most likely to be used in two applications. Firstly when adding a cushion to a chair, use polyurethane flexible foam, and secondly when drilling and shaping a transparent panel, it is much easier to use plastic. For example, when making the CD rack project (see pages 200–5), plastic sheets need to be cut to size and drilled. For the sheets, use either acrylic or polycarbonate, which can both be worked easily, using a combination of timber and metalworking tools.

Plastic sheets are sometimes available from do-it-yourself stores or specialist plastics suppliers. It is best to store plastic upright on edge, ensuring that the sheets cannot fall or be knocked over.

*Leather upholstery is here combined with timber to luxurious effect.*

35

# DESIGN AND CONSTRUCTION

*Vavonna burr veneered panels offer a striking contrast to the solid ebony body of this music cabinet, designed by Declan O'Donoghue.*

with additional coating, can build from a matt to a gloss finish. A major feature of oil finishes is that they retain the tactile quality of the timber and can be easily rejuvenated if bruising or stains have to be removed. White polish, or sanding sealer, will seal timber surfaces with very little colour change. Wax polishes can be applied to unfinished and treated timber. They can be clear, slightly tinted, or coloured with proprietary

pigments to use as a grain filler in order to accentuate an open grain pattern.

Further options for finishes can change the natural colour of solid timbers by bleaching, dying or fuming. Bleaching and dying are achieved with proprietary products, while fuming is done with ammonia in a sealed container, and should be handled with great care. Oak timber is especially responsive to fuming, increasing in darkness the longer it is exposed to the fumes.

Open-grained timbers such as oak and ash can be given a limed effect by being coated with either a proprietary liming paste, or with white or coloured paints. The coating is wiped from the surface across the grain before it has dried, leaving the open grain filled. Coloured paints can be used on most timbers to accentuate the grain of coarse-textured timbers, or to fill the grain to provide an even finish.

## Veneering

Veneers add a surface to board materials or solid timber where a particular colour, grain pattern, or exotic appearance is required. They are cut to different thicknesses to meet specific

*A chequer pattern made of veneers.*

*An intricate example of marquetry.*

requirements of decoration or durability. Most are knife cut with the grain and laid in sequence, slipped or book-matched to create repeating patterns. Plain veneers, often of sycamore, are also available dyed in a variety of colours. Decorative or plain-coloured stringing, inlaid in either solid timber or veneered surfaces, can be used to create linear designs and borders. End-grain veneer is cut square or obliquely across the grain to feature growth rings. Often cut from a branch of laburnum or yew and laid in sequence in a grid formation, these are referred to as oysters.

Marquetry is a technique of laying veneers of contrasting colours into a surface, which offers still more opportunities for decoration. Marquetry introduces colour and shading effects, which can create three-dimensional illusions.

## Bending and laminating

Techniques of bending and laminating timber have been used to great effect and economy in furniture design and manufacture. Both techniques are used equally in industry and in small workshops, differing from one to the other only in their scale of operation. Bending timber is a very ancient craft that has been used in furniture making for hundreds of years. In industry, very complex shapes can now be achieved, while it is possible for the home woodworker to make simple bends. Timber used for steam-bending need only be partially seasoned and prepared for bending with minimal waste and energy.

The technique of laminating was developed in the twentieth century to produce shaped components. A series of veneers, or laminates, are glued together – with the grain of each running in the same direction – in a mould that will give the required shape. Preparing laminates of thin slices of solid timber has a high waste factor to set against

the final effect. More economic methods use, for example, plywood with a face veneer.

Both bending and laminating offer enormous scope for structural and decorative forms in furniture, whether linear or in broad planes.

### Decorative joints

There are various decorative joints, including through mortise and tenon, and dovetail joints. End grain and long grain timbers are often combined to emphasize the joint, or wedges of two contrasting timbers can be used to enhance the decorative effect.

### Shaping and carving

Router cutter profiles offer further scope for imaginative decoration. Straight or curved lines with an even depth, or tapering, from a simple jig, are starting points to explore techniques, shadow effects and different grain patterns. Traditional hand-carved motifs, cut with chisels and gouges, are also worth considering.

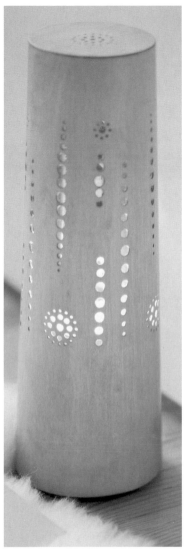

*Carving can also be used to create curved shapes and decorative effects.*

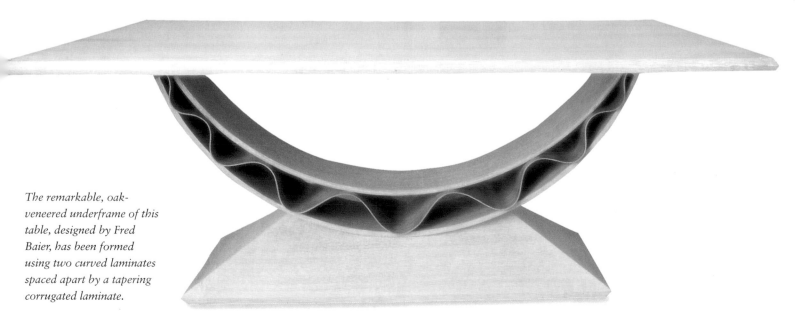

*The remarkable, oak-veneered underframe of this table, designed by Fred Baier, has been formed using two curved laminates spaced apart by a tapering corrugated laminate.*

*Opposite: A proliferation of decorative metal fittings brings distinctive style to this otherwise plain Japanese chest.*

With preforming, a series of veneers or laminates with the grain at right angles can be formed into shaped sheets. Generally it is only possible to form single curvatures, although double curvatures can be achieved with specialist presses. Timber is one of the materials that cannot be cast as such, but shapes can be made industrially by using chips and fibres that are pressed in metal-matched moulds. Another shaping technique is that of papier-mâché, which predates modern glass fibrework.

### Using contrasting materials

Introducing different materials into a piece of timber furniture can have a big influence on the overall character and tactile qualities of a piece of furniture.

For hard surfaces there are the different colours of slate and the wide, often dramatic, choice of marble colours and patterns. The many forms of glass bring a delicate quality – clear, tinted or silvered, with polished bevels, square or profiled edges.

Fabrics, available in an infinite variety of colours, patterns and weaves, offer a sometimes bewildering choice of materials and should therefore always be considered with care. Felt, cane or rush are other options. Leathers can be both supple or stiff, and also come in a wide range of colours.

### Developing an individual style

Look at furniture, in your own home or in illustrations, to discover what approaches to design you find sympathetic to your taste. Note how furniture relates to interiors and vice versa. A scrapbook of sketches will become a valued reference

*Bevelled glass panels transform the top of this dressing table, designed by Martin Grierson.*

of forms and details, colour, decoration and structure, and will help to develop a way of regarding furniture from the many aspects that combine to create 'good design'.

*A machined linear profile running at 45 degrees gives this elm cupboard door, designed by Matthew Burt, a modern look.*

*This contemporary-looking 'Daybed', designed by Mies van der Rohe, combines leather, metal and wood in a stylish amalgam of materials.*

# DESIGNING FOR YOURSELF

*Once you understand the basics of construction and have explored the possibilities of design, you may feel ready to try designing your own furniture and will need to know how to turn your ideas into practical drawings.*

## Tools for drawing

If you have developed your skills to the point of wanting to design your own furniture, you will need to invest in some drawing equipment – including a flat-square-cut drawing board, a large set square for drawing vertical lines, a T-square for drawing horizontal lines, a compass, a protractor for drawing angles, French curves for drawing curved lines and a scale rule.

*The finished folding chair, for which the drawings are shown opposite.*

## Working drawings

Working drawings show how a piece is made and are critical in furniture making. The drawings in this book are more decorative than standard working drawings, with colour, grain and shadow added. The metric and imperial measurements given in the book are not direct conversions so it is important to follow either one system or the other but not a mixture of the two.

### Views

Working drawings follow a convention that is understood worldwide. A working drawing presents a piece in a series of different views. The plan presents the view from the top, the front elevation presents the view from the front and the side elevation presents the view from the side. Sections show the internal structure, such as the

details of joints, by showing the piece as though it has been cut through on a particular axis. It is sometimes easier to combine an elevation with a section.

### Perspective drawings and details

The drawings for each project also include a perspective drawing, which attempts to show how the piece will appear visually. Perspectives are useful in showing how things fit together, particularly if they are either exploded to show the parts separately or sectioned, when some parts are removed to make a construction clearer. Details of important joints or particular features of a piece are also given where relevant.

### Scale

For a working drawing to be really useful, it needs to be drawn to scale. It may be drawn full size (or 1:1). Usually,

*Detail of tongue and groove joints from the dining table (see pages 218–22).*

FRONT ELEVATION

SECTIONAL SIDE ELEVATION

SINGLE-POINT
PERSPECTIVE

PLAN

however, the piece itself is of such a size that the drawing must be smaller, in which case you must scale it down. For example, when using metric measurements, one-fifth full size (1:5), where 10mm represents 50mm, is the most common scale. One-tenth full size (1:10) and sometimes one-twentieth full size (1:20) are also used.

For imperial measurements, the most common scale is 1:4, where ½in represents 2in. When using a scaled drawing, a special rule called a scale rule is used so that the dimensions of the actual piece can be read from the drawing.

A scale is not given on the drawings that are featured in this book, but annotated dimensions are given throughout. These accurate, full size dimensions will remove the possibility of doubt and mistakes if you come to make the piece yourself.

## Models and mock-ups

Once you have designed your piece it is a worthwhile idea to 'try out' the design before you start to build it. This can be done by making either a scale model – for example, using balsawood – or a full-sized mock-up – using fibreboard. By making a scale model or mock-up, you can check all the dimensions and proportions of the piece.

# TOOLS AND TECHNIQUES

# THE WORKSPACE

*If you are new to woodworking and furniture making, it is important to spend time planning the design of your workspace. Initially you may use existing spare space so that some basic projects can be constructed before you commit to longer term spaces and equipment. In this case, it is worth adapting a sturdy table as a workbench and obtaining some basic tools as a starting point.*

When you are sure that you want to develop your skills you will need to set up a dedicated workshop, which will include a good quality workbench, a range of vices and various hand, power and machine tools.

### Planning a workshop

A clean, well-planned, dedicated workshop will provide a safe, effective and pleasurable environment in which to develop and

refine your woodworking skills. To have a fully dedicated space for woodworking may not be feasible, unless at some time you graduate from hobby to professional work. However, it is possible to adapt and dedicate spaces

*A well-designed and fully equipped workshop is essential for a woodwork enthusiast.*

such as sheds and garages. Circumstances will dictate the size that will be available to you, but with due consideration, and accepting that you will need to move machinery, most spaces can be made to accommodate a workshop area. Whether you decide to adapt or dedicate space for your workshop, all of the principles of workshop design described here need to be considered.

## The floor surface

The floor needs to have a finish that will enable you to keep it clean and even – a concrete floor painted with floor paint will serve well. The place where you stand at your workbench benefits from having a slightly less hard surface. Industrial-type rubber flooring works well for this.

## Power sources

Almost all mechanical equipment is powered by electricity, and so it is essential that the power supply meets all of the necessary regulations and that its distribution is suitable and safe to run your power and machine tools. In industry, machines use three-phase electricity, but in most domestic situations the power is single phase. Although second-hand commercial machines may be cheap, problems can arise in connecting them.

## Lighting

It is best to have as much natural lighting as you can. North-facing is preferable, but if this is not possible and you have direct light, you may need blinds to stop the sun's glare. This will no doubt have to be supplemented by artificial light. Fluorescent lights can give an even illumination, but spotlights can be very useful over the workbench and your machinery.

## Heating and humidity

Some form of heating is usually necessary depending upon the climate. Furniture makers are always concerned about the fact that timber moves and, ideally the workshop should be at the same temperature, and definitely the same humidity, as the environment where the completed work will stand.

## Access

As long as the pieces made are small scale, access might not be a problem. However larger pieces will need to be moved out of the space when completed and inaccessible places can give rise to severe problems. Try to select a place where materials and equipment can be moved in and completed furniture moved out. Attic or basement areas therefore may not be suitable.

## Security

As your facilities develop ensure that your valuable tools are secure because they will be very expensive to replace.

## Storage requirements

It is convenient to have many tools, particularly hand tools, hung on the walls near the bench. However, hand power tools should always be stored in cupboards for safety reasons, and drawers are needed for many of the smaller tools to keep them tidy.

*Ensure that you have the necessary power supplies and a heat source, such as this wood burner.*

You will collect many types of materials. Hardwood planks are best stored in a similar way to that found in a good timber yard – horizontally with sticks in between each board and away from sunlight or direct heat sources. Softwoods can often be found at the suppliers stored vertically, but this is best avoided unless it is absolutely

*It is best to store tools safely near your workbench.*

*Use a bench shelf for the most useful and commonly used items.*

*Wherever possible, store tools safely out of the way on a wall.*

necessary. In general ensure that the workshop is dry and well ventilated so the wood does not gather moisture. Manufactured boards should be stored in a vertical stack against a wall or partition.

As you work, you will find some material will be waste but other, particularly exotic, timber may be worth retaining for future jobs. It is useful to have some boxes or bins where you can keep small pieces of

wood for this purpose. Ensure however that this is undertaken methodically so that you know where to find different wood types quickly and easily.

Sundries such as fittings, adhesives and polishes can be stored on open shelving or in cupboards. Remember, however, that if you are going to have large quantities of finish, it should really be stored outside the workshop in order to reduce the risk of fire.

*Power tools will soon become covered in dust if left on a bench. Store them in boxes under or near the bench.*

*Label and store containers safely.*

# Health and safety

Always be aware of the possible problems, but work with caution and confidence. Make sure that you have a first-aid box available.

## Fire

Your workshop should have anti-fire measures built into it. A fire extinguisher or fire blanket should be at hand, and fit a smoke detector. Prevention though is better than cure, and so ensure that dust and shavings are removed daily and that you do not smoke. Also make sure that there are no sparks from electrical or other equipment.

Some materials may be inflammable, and so store large amounts of such material outside in a metal fireproof box, and only bring enough material into the workshop to complete the job in hand. When using finishing oils applied by cloth, always unfold the cloth and leave it outside – otherwise it could self-ignite.

## Fine dust and chemical fumes

When work is generating fine dust or chemical fumes, ensure that you wear a face mask or respirator, and use safety goggles whenever your eyes may be vulnerable. Some form of extraction is needed when you progress to machine tools and this is also useful for many of the hand power tools. With machines such as table saws and planer/thicknessers, extraction is very important.

Most of your finishing may well utilize oils and waxes, but if

*For your health and safety, always use a dust extractor of some kind when working with power tools.*

you are working with solvent-based finishes that generate noxious fumes it is better to have a part of the workshop specifically dedicated as a small finishing or spray booth. Then you can fit an efficient extractor to remove fumes. In this situation you should always wear a suitable mask.

## Noise

When using machines or processes that generate high noise levels always wear ear defenders or plugs.

## Hand tool safety

Accidents can happen, and so be aware when procedures could be dangerous and take special care.

## Machinery safety

With any woodworking machinery safety is paramount. Follow these guidelines:

• Never make adjustments without turning off the power.

• Always follow the manufacturer's instructions for the specific machine.

• Inspect the machine before you switch it on and always check the machine after making adjustments.

• Always use the guards supplied.

• Never attempt to machine small items without adequate jigs.

• If anything happens to your piece of work, switch off the machine before attempting to rectify the situation.

• Most importantly, when using any cutting machine, be it a table saw, portable power saw or router, wear safety glasses. Safety glasses are also recommended for any drilling operation and nailing, particularly when using large nails.

Dust mask

Ear defenders

# THE WORKBENCH

*A good, sturdy workbench is an essential element of a woodworker's workshop. A thick, hardwood top is best to use as a work surface, and the underframe should also be of a sturdy hardwood.*

Ensure the worktop is level. The usual height for a workbench is between 800mm (32in) and 850mm (34in), although different heights can be made to order.

## Workbench fittings

The workbench should be fitted with well-machined vices. Many workbenches have both side and end vices already fitted. However, if you need to

purchase and fit vices separately, the most important vice is the main woodworker's vice. Buy as big a capacity as you can afford, and fit the vice as close as possible to one of the legs of the underframe, as this will prevent any flexing of the worktop when the working timber is cramped in the jaws of the vice. It should also be properly set into the bench so that, when the wooden vice cheeks are applied, no metal shows and the top of the vice is

*A large woodworking vice is useful for holding work securely.*

perfectly flush with the top. You will need to drill large holes or cut mortises in the worktop so that a bench stop can be fitted. These are normally used with an end vice, which can be useful for cramping small jobs as well as holding the work.

Most workbenches are made with a tool well, which enables a large work piece to be moved across the worktop without sweeping hand tools onto the floor. Many workbenches also come with a drawer or cupboards for the storage of tools or materials underneath.

The workbench project featured later in this book (see pages 188–92) would be a good investment. It has a strong underframe with some substantial timber for the main working area, a ply well for tools and a deep backboard to make the structure rigid.

*Try to make a workbench one of your first major projects (see pages 188–92).*

Saw horse

Folding bench

## Other types of bench

Proprietary folding benches can also be bought. Although not substantial enough to be your main bench, they can be useful in the workshop if you need to undertake work such as fitting away from your base.

Saw horses, or trestles, are also useful when initially cutting sheets of manufactured board.

## Maintaining your bench

A workbench needs to be well-maintained to provide good, long-lasting service. Here are a few tips for good maintenance:

• Support the work piece away from the work surface, using padded strips of timber. This will protect the work surface as well as the piece that you are working on. Specialized rubber mats are available that allow nails, screws and working debris to fall through the mats to the work surface. As an alternative to these mats, a layer of hardboard can be placed on the worktop surface and changed when it becomes damaged.

• Clean the work surface down regularly with a banister brush to remove debris.
• Avoid using carpet as a surface protector as it can trap and hide nasty abrasive materials, such as glass fragments, small nails and screws, in its surface.
• Avoid nailing anything into the surface of the workbench if possible. Try to use a cramp or screws instead.
• When drilling, always make sure that you use a piece of scrap material between the work piece and the worktop.
• Check that the surface of the worktop is straight and without twist. This can be achieved with winding sticks, which are parallel pieces of timber. Set the timber edge up at either end of the workbench and sight across the top edges to test. Alternatively, you could use a spirit level and a straightedge to test for level. Adjust the workbench with chocks to set the worktop true and flat.

## A temporary workbench

If you have only just started woodworking you may want to make a temporary workbench initially rather than investing in a permanent one straight away.

In this case you will need to find an existing table, which has a strong structure, and make a temporary top.

Take a sheet of manufactured board, 25mm (1in) thick, and cut it to a size that is 150mm (6in) larger than the existing table all the way round. Fit some baize – a soft, usually green, woollen fabric, resembling felt – to the underside and make four corner blocks so that the surface will not move out of position. On the edge where you wish to work, fit another strip of board approximately 300–400mm (12–16in) – the same length as the base board – and glue this board into position.

You should have enough room to fit a small vice and it would be advisable to use a couple of G-cramps to hold it in place and ensure that it is stable. This should give you a surface that enables you to start work.

Ideally the workbench should be level with your waist, and so you may have to make some chocks for the legs.

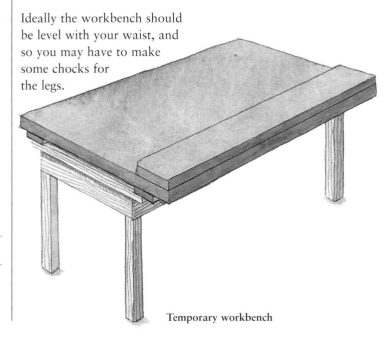

Temporary workbench

# THE ESSENTIAL TOOL KIT

*If you are a woodworker with experience you will already have a set of tools, but if you are starting this pleasurable journey you will need to begin by purchasing some basic tools. The list below is a reasonable starting point.*

It is good practice to extend your tool kit by purchasing reasonably priced tools as they are needed for a particular job, and also to have a longer term plan for expensive tools, power tools and machine tools. Within your budget always purchase the highest quality that you can afford since they will last longer and will be easier to use. A good list of hand power tools would include a power drill, jigsaw, orbital sander and router. Machine tools would include a pillar drill or drill press, a table saw, a bandsaw and a planer/thicknesser.

Below is a summary of the tools that you will need as you begin your woodworking journey.

## Measuring and marking tools

The importance of accurate measuring and marking out is stressed often throughout this book, and it is advisable to obtain the best quality tools available on the list. The most important are:

### Beginner's tool kit

A  jack plane
B  beech mallet
C  try square
D  marking pencils
E  sliding bevel
F  screwdrivers
G  pin hammer

H  file
I  coping saw
J  G-cramp
K  basic cabinet scraper
L  gooseneck cabinet scraper
M  chisel

N  marking knife
O  marking gauge
P  tenon saw
Q  panel saw
R  folding plastic rule
S  steel rule

• For workshop-based furniture making, a folding rule is useful, but if you need to do a lot of site work a steel tape can be more useful.

• A good-quality, accurate steel rule – 30mm (12in) long – is essential for measuring and marking work.

• Pencils need to be hard enough to give a precise fine line, but soft enough to be seen. A 2H grade will be adequate.

• Some people favour a marking knife that is ground on one face only, but a more traditionally sharpened blade is usually preferable.

• A good-quality try square or combination square is essential. A combination square is a more expensive option, but is preferable since a good-quality tool will give much better results and will last longer if cared for. If funds are tight, however, a good-quality try square will suffice.

• A traditional sliding bevel will suit well.

• You will need other gauges later, but a good marking gauge will suffice at first. If you buy a mortise gauge as well, ensure that it is the type with a screw adjustment for setting the space between the points rather than a simple slide.

## Sawing tools

• A good-quality panel saw cuts both solid timbers and manufactured boards.

• A back saw, a small tenon saw or large dovetail saw will be needed for fine work – 200mm (8in) will be suitable.

• For curved cuts, a coping saw is essential.

• Even though most power tools will be added to your kit at a later date, if you wish to undertake large-scale or a large amount of work, then a jigsaw will be a welcome addition. The jigsaw removes much hard work, and can cut both solid timber – up to 50mm (2in) plus – and manufactured board, and also helps with some finer work. Metal blades are also available.

## Surfacing tools

• A jack plane is the most useful to start with.

• A cabinet scraper, for fine finishing on difficult timbers, is a must.

## Cutting tools

A range of bevel-edge chisels – 6mm (¼in), 12mm (½in) and 25mm (1in) – will suffice at first.

## General tools

• Small cordless electric drills are now so reasonably priced that they are the best tool for early drilling jobs. You will need a range of drill bits: twist drills from 1–12mm (¹⁄₃₂–½in) or dowel bits from 3–12mm (⅛–½in). There may be a need to drill holes larger than 12mm (½in) and a set of spade bits from 12–40mm (½–1½in) will tide you over until you can afford more expensive bits.

• Buy a small power router with basic cutters.

• For initial shaping work, rasps will suffice until spokeshaves are needed.

• A pin hammer is good for fine work. Heavier hammers will be needed later.

• A beech mallet is essential for both joints and assembly.

• Both cross-head and slot screws are now used, and so buy a screwdriver that accepts different-sized heads – or use screw bits in your power drill.

• A hacksaw and a range of small files will cover jobs where some modification to metal parts is necessary.

• Holding and assembly tools, including sash cramps and G-cramps, are essential. Purchase a small set of four light sash cramps – 800mm (30in) – as a start, and two 250mm (10in) and four 150mm (6in) G-cramps.

### More advanced tools

Once you have the basic tool kit, the following are worth considering:

• An orbital sander will help you with finishing large surfaces.

• A floor or bench-mounted pillar drill (or a large electric drill and a drill stand) is a very useful addition to the workshop.

• A table saw is useful for many precise operations.

• A belt sander is also useful, but it is essential that you get this bench mounted.

• A bandsaw will enable you to cut curved components and thicker pieces of timber.

• A planer/thicknesser means that you can purchase sawn timber, and ensure that work is straight, flat and to the correct thickness.

*A selection of chisels is an essential part of your tool kit.*

# MEASURING AND MARKING

*Accurate measuring and marking are vital in achieving quality work. Even the slightest inaccuracies in the early stages will inevitably lead to complications later. There is an old craftworkers' saying: 'measure twice, cut once'.*

## Tools

As with any aspect of woodworking, the range of equipment available for measuring and marking is vast. However, some tools are more useful and adaptable than others, and so it is worth finding the best ones that can be trusted for the job. A rough measurement is adequate for converting planks into slightly oversized pieces, but precise measuring and marking are essential in tasks such as preparing to cut specific lengths of timber or waste from a joint.

### Rules and measures

A **folding wooden** or **plastic rule** or a **retractable steel tape measure** are equally suitable for the initial marking out of length, but are not accurate enough for precise marking. A **metal steel rule** is best for precision marking. A 300mm (12in) rule is essential and a longer one in excess of 600mm (24in) is also useful. Buy a quality rule that has accurately marked measurements. A **steel straightedge**, at least 600mm (24in) but preferably 800mm (32in) long, is useful for marking straight lines or checking the flatness of a surface. A **vernier gauge** is useful for measuring small dimensions. A small plastic one that will measure to $\frac{1}{10}$mm ($\frac{3}{200}$in) is adequate.

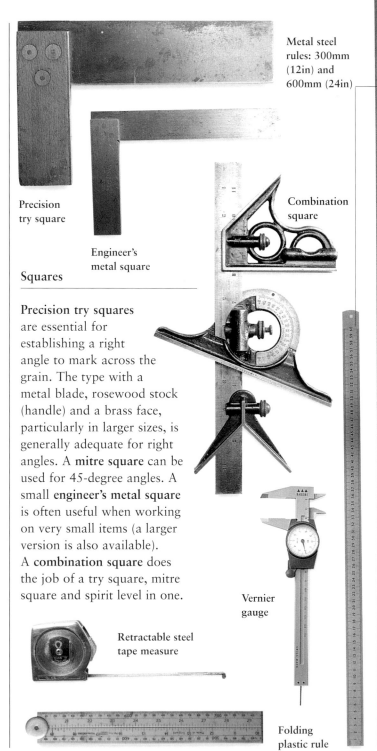

Precision try square

Engineer's metal square

Metal steel rules: 300mm (12in) and 600mm (24in)

Combination square

### Squares

**Precision try squares** are essential for establishing a right angle to mark across the grain. The type with a metal blade, rosewood stock (handle) and a brass face, particularly in larger sizes, is generally adequate for right angles. A **mitre square** can be used for 45-degree angles. A small **engineer's metal square** is often useful when working on very small items (a larger version is also available). A **combination square** does the job of a try square, mitre square and spirit level in one.

Vernier gauge

Retractable steel tape measure

Folding plastic rule

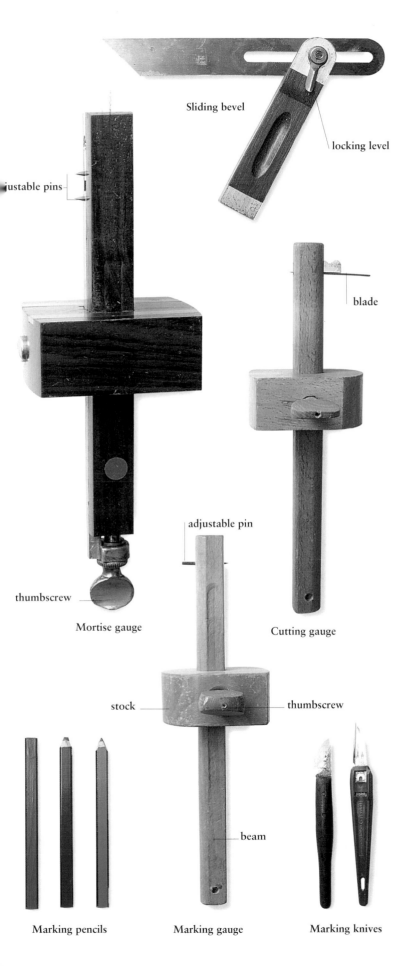

Sliding bevel

locking level

adjustable pins

blade

thumbscrew

Mortise gauge

adjustable pin

Cutting gauge

stock

thumbscrew

beam

Marking pencils

Marking gauge

Marking knives

## Sliding bevels

A **sliding bevel** is necessary for marking out dovetail joints and for other angled work. They are available with a wooden handle or all in steel, the engineer's version. The screw allows the sliding bevel to be set at the required angle with the aid of an accurate protractor.

## Pencils

**Pencils** can be used for precision marking if they are fairly hard and can be sharpened to a good point or chisel edge that will last. It is best to use a pencil mark for rough guidance and for setting out; use a marking knife to make a cut line when greater accuracy is required, such as when marking joints, or for sawing or chiselling.

## Marking knives

**Marking knives** are much more accurate than pencils and provide a slight indentation for saw teeth. Always use a knife for marking across the grain, running the blade along the waste side of the desired line.

## Gauges

A gauge is the best tool for marking along the grain and there are several types available. Each has an adjustable marking device that can be set at the required measurement and used to score a line. A **marking gauge** has one steel pin, whereas a **mortise gauge** has two independently adjustable pins for marking the position of mortise and tenon joints. A **cutting gauge** has a small blade that is most suitable for cutting lines across the grain.

## Measuring equal divisions

You can divide a piece of timber or board into equal divisions, where the actual width of the divisions is not vital, without using mathematics. Lay a rule at an angle cross the surface so that clear increments mark out exactly the required number of divisions.

## Using a bevel to determine a ratio

Bevels can also be used to determine a ratio – for example, on dovetail joints. For a ratio of 1:4, square a line across from the edge, measure up four units – say 40mm (2in); on the edge of the board measure one unit – say 10mm (½in). Then join the two points up with the blade while the stock is against the edge.

# Preparing the tools

All measuring and marking tools should be used with care or their accuracy can be affected.

## Checking a try square

1  To check that a try square is accurate, lay it on a piece of board that has a straight edge. Position the metal-edged stock along the straight edge.

2  Mark a line on the board face against the try square blade, at right angles to the edge. Turn the square over and mark another line a short distance from the first. If the lines are parallel, the square is accurate. If not, repairs can be difficult so it is best to replace the tool.

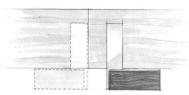

*Check with a try square.*

## Adjusting a sliding bevel

1  Make a mark on the edge of a board and use a protractor to make a second mark at the desired angle. Join the marks to give a line on the face of the board that is at the correct angle to the edge.

2  Loosen the screw on the sliding bevel and align the outer edge of the bevel along the angled line. Retighten the screw to set the bevel.

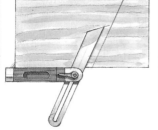

*Adjusting a sliding bevel.*

# Preparing the timber

Before measuring and marking the timber for a project, it is important that it is perfectly flat, square and straight.

## Checking timber

1  Check the surface is free from pits or bumps by running a straightedge across it. If the surface is not flat, it should be planed true – perfectly flat – before the timber is measured and marked (see Planing, pages 74–81).

*Use a straightedge to check for flatness.*

2  You can check that the timber is straight by positioning two steel rules across each end. Now sight along the timber and, if the two rules appear parallel, the timber is straight.

*Check that the timber is straight.*

## Marking the faces of timber

1  Make the face-side mark (usually a scroll shape) on the timber surface, towards the edge to be planed next.

*Face-side mark.*

2  Plane the edge straight and at right angles to the face side. Check with a straightedge and try square.

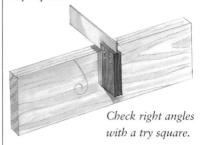

*Check right angles with a try square.*

3  Apply the edge mark, conventionally a 'v' shape, on the face edge.

*Apply edge marks.*

# Taking measurements

Measurements of timber and the accessible parts of projects can easily be taken with a steel rule. Simply position the end of the rule on one edge of the surface and read off the required dimension at the other.

## Measuring awkward spaces

Some measurements can be difficult to take because a rule cannot be held in the best position for accuracy. For example, measuring across the internal diagonal of a frame or cabinet, in order to check for squareness, can be a tricky task.

1  Cut two strips of timber that, when overlapped, will span the distance to be measured. Cut a bevel at one end of each strip.

2  Hold the strips together, positioning the bevelled ends in each corner. Mark a line on each strip to show where they meet.

*Use bevelled strips across diagonal.*

3  Place the strips on a flat surface, match up the lines and measure from point to point. Alternatively, measure from the line to the point on one strip and add it to the total length of the other strip.

## Marking rough measurements

For approximate measurements parallel to the edge of the timber, you can make the marks with a pencil and improvize a gauge by using a finger or rule.

### Gauging with a finger
1  Hold the pencil between your thumb and index finger. Rest another finger on the edge of the timber so that the pencil is at the required distance from the edge.

2  Keeping the hand and pencil steady, run the pencil along the timber to make a line parallel to the edge.

*Gauge a line with your finger.*

### Gauging with a rule
1  You can also use a rule as a gauge. Place the rule on the timber surface so the end is the required distance from the edge.

2  Hold a pencil against the end of the rule and use your other hand to keep the rule at the correct distance from the edge. Run the rule and pencil along the timber length to make a line parallel to the edge.

## Marking precise measurements

Precision is best achieved with a marking knife or a gauge, which will give a clean indentation for positioning a chisel or saw.

### Using a marking knife
1  Hold a rule or try square firmly in place and position yourself so that you can see where the edge meets the timber.

2  Position the knife blade flat against the edge of the rule or square and mark the timber by pulling the knife along the edge with care.

### Using a marking gauge
1  Use a rule to set the position of the stock to the correct distance from the pin or blade and lightly tighten the thumbscrew. Check this against the timber and make any required adjustments by tapping the gauge on the workbench. To increase the gap, tap the base of the beam; to decrease it, tap the beam at the head. When the pin is in position, tighten the thumbscrew.

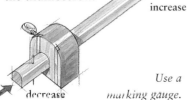

increase

*Use a marking gauge.*

decrease

2  Position the stock against the face edge, with the pin just touching the surface of the face side. Slightly rotate the marking gauge and run the stock along the edge.

### Using a cutting gauge
You can use a cutting gauge in the place of a marking gauge in order to achieve a cut line. This tool is used in the same way, but the blade must be very sharp and firmly inserted in the beam.

*Gauge a line with a marking gauge.*

### Using a mortise gauge
One pin is fixed in position while the other is attached to an adjustable metal bar. The pins must first be set to the correct distance apart – that of your chosen mortise chisel. Then, the stock may be adjusted along the stem, and tightened with the thumbscrew. The gauge is then ready to mark two parallel lines along the timber.

*Set the pins to the correct position.*

### Finding the centre point

Marking gauges can also be used to find the central point on a piece of timber. Set the pin to approximately half the surface width. From each side, make a small mark with the point. Keep adjusting the stock by tapping the beam, as described above left, and repeat the operation until the marks line up from each side, at which point the mark is perfectly central.

# BASIC SAWING

*Some saws can be used to cut timber into manageable sizes, and others to cut*

*intricate joints and shapes. It is useful to separate the skills into basic sawing,*

*which is discussed here, and fine sawing, which is discussed on pages 82–5.*

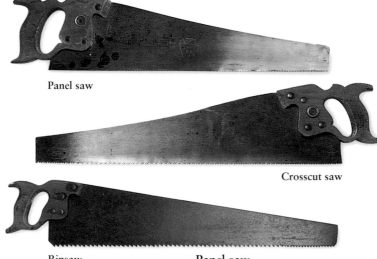

**Panel saw**

**Crosscut saw**

**Ripsaw**

**Panel saw**

## Saw teeth

The teeth on saws differ to suit the type of sawing that is to be undertaken. However, all but the smallest saws are sharpened and set in a specific way. Each tooth has a leading edge, which makes the cut, and a less upright side known as the trailing edge. The shape produced is known as the pitch. The teeth are also set – that is, bent firstly to one side, then to the other – so that the cutting is more effective and the blade does not bind in the cut. The cut that the saw makes is called a saw kerf.

## Hand saws

There are three main types of hand saw – the **ripsaw**, the **crosscut saw** and the **panel saw** – and all taper in length to assist the blade's movement. The main difference between each of the saws lies in tooth size. Large teeth remove a lot of material, whereas smaller teeth make smaller, finer cuts. Tooth size is generally measured by the number of teeth per 25mm (1in), and is expressed as teeth per inch (tpi). This applies where teeth are measured from the base of one tooth to another but, if you are calculating from point to point instead, the measurement is described as points per inch (ppi).

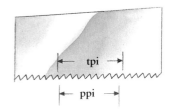

*Saw teeth are measured as tpi or ppi (teeth or points per inch).*

The panel saw has much finer teeth than ripsaws and crosscut saws, with a tpi of about 10–12. It can be used on solid timber, and is also more suitable than the other saws for cutting manufactured board because of the finer teeth.

## Crosscut saw

The crosscut saw is designed for cutting solid timber across the grain. The leading edge has a greater pitch than on a ripsaw and the teeth are sharpened at an angle so that each tooth has a knife-like cutting edge. These saws have more tpi (8–9) than ripsaws and, while many experienced craftworkers will use both types of saw, most enthusiasts find that possessing one crosscut saw is adequate.

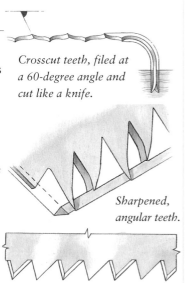

*Crosscut teeth, filed at a 60-degree angle and cut like a knife.*

*Sharpened, angular teeth.*

## Ripsaw

The ripsaw is normally the largest of the hand saws. It is sharpened for cutting timber along the grain and thus has few tpi (4–5). Each tooth has an upright leading edge, which is filed to a chiselled point at 90 degrees to its face.

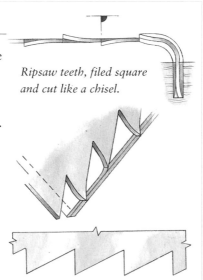

*Ripsaw teeth, filed square and cut like a chisel.*

*The teeth of the ripsaw are squared off.*

## Using a hand saw

All of the saws described left are generally used for cutting material to an approximate size. For this reason, an allowance of about 3mm (⅛in) for planing is needed. Bear this in mind when marking out the cutting lines, both along and across the grain. Always hold the saw firmly, with the index finger pointing in the direction of the cut. This will help to prevent the handle twisting with the movement of the blade.

*The correct grip for a handsaw.*

1  Mark out the lines to be cut, both along and across the grain. Cuts along the grain or in manufactured board are generally easier if the material is supported horizontally on saw stools or trestles.

*For cutting along the grain, support the timber horizontally on trestles.*

For cutting short pieces of timber along the grain, it may be possible to put the timber in a vice, so that it can be cut vertically.

*Cut short pieces of timber along the grain in a vice.*

For cutting across the woodgrain, it may be more convenient if the timber is cramped to a workbench.

*Cramp the timber to a bench to make cuts across the grain.*

2  Use your thumb in order to locate and steady the saw on the waste side of the cutting line and make some short strokes to begin the cut. Take care to keep your thumb away from the teeth of the saw.

*Use your thumb to steady the saw as you start the cut.*

3  Remove your thumb once the saw has started a small kerf in the timber. Continue to apply pressure to the handle so that you guide the saw along the cut.

4  Gradually increase the length of the strokes that you take and build up a steady rhythm, ensuring that each forward cut stays on the waste side of the line.

5  On some timbers, the cut can begin to close as you work further down the length of the timber. This may cause the blade to bind and interrupt the flow of movement. Insert a small wedge in the saw kerf, so that the timber remains separated. You could also add a little wax or even soap to the side of the saw to act as a lubricant and help it slip through the cut.

*Cut along the grain with a wedge in the kerf to separate the timber.*

### Cutting cleanly

Generally, sawing along the grain of the wood should not present too many problems with splintering or splitting. However, sawing across the grain can cause the grain to fracture and break out on the underside. This should not be a cause for concern when you are sawing prior to planing, because the damage will be removed later as the timber is refined. However, precautions need to be taken when you are cutting after the timber has been planed true and to size.

If breakout is a particular problem, you could use a finer toothed saw and/or lower the angle of the saw as you work – especially when you are working on veneer board such as plywood.

### Sharpening a saw

Saws should be sharpened regularly to ensure that they cut smoothly and accurately. While traditional craftworkers used to sharpen their own saws, many modern woodworkers take their tools to saw doctors. These people specialize in saw sharpening, and work with machines or, for very fine saws, by hand. Some modern saws, especially cheap ones, may have hardened teeth that can only be sharpened by machine, while others must simply be replaced when the teeth become too blunt. It is therefore more economical in the long run to buy quality tools that can be serviced regularly, rather than constantly replacing them.

### Sawing manufactured board

Use a panel saw to cut manufactured board. Hold the saw at a low angle to prevent breakout on the bottom face, especially on veneer-faced boards. Steady the work with a cramp or your knee.

## Safety first

- Always tie long hair back and don't wear loose clothing.

- When using power tools, follow the instructions provided by the manufacturer.

- Cut carefully and do not force the blade – let the saw do the cutting.

- Never lift tools by the lead or disconnect by pulling the lead.

- Before changing blades or making any other adjustments, check that the tool is disconnected from the power supply.

- Don't use faulty tools.

- Always wear the correct protective gear – for example, safety glasses, dust mask and ear muffs.

- Ensure that the work is held firm and the saw blade will not cut any unnecessary objects such as the saw stools.

- Place the power lead over your shoulder so that it is behind both you and the saw.

- If possible, use safety cut-offs such as a residual current device.

- Keep all body parts away from the blade, especially hands, which should never be in line with the cut.

- Only use a tool for the purpose for which it was designed.

- Allow the tool to reach full speed before working it.

- Keep tool cutters and blades sharp.

- Always ensure that you have set the machine correctly.

- Whenever possible, use fences, jigs and other guides, keeping your hands away from the cutters at all times.

# Power saws

There are two main types of power saw – the hand-held saw and the machine saw. Although these tools are unlikely to remove the need for hand tools and careful, skilled craftwork, they are versatile and can be useful for some woodworking tasks. For example, power saws are ideal for cutting heavy or large pieces of timber, which would need a lot of effort if sawn by hand. The jigsaw is also good for intricate work, helping to ensure accurate and precise cuts.

### Hand-held power saws

The **jigsaw** is particularly useful for initial rough cutting timber both along and across the grain, as well as manufactured board. It can also be used for finer work, giving accurate and precise cuts. The tool can be used with a variety of blades, all of which are designed for cutting different materials and producing different results. Most blades cut with a vertical – or reciprocating – motion, although some advanced saws can have an orbital action. The blade always cuts on the upstroke and can saw solid timber up to 50mm (2in) thick. Some varieties have different speeds so that they can be used on plastics and soft metals.

Many woodworkers also use a **circular saw** for cutting solid timber and manufactured boards. Light and portable, the saw is suitable for site work, but a hand saw or jigsaw are usually adequate alternatives in the workshop and are much safer to use. However, the circular saw can be useful if it is mounted in a stand as a first table saw. The saw consists of a sole plate that will rest on the work, a saw guard to prevent accidents, a fence for parallel cutting and a tilt mechanism for angled cuts. Unlike jigsaws, circular saws are always used for straight cuts, though the blade can be set to cut right through the material, or work to a set depth.

### Using a jigsaw

Jigsaws can be used to cut freehand straight or curved lines, or in conjunction with fences and guides that direct the cut. However, always ensure that there is nothing in its path that is likely to foul the blade.

1 Hold the jigsaw firmly by the handle with one hand. Use the other hand to support the weight of the timber or board, or cramp the work down.

2 Start the saw and bring the blade up to the edge of the work, resting the sole plate on the work; ease it through the board. Always saw on the waste side of the cut lines – the blade cuts on

the upstroke, which can cause grain breakout that will need to be cleaned up later.

*Starting the cut from the edge.*

3 Work slowly, firmly and smoothly, avoiding any sudden changes in direction that may cause the saw not to cut true or the blade to break.

### Making internal cuts
1 Measure and mark out the shape on the timber.

2 Drill (see Drilling, pages 96–100) a starting hole in the waste area, large enough to accommodate the blade of the jigsaw.

3 Insert the jigsaw blade through the hole and use the tool to cut the shape in the normal way.

*Use a jigsaw to make a neat internal cut.*

### Machine power saws

Like hand-held power saws, machine power saws can make light work of large pieces of timber and board. They can also be set to levels of accuracy for repetitive work that can be hard to achieve with hand-held tools.

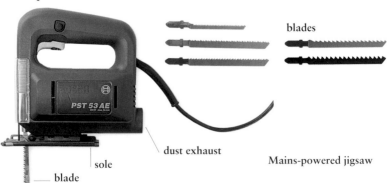
blades
dust exhaust
sole
blade
Mains-powered jigsaw

The **table saw** is the most popular kind of machine tool. This is basically a machine with a rigid, flat table through which a circular saw blade projects. Behind the blade is a riving knife. The blade can be set to produce different depths of cut and in most models can also be angled. The machine has a secure fence against which parallel cuts can be made, and adjustable fence slides, set in grooves, for crosscutting. There are many types of saw blades, which means that the machine can be used to make both quick cuts as well as precise saw cuts. Always operate the saw with extreme care, checking that it is set correctly, with all the necessary guards in place, before beginning any work.

Table saw

**Radial-arm saws** can be used to perform many tasks in woodwork, including crosscutting and jointmaking. They can also be used for ripping timber, although this can be hazardous so always use extreme care. Some machines may also be set up with a sanding disc. Specialized machines that are dedicated to a specific task often perform better than ones that do multi-tasks.

Radial-arm saw

**Bandsaws** (see page 85) are another useful machine for cutting, especially shaped work.

A **mitre saw** is used for precision cutting of angles and square ends. It is used for cutting mitre joints for skirtings, architraves and picture frames. The saw assembly and motor are hinged on an arm, which is lowered to cut the timber. The arm is spring-loaded to return the saw to the 'up' position. The saw has a fixed top guard that covers the blade and a lower guard that retracts as the arm is lowered onto the work. The mitre saw can be turned to make angle cuts. Most saws turn at 45 degrees to each side, and some turn up to 60 degrees.

Other types of mitre saw include **compound** and **compound slide saws**. These allow the motor assembly to turn both vertically and horizontally.

### Using a table saw

**1** Check that the table saw is set to the correct adjustments before turning it on. To cut timber into parallel pieces, set the fence to the required distance from the blade; ensure the blade is at the correct height.

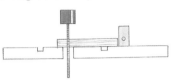

*Set the fence securely so that it is at the right distance from the blade.*

*Saw the timber into parallel pieces.*

**2** To crosscut, set the adjustable fence to the required angle. Mitres and specific angles can also be cut by setting this fence, or by canting the blade. Hold the timber against the crosscut fence. Slide the work towards the blade and cut steadily. Once cut, slide the work away from the blade before bringing the crosscut fence in front of it.

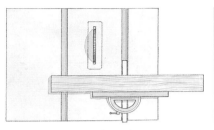

*Make angles and mitres with the fence.*

**3** Use push sticks, spare battens, to feed timber through the blade, so that you can keep hands clear of the blade. This should have a notch cut in the leading end to hold the timber down while pushing it forward.

*Use push sticks as a safety measure when using a table saw.*

**Mitre saw safety**

• Check that the guard is working correctly.

• Use the vice at the base of the saw to hold your work.

• Ensure the tilt adjustments are tight.

• Never 'cross hands' when operating the saw.

• Always use the correct saw blade.

# SHARPENING

*Effective woodworking relies on tools that have sharp cutting edges. This is particularly important for hand tools, such as planes, chisels and gouges, as well as the blades and cutters in machine tools.*

The following description of sharpening uses a wide chisel to demonstrate the process, but exactly the same methods are used for plane blades and narrow chisels, although the grinding angle for narrow chisels is smaller: for wide chisels and plane blades, the angle is 25–30 degrees, and for narrow chisels the angle is 20–25 degrees.

Sharpening is carried out in two stages: the blade is first ground to an angle and then it is honed in order to achieve the sharpest edge.

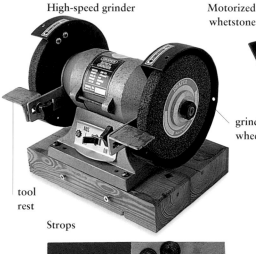

High-speed grinder

Motorized whetstone

stone disc

grinding wheel

tool rest

Strops

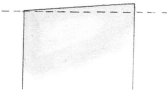

Grinding wheels

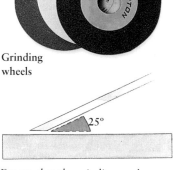

## Grinding

Chisel and plane blades can be ground to an angle using a high-speed bench grinder or a slow-speed motorized whetstone.

### High-speed grinder

**High-speed grinders** are a quick means of grinding an angle. The blade is held against the rotating wheel. The wheels are usually made from aluminium-oxide and rotate very fast, at around 3000 rpm or more. Make sure that heat does not build up; otherwise the temper of the blade will be removed, rendering the tool useless. If this happens, the metal will change colour. Cool the blade very frequently in water.

1  Always wear safety goggles when using a grinder even though the tool has protective spark deflectors. Before grinding a bevel, check that the cutting edge on the blade is square by holding it against an accurate try square. If it is not square, sharpen the edge on the grinder, before moving onto the bevel.

*Ensure that the cutting edge is square before you start on the bevel.*

2  Hold the tool at the correct angle to ensure that you will achieve the correct bevel. For a wide chisel, this is about 25 degrees. Then, adjust the tool rest to match.

25°

*Ensure that the grinding angle is correct before you start.*

3  Switch on the grinder, and hold the blade between your index finger and thumb. Position the blade on the rest, ensuring your fingers are well clear of the wheel. Move the bevel forward until it just starts to grind. Move the tool from side to side over the face of the wheel to sharpen the full width.

25°

*Start grinding, keeping the angle steady at 25 degrees.*

**4** Inspect the sharpened edge often to check that it remains square and at required angle.

## Motorized whetstone

Use a motorized whetstone for the same job. This has a horizontally or vertically mounted whetstone, turning at under 500 rpm, which is lubricated by a stream of water or oil. The slower speed and in-built lubrication help to ensure good control, while removing the risk of drawing the temper.

**1** Check that the cutting edge of the blade is square. Bring the tool down firmly onto the stone at a 25-degree angle.

*Grind the chisel on the whetstone at an approximate angle of 25 degrees.*

**2** Inspect the bevel often to ensure that it remains square and at the required angle. The grinding process generates a burr, which will be removed by honing.

## Honing

Honing produces the final cutting edge on the tool blade. It is achieved by rubbing the ground tool edge up and down a stone that is lubricated with oil. This produces a second bevel, which will give the sharp, cutting edge.

## Oilstones

Most people starting out in woodwork use an oilstone made from synthetic materials such as aluminium-oxide or silicon-carbide. These are available in coarse, medium and fine grades and are the cheapest varieties on the market. However, as you develop your woodworking skills there are some suitable alternatives. For example, natural stones such as Arkansas have a range of hardnesses, while some woodworkers prefer to use Japanese waterstones. There are also manufactured sharpening stones that have hardened particles bonded into them.

*Japanese waterstone*

*Oilstone housing tray*

### Honing sequence

The grinding of the chisel blade will have produced a bevel of 25 degrees. To ensure the tool is ready for use, this bevel now needs to be sharpened or honed to an angle of 30 degrees.

*The honing angle must be 30 degrees.*

**1** Place the edge of the blade flat on the stone, bevel side down. Hold the blade firmly in one hand and place your other hand on the top of the blade. Lift the tool slightly to give the correct honing angle – five degrees more than the grinding angle.

**2** Work the bevel by rubbing the blade firmly up and down the stone, ensuring that the whole cutting edge is in contact with the stone.

*Make the bevel by honing the chisel at an angle of 30 degrees.*

**3** When you have produced a bevel of about 1mm (¹/₃₂in), continue the same process on a finer stone. The rubbing action will cause a burr to form on the back of the blade. To remove it, turn the tool over and make a few light strokes, holding the blade perfectly flat. This removes the burr and leaves a sharp edge.

*Create a sharp edge by removing the burr.*

### Honing a narrow chisel blade

Use a zig-zag or figure eight action. Move the chisel along the stone to ensure that its surface does not become unevenly worn. If you find this process difficult, honing aids that hold the blade in a given position are available, but it is worth persevering to develop this skill yourself.

### Truing stones

After a great deal of use, an oilstone will become hollow. This makes it difficult to keep a square edge on chisels or blades; therefore, it needs to be flattened. Grind the surface with carborundum powder and oil or water, on a sheet of glass. Continue to rub the face of the stone until it is flat.

### Using a leather strop

A leather strop helps to remove any trace of a burr and leaves an extremely sharp blade. Hold the blade, and 'wipe' the honed bevel away from the sharp edge. Then turn the tool over and do the same to the back. You should now have a razor sharp edge. If a fine, shiny line along the cutting edge appears on the blade, continue sharpening.

## Planer/thicknesser or combination planer

These machines come in a variety of sizes, so aim for one that is adequately large – a width in excess of 200mm (8in) is best. A planer with long infeed and outfeed tables is also preferable.

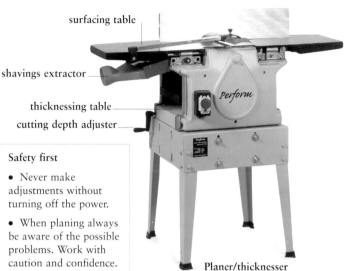

**surfacing table**

**shavings extractor**

**thicknessing table**

**cutting depth adjuster**

*Planer/thicknesser*

### Safety first

• Never make adjustments without turning off the power.

• When planing always be aware of the possible problems. Work with caution and confidence.

• Always follow the manufacturer's instructions for the specific machine.

• Inspect the machine before you switch it on – always check and recheck adjustments.

• Always use the guard supplied.

• Never attempt to plane short or thin pieces without using adequate jigs.

• The material you are planing must be at least as long as the distance between the two feed rollers.

• Feed only one piece of board through the machine at a time.

• Never try to remove too much material in one pass – it is better to use several fine cuts.

• If anything happens to your piece of work, switch off the machine before attempting to rectify the situation.

The surfacing part of the machine has two tables – the infeed table and the outfeed table. A rotating cutter block with sharp cutters is located beneath the gap between these two tables. The infeed table is adjusted to produce different depths of cut, and the outfeed table is appropriately adjusted, so that it is level with the top of the cutters.

A guard covers the cutter block and is adjusted to accommodate the thickness of the timber, so that the board safely passes beneath. The fence enables edges to be planed and can be tilted at an angle for bevelling. The thicknessing part of the machine is similar to an old-fashioned mangle. The cutter block and the feed rollers are at the top and the feed table is adjustable in height so that the timber can be planed to an exact thickness.

*Section of planer showing surfacer and thicknesser.*

### Cutter block and cutters

To achieve the best quality finish, ensure that the cutters are very sharp and that they are correctly installed in the cutter block. High-speed steel cutters can be used, but if there is a lot of planing to be done, tungsten carbide-tipped knives are preferable. Most cutter blocks have provision for two cutters whereas larger, industrial machines tend to take three or four. Always follow the manufacturer's instructions for fitting the cutters into the block.

*The cutter block.*

Always double check to ensure that the cutters are tightened in position and that the power is off. When fitting the cutters into the block you must adjust them so that all cutters and all parts of the cutting edge are working together. So, when inserting the knives ensure that they project from the block evenly. Positioning a perfectly straight piece of timber on the outfeed table should make this easier.

*Fit the cutters and tighten in place.*

## Surfacing with a combination planer

It is essential to adopt the correct stance when surfacing – planing the face side – with a planer. This is both for safety reasons and to ensure that you apply an even pressure when passing timber across the plane.

1 Stand to the right of the table and position your right hand flat on the work.

2 Feed the work under the guard, maintaining pressure with your right hand. As it emerges, shift your body weight slightly and use your left hand to apply pressure to the work on the outfeed table.

3 Continue to feed the work through, with pressure on both ends, before shifting your right hand to the work on the outfeed table.

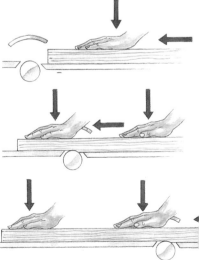

*Apply varying pressures to your work while surfacing.*

### Planing the face side

1 Adjust the infeed table to determine the thickness of the shaving that will be planed. Slide the bridge guard into place over the cutter block.

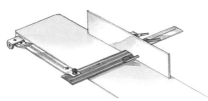

*The two tables, fence and guard.*

*Change the thickness of the cut by adjusting the infeed table.*

**2** Position the timber on the infeed table and raise the guard so that the timber can pass beneath. Stand to the side of the infeed table and, with the machine switched on and at operating speed, apply pressure to the board so that it does not rock. Slowly feed the timber through the planer. As the piece passes under the guard, transfer pressure to the outfeed table so that the cut will give the flattest possible surface.

**3** Continue to apply pressure until the whole of the piece of timber has passed through the planer. Then lead the piece through again and continue doing so until the surface is flat. If the timber is cupped or bowed, make several passes to make the board stable on the planer tables, prior to achieving a finished surface.

### Planing the face edge

**1** With the machine switched off, check that the fence is at a right angle – 90 degrees – to the tables. Or, for a bevelled edge, set the fence to the required angle. Lower the guard and slide it across, so that the timber can pass between it and the fence.

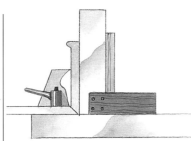

*Set the fence at a 90-degree angle for the face edge.*

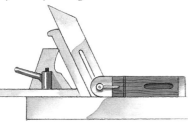

*Set the fence at the appropriate angle for a bevel.*

**2** Switch the machine on and position the timber on the infeed table. Hold the face side firmly against the fence and feed it over the cutter block, passing it from one hand to the other.

*Pass the timber from hand to hand as you feed it over the cutter.*

### Thicknessing with a combination planer

With a perfectly flat face side and face edge, it is now possible to plane the board to the required width and thickness.

**1** Remove most of the excess material with a table saw in order to help make the board manageable.

**2** Ensure that the surfacing tables are correctly adjusted and that the cutter-block guard and shavings deflector are in position.

**3** Stand slightly to one side of the machine. Position the board on the infeed table and use push sticks to feed it through the thicknesser – keep your hands away from the rollers.

*Use push sticks when the timber nears the base and the feed rollers.*

**4** As the board moves across the rollers, move to the other end of the machine to receive it. Do not force the board by pulling or put your hands anywhere near the rollers – make sure that you wait for the board to feed through naturally, keeping your hands well away.

### Planing thin pieces to width

Very thin pieces of timber can be difficult to plane to width because they may not stay upright. Either make a special jig to ensure their stability or carry out this operation using the same method described in 'Surfacing with a combination planer', having first sawn almost to width.

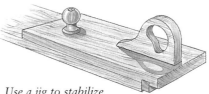

*Use a jig to stabilize very thin material during planing.*

### Planing the face edge of thin timber pieces

To plane the edge of thin timber, use a special jig to hold the wood safely. Set the machine fence at the correct angle (as above) and take extra care.

Turn to pages 150–2 and use the small shelf exercise in order to practise and develop your planing skills.

### Dust/chip extraction

Even small machine planers produce a lot of waste chips. Most machines have attachments whereby an extraction unit can be fitted to remove this waste, thus keeping both the job and surrounding air clear. Although the unit is normally a separate investment, most woodworkers find that it is well worth the additional expense.

# FINE SAWING

*In addition to rough sawing timber to size, you will also need to be able to perform much finer saw work. This section looks at the tools and skills needed for fine work, such as cutting precise joints and difficult shapes.*

## Hand tools

There are many saws available to the woodworker for fine cutting.

### Backsaws

Backsaws are used for precise work. They have a strip of brass or steel that is cramped to the top of the blade – this both keeps the blade straight and adds weight to the tool, to help make cutting easier.

A **tenon saw** is the largest of the backsaws. Its blade ranges between 250 and 350mm (10 and 14in) in length, with a 12–14 tpi. As its name suggests, this saw is used mainly for cutting fairly large joints, particularly tenons.

A **dovetail saw** is similar to a tenon saw, though it is slightly smaller. The blade is about 200mm (8in) long, with 15–21 tpi. The teeth on this saw are generally set very fine. Again, its use is quite specific – for cutting dovetails and other fine sawing work.

A **bead saw,** or gents saw as it is sometimes known, is designed for very delicate work. It normally has a straight handle and is a much finer backsaw than the dovetail. The blade is about 150–200mm (6–8in) long, with 15–25 tpi.

Tenon saw

Dovetail saw

Bead saw

### Curve-cutting saws

There are several saws used for cutting curves.

The **bow saw,** although not used very much these days, is a traditional curve-cutting saw that has a lightweight timber frame. The removable blades are between 200 and 300mm (8 and 12in) long with 8–16 tpi. The blade is tensioned with a tourniquet and can be turned through 360 degrees.

A **coping saw** has a sprung metal frame, which holds the blade in position by tension. The handle turns to add or release tension. The blade is 150mm (6in) long, with approximately 15 tpi. The blade is very narrow, and can be disposed of when blunt as it is inexpensive to replace. The blade can be revolved in the frame by turning the end fittings. Unusually, this saw cuts on the pulling stroke.

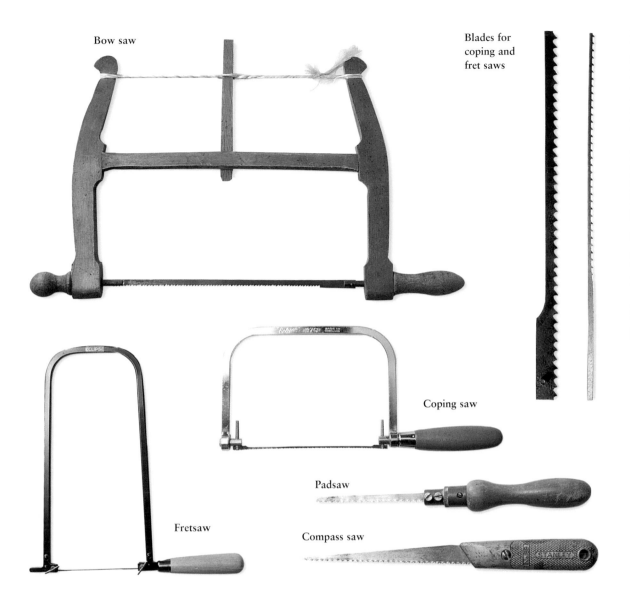

Bow saw

Blades for
coping and
fret saws

Coping saw

Padsaw

Fretsaw

Compass saw

**Hand power tools**

The best hand power tool for fine sawing is the jigsaw (see page 70). This is able to saw relatively tight curves, both externally and internally, and with care can handle quite intricate work. The main problem is that the saw cuts on the upstroke and, when cutting across the grain, this can cause grain breakout or pickup. The tool must be held flat against the surface of the work, and always cut on the waste side of the line.

---

A **fretsaw** is similar to the coping saw but it has a deep throat in the steel frame and is designed for cutting very tight curves. The blade is 150mm (6in) long, with approximately 15 tpi. The fretsaw uses very thin blades – as thin as 3mm (¹⁄₈in) – that are held in with thumbscrews at both ends and are quite fragile.

A **padsaw**, or keyhole saw, is used for internal cuts when a bow saw is unable to reach the area to be cut. It has a straight handle, which can be more comfortable for some tasks. You may come across a compass saw with a shaped or straight handle, which performs the same operation as the padsaw.

### Using a backsaw

Backsaws are generally used for fine, accurate saw work.

1  Measure and mark out the lines with a marking knife.

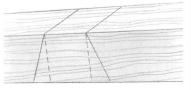

*Use a marking knife to mark out the saw lines on your timber.*

2  Secure the work in a vice. Use the tip of your index finger to position the saw blade on the waste side of the cut line. Begin with a few backward strokes, guiding the saw with your finger.

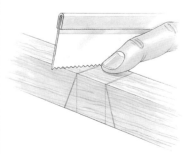

*Start the cut on the waste side and guide the saw with your finger.*

83

## Japanese saws

*Japanese tools have become increasingly popular with Western woodworkers in recent years. Japanese saws have superb cutting performance and cut on the pull stroke rather than needing pressure to cut like European saws do. The range of Japanese saws shown here includes the most commonly known example to Westerners, the ryoba noko (double-edged saw), shown in the centre. It is used for work where both crosscutting and ripping are necessary. A small ryoba noko is often employed in the making of cabinets or when framing doors. The unusual-looking saw on the left is known as azebiki nokogiri and it has a short blade with curved edges. The curves allow the woodworker to begin in the centre of a piece of wood, which can be extremely useful. It is also used to cut sliding dovetails.*

**3** Extend the strokes along the cut line, keeping to the knifed mark. The saw cuts on the forward stroke, and so release pressure on the return stroke. Guide the saw on the forward stroke; the weight of the back strip aids the actual cut.

## Using a bow saw

**1** Begin by fitting the blade into the bow saw. Do this by loosening the tourniquet and positioning the blade in the slots in the handle rods. Carefully insert the pins through the holes in the blade and rods and take up the slack on the tourniquet.

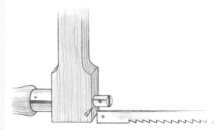

*Fit a blade in a bow saw.*

**2** Turn the handles to adjust the blade to the required position in relation to the frame for the intended cuts. The blade may be revolved as for a coping saw.

*Turn the handles to adjust the blade position.*

**3** Tension the blade by twisting the tourniquet with the central piece of timber – the toggle. Ensure that the toggle is sitting against the central rail.

**4** Hold one end of the saw with both hands. It is vital to have a proper grip on the tool, with the index finger of the first hand extending in line with the blade. Even though the saw has a handle at both ends, it is normally used holding one end only with both hands; take careful strokes making sure that you keep to the line.

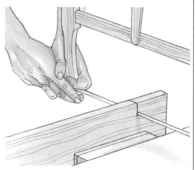

*Hold the bow saw correctly.*

## Using a coping saw

**1** To replace a blade, unscrew the handle to bring the pins closer together and release tension. Insert the blade in one end and slightly flex the frame against the bench; insert the blade in the other end and tighten by turning the handle.

*Flex the coping-saw frame and fit the blade.*

**2** Secure the piece of timber in a vice, grip the handle of the saw firmly and position the blade on the waste side of the cut line. Pull the saw towards your body in order to make the cut.

*Pull the coping saw towards you as you make the cut.*

**3** To change the direction of the blade or to prevent the frame from falling foul of the edge, loosen the handle slightly, rotate the blade in the frame, and retighten before continuing with the sawing. This allows the frame to be turned over the nearest edge without changing the cutting direction.

## Using a fretsaw

**1** To fit a blade, loosen the thumbscrews at each end and insert the blade. As you retighten the thumbscrews, spring the frame closed; this will give the blade tension.

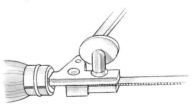

*The fretsaw blade.*

**2** Cramp the timber to the bench with the work area overhanging, and sit so that you are near the cutting area.

**3** Position the blade on the waste side of the line, so that it cuts on the downstroke and you can cut to the marks on the top surface. These saws cut with a pulling action, not pushing as other saws do.

*Use a pulling action with a fretsaw.*

## Using a compass saw or padsaw

1  To make an internal cut, drill a hole in the marked area of the piece, on the waste side.

2  Insert the saw blade and use the forward thin edge of the blade to start the cut. Gradually increase the length of the strokes.

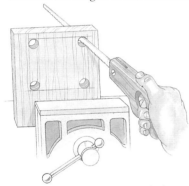

*Use a compass saw to cut a hole.*

## Bandsaw

The best machine tool that you can use for intricate, fine sawing is a bandsaw. Unlike most other types of machine saws, this has a continuous band of metal with teeth on the leading edge. The band runs around two or three wheels and the blade passes through a slot in a machine table.

The blade is tensioned by the top wheel, and it is powered by a motor working on the bottom wheel. Various thicknesses of

blade and different sets of teeth mean that quite small curves can be sawn, and the large blade makes it an extremely good general-purpose machine. The machine is supplied with various fences but, once mastered, it is often easier to use by sight than with guides or fences.

### Using a bandsaw

1  Before starting the machine select the correct blade that you need for the job. It is important to check this for faults before you start work. The blade needs to be tensioned and the top wheel needs to be tracked in order to keep the blade running in the centre of the wheel. A hand wheel or knob tilts the top wheel to align the blade. Set the guide blocks so that they just miss the sides of the blade; usually there is a set above and below the table.

2  Next, the friction wheel needs to be set approximately 2–3mm ($\frac{1}{16}$–$\frac{1}{8}$in) from the back of the blade – too far back and the blade may come off, while if you put it too far forward, it could break the blade.

3  Once the saw is set up test run it for 5 to 10 seconds on full speed; stop the saw and check that the blade is still set in the correct position; adjust as required.

4  Before sawing, adjust the blade guides so that there is only about 3mm ($\frac{1}{8}$in) between them and the work.

5  Switch on the machine and align the saw blade with your marked line, ensuring it is on the waste side.

6  Carefully feed the work into the blade, constantly checking that it is following the line.

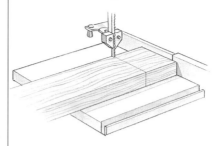

*Carefully feed the timber into the blade of the bandsaw.*

7  At the end of the cut, use a push stick to feed the remaining edge of the work through the blade. Always ensure that your fingers are out of the way when the saw breaks through.

### Safety first

• Wear the appropriate safety equipment.

• Always ensure that the blade is properly tensioned, and that the blade guides and rear thrust wheel are properly positioned.

• Never force the work. The blade should be sharp enough to do the cutting; you are only directing its path.

Turn to pages 153–5 and use the letter rack exercise to practise fine sawing.

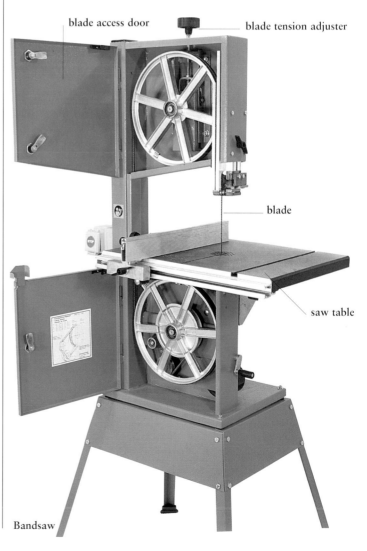

blade access door

blade tension adjuster

blade

saw table

Bandsaw

## Using chisels

### Paring horizontally

1 Lay the work flat on the bench and secure it with G-cramps or, if it is a suitable size, in the vice.

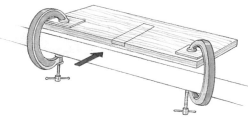

*Secure the work on the bench, ready to be pared horizontally.*

2 Stand with your chest and shoulders at right angles to the board, with your legs apart and the elbow of your dominant hand tucked into your body.

*The correct stance to adopt when paring horizontally.*

3 Hold the chisel handle in your dominant hand. Hold the blade between the thumb and forefinger of your other hand, behind the cutting edge. Apply pressure with the forearm of

your dominant hand in order to make the chisel cut. Use the other hand to steer and guide the direction of the chisel.

*Hold the blade between your thumb and forefinger for horizontal paring.*

*Guide the chisel carefully and pare away the waste.*

### Paring vertically

1 Place the work on the benchtop and secure in position with a G-cramp. It is preferable to fix a piece of spare timber underneath the work.

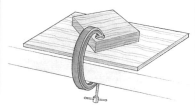

*Secure the work on the bench, ready to be pared vertically.*

2 Bend over your work so that your shoulder is directly over the chisel, and apply a controlled, downward pressure on your hand. This action will help you to keep the chisel straight while cutting.

*The correct stance to adopt when paring vertically.*

3 Grip the handle of the chisel firmly by placing your thumb over the end of it. Use the thumb and forefinger of the other hand to control the blade carefully as before when paring horizontally. Apply firm downward pressure in order to chisel out the waste.

*Control the blade with your thumb and forefinger.*

*Apply a downward pressure as you chisel away the waste.*

## Cutting mortises with a chisel

**1** To remove the bulk of the waste, hold the chisel in one hand with the blade positioned between the gauge lines – approximately 3mm (⅛in) in from the end of the mortise – and apply pressure. Repeat several times along the mortise to chop out the initial layer.

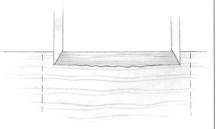

*Remove the first layer of waste from the mortise.*

**2** To remove deeper levels, strike the handle of the chisel squarely with a mallet. Do this first at each end of the mortise, with the bevel facing the centre of the recess. The chisel will cut straight down. Then hold the chisel at a slight angle a little further in from the end and strike the chisel with the mallet. This will raise the waste from the bottom of the mortise. Lever out the waste and continue these steps until the required depth has been reached. If cutting a through mortise, work from both sides.

*Use a mallet to raise the waste from the bottom of the mortise.*

**3** Finally, finish the mortise by cutting it back to the required shoulder lines. Do this by paring away the waste to the end of the mortise using the technique shown in 'Paring vertically' opposite. It is important that you keep the chisel square during this process.

## Using gouges

Use gouges in the same way as chisels, ensuring that the cutting edge is sharp. Use the in-cannel gouge when you are trimming curved shoulders, and the out-cannel gouge for hollowing out shapes.

*Use an out-cannel gouge for hollowing out shapes.*

Turn to pages 156–7 to practise chiselling to make animal shapes.

*Examples of chiselled shapes – see pages 156–7 for instructions.*

# GROOVING

*Grooves are long narrow channels cut either along or across the grain. They can be used for joints that fit pieces of timber together or for decorative effect. Grooves are often used to hold drawer bottoms and cabinet backs.*

## Hand tools

Before power tools were introduced into the workshop, grooves were cut with a hand plough plane, or one of the more complex tools that derived from it, such as the combination plane (see page 75).

The plough plane has cutters ranging from 3–12mm (⅛–½in), which are held with a screw at the correct cutting angle. The tool is fitted with a depth gauge and a fence, which means that it will only cut straight grooves parallel to a given edge. The combination plane has features that make it suitable for tongue and groove work, while the multi-plane has extra cutters for mouldings.

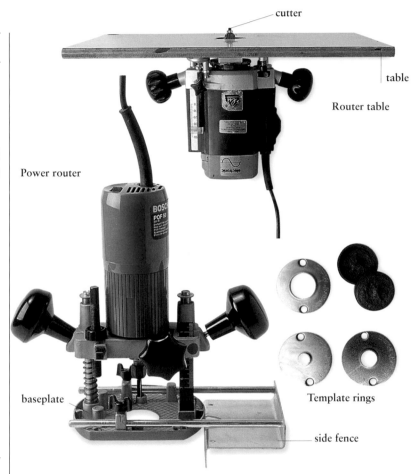

Power router

Router table

cutter

table

baseplate

Template rings

side fence

## Power tools

Good quality hand power routers can be used for carrying out grooving and operations such as rebating and moulding. For people starting out in woodwork, a small power router is ideal because it is more versatile than a plough plane.

### Power routers

**Power routers** consist of a motor held in a mounting, beneath which is fixed a collet to hold varying sizes of cutters.

The baseplate guides the tool over the work surface and is fitted with cramps for securing rods and accessories. The depth stop is used to adjust the projection of the cutter from the baseplate, while the handles are used to steer the tool.

Most large routers work by a plunging action. The motor body rises and falls on a pair of columns and the cutter is plunged into the timber, before being retracted at the end of the job. The motor size varies but all routers give a speed without

load of between 22,000 and 27,000 rpm. However, because the speed drops as soon as the cutter touches the work, high-powered motors are preferable for high-quality finishes.

The collet accepts the shank of the router cutter and can be found in several sizes. The lightest routers have collets of either 6 or 8mm (¼ or ⅜in) in diameter, while larger machines have a capacity of 12mm (½in). The larger the collet capacity, the larger the size of cutters that can be fitted.

*Groove-forming cutters*

*V-grooving cutters*

*Plug cutter    Dovetail    Combined
            cutter      cutter*

*Edge-forming cutters*

## Router cutters

While high-speed steel cutters are adequate for most jobs, tungsten-tip cutters maintain their sharpness for longer. However, when these cutters do need sharpening, they must be sent to a specialist. There is a wide range of cutters available,

and these can be categorized as either groove-forming (straight) or edge-forming (moulding).

**Groove-forming cutters** come in a range of styles. Straight cutters cut square grooves, while V-grooving cutters create a V-shaped indent, largely for decorative work. Veining and core-box cutters produce round-bottomed grooves, while a dovetail cutter is used for dovetail housings and joints.

**Edge-forming cutters** can have pin- or ball-bearing race guides. The latter is preferable as it reduces the risk of damage along the edge of the timber. The most common types are rebate, chamfer, rounding and trimming varieties. For shaping edges, cove, ogee and beading cutters create decorative edges along the timber.

## Router table

One main advantage of the router is that it can be mounted upside down in a frame so that the cutter projects from the surface, with safety fences in place. This is a very useful and safe way of working. Instead of taking the router to the work, the timber is fed over the router, in the direction of the cutter.

Proprietary **router tables** can be bought, but you can also make one using material such as plywood. Cut and construct a

*Construct a homemade router table.*

box with one open side so that the router is readily accessible. Cut a hole in the top of the box for the cutter to protrude through and fix the router baseplate in the box, directly below the hole in the top.

### Biscuit jointers

Even though the furniture maker can use the jointing methods described previously, if you need to make a lot of cabinets or boxes, the biscuit jointer is a very useful tool.

The **biscuit jointer** is a small circular saw that cuts slots into both faces of a joint. A timber oval – the biscuit – available ready-made of compressed beech, is inserted into the slots. The biscuit joint is often used in place of tongues and grooves or dowel joints and can even replace some traditional cabinet- and drawer-making joints.

The biscuit jointer can make butt joints, both from edge to face and from edge to edge, as well as mitre joints. It can also be used to cut small grooves and to trim panel edges.

Biscuit jointer

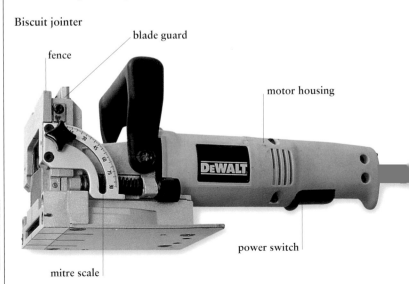

fence

blade guard

motor housing

power switch

mitre scale

## Dust extraction

Routers produce a lot of very fine dust, so try to have some form of extraction system as you work. Many machines have a facility for attaching extraction tubes, so take advantage of this whenever possible. You should always wear safety glasses and a dust mask is also advisable.

## Cutting housings

Provided the router is fitted with sharp cutters, the action of routing across the grain – cutting a housing – is very similar to that of routing with the grain. However, you may encounter problems with certain types of grain as an open texture or dry timber may split or chip easily. In this case it may be necessary to work to a marking knife line, although this should not normally be necessary.

## Safety first

• The router is generally a very safe machine, but remember always to keep your hands away from moving cutters.

• Always switch the machine off and wait for it to stop completely before laying it down on a bench.

• If you need to make adjustments, disconnect the machine from the main power supply.

• Wear safety glasses and a dust mask, and secure your work.

## Using a power router

Compared with some tools, power routers are relatively safe to use, provided you maintain them properly and follow the manufacturer's instructions.

### Fitting a cutter

When fitting a cutter into a collet, first unplug the router from the electrical supply.

1  Lock the spindle, using either the button provided, or the metal rod that passes through a hole in the spindle. Some routers have two spanners – one for the spindle and one for the collet nut.

2  Use a spanner to loosen the nut and unscrew the collet.

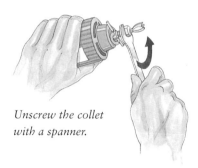

*Unscrew the collet with a spanner.*

3  Insert the cutter into the collet, carefully pushing it home into position. Be careful not to cut your fingers.

*Insert the cutter with the retaining nut into the collet.*

4  Then, tighten the collet nut using the spanner and unlock the spindle.

5  Use your fingers to check that the cutter is tight. Test run the router, so that it gains full speed for 5–10 seconds. Turn off the router and recheck the cutter.

### Cutting grooves with a side fence

To produce a straight, grooved line, parallel with the edge of the timber, use a side fence. This should be positioned to the right side of a clockwise-rotating cutter, so that the force of the blade does not pull the fence too much towards the work. It is a good idea to test run a scrap piece of timber first before routing your work.

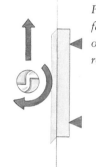

*Position the fence to the right of the clockwise-rotating cutter.*

1  Choose the required cutter for the job and insert it into the tool as explained above.

2  Adjust and lock the fence in the correct position.

3  Set the depth of cut so that the cutter will only plunge as far as you require. In many instances, it is better to make deep cuts in small stages. This will help to prolong the life of the cutter and prevent the machine from over-heating.

4  Hold the router firmly, using both handles. Switch on the machine, with the router motor in position above the base. Twist the locking handle to unlock the router body and plunge the cutter into the work to the preset depth. Lock the router into position.

*Cut a groove, using a router and side fence.*

5  Continue the cut to the end of the piece of timber. To make a stopped groove, plunge the router at the start mark, guide the tool until the cutter reaches the end mark, and release the plunge mechanism.

### Cutting a groove using guide battens

Guide battens can be used for making grooves that are some distance from the edge of the timber. You can use any straight pieces of timber that are long enough to project beyond the start and finish marks of the groove.

1  Using G-cramps, fix the guide battens to the work. The cutter needs to line up with the centre of the router base, so that the groove will end up being midway between the battens.

2  Select the required cutter and fit it carefully into the power router.

3  Plunge the router and cut as before. Remove the battens when finished.

*Cut a groove, using a router and side battens.*

## Cutting edge mouldings

Edges are moulded for decorative effect or to soften sharp corners.

1 Select the required cutter and insert it in the collet. Use moulding cutters with a bearing at the tip, rather than a simple steel tip, as this reduces the risk of burning the timber.

2 Fit the fence securely, bearing in mind that the cutter will tend to draw the fence to the edge.

3 Cramp the work to the bench as shown below, ensuring that nothing is obstructing the fence.

*The edge to be moulded needs to overhang the bench sufficiently.*

4 Plunge the router to the correct depth, lock and start the motor. Bring the cutter up to the edge of the timber and, holding the fence or bearing against the work, cut the moulding, moving from left to right.

## Routing with a template

In addition to using fences and battens, shaped edges and internal shaping can be carried out using a template. Most routers have a collar or ring that can be fixed to the tool's faceplate, which will act as a guide when using a template. The diagram shows a section of the collar and the cutter, and how the aperture along the edge and inside the template has to account for the differences in diameter. For example, a 10mm (³/₈in) cutter with a 16mm (⁵/₈in) outside diameter collar will need the template cut 3mm (¹/₈in) bigger than the finished cut out.

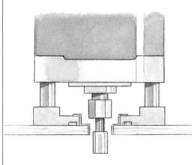

*The collar and template.*

1 Mark a template on a piece of 6mm (¹/₄in) medium density fibreboard. Draw out the whole pattern that you want to reproduce, with the outer line representing the edges of the final job. Remember you can cut shaped external or internal edges. Now measure the cutter and the collar to determine the differences in diameter, as described above.

2 Make the template, cutting as closely as you can to your second line with a bandsaw or jigsaw. Finish off with a rasp, file or sandpaper.

3 Fix the template in position. If the surface has not been finished, you can use pins to secure it. If any finish or veneer

has been applied, use double-sided tape. In some instances, depending upon the desired shaping, it may be possible to use G-cramps.

4 Switch the router on and plunge the cutter to the required depth; guide the collar against the template as you rout around the edges.

## Cutting joints

The router is a versatile tool that can be used to cut many types of joints – even some of the complex ones such as mortise and tenons and dovetails. Unless you need to cut a vast number of joints, these can be done by hand. However, any joints based on rebates and grooves, such as tongue and groove, lap and housing joints (both barefaced and dovetail) are very suitable for the router.

## Using a biscuit jointer

The instructions below show you how to make a simple butt joint.

1 Set the cutting depth to suit the biscuits you are using, and adjust the fence so that the blade aligns with the centre line on the first component. Press the fence against the work.

2 Start the machine and plunge the blade to make a cut. Use the same procedure to cut the rest of the slots. Then cut those on the edge of the second component.

3 To assemble the joint, spread adhesive into the slots and insert the biscuits. The adhesive will make the biscuits swell, producing a very strong joint. You will need to work rapidly to apply the adhesive, insert the biscuit and cramp the joint.

**Expert tip**

When moulding the edges of solid timber panels, particularly across the grain, there may well be some breakout at the end of the pass. For this reason, use the tool on the two sides of the end grain first. Then, as you mould the long sides, this breakout should be removed.

Turn to pages 158–9 where the hot plate stand will give you practice in grooving.

**Machine tools**

A machine tool equivalent of the power router is a large industrial machine with a fixed head containing the motor with larger capacities and speeds. Nowadays the hand power tools are so efficient that you may never need to investigate the machine alternative. Another industrial machine is the spindle moulder, and again the power router is so efficient for most purposes that this industrial equivalent will not be necessary.

# SHAPING

*The ability to shape curved surfaces and edges moves furniture away from the solely functional. When you want to introduce a freer approach to your work, you will need to use the tools and techniques described in this section.*

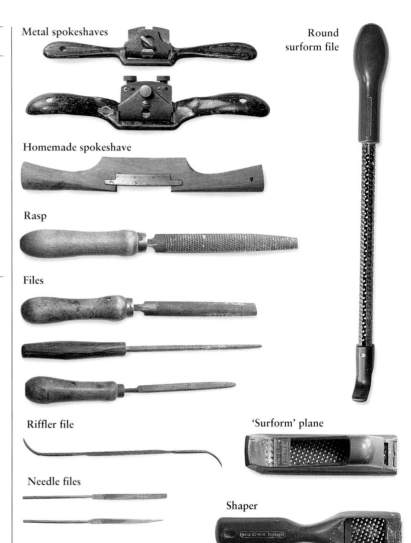

Metal spokeshaves

Homemade spokeshave

Rasp

Files

Riffler file

Needle files

Round surform file

'Surform' plane

Shaper

## Using a second-cut file

The distribution and size of teeth on rasps and files determine the degree of coarseness – or cut – of the tool. A bastard cut is the coarsest, a smooth cut is the finest and a second cut is in between the two.

## Drawknives

A traditional tool used by chairmakers, wheelwrights or coopers, drawknives have similarities with axes, and remove timber very quickly. They do not produce a very refined finish, and are most suitable for initial shaping before using a plane or spokeshave. The tools are now not really in general use, and tend to be found only in specialized trades. The one pictured here is a curved drawknife.

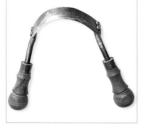

## Shaping tools

Even though some work on convex and other curved surfaces can be carried out with planes and chisels, narrow edges require a smaller tool to prevent slipping. Spokeshaves are ideal for such work. Rasps and files are also used for shaping work, particularly when curves are tight.

### Spokeshaves

Although spokeshaves are ideal for shaping, they can be quite difficult to control and will require some practice. There are two main types – one for convex shapes and the other for concave. Spokeshaves are usually made of metal but, traditionally, furniture makers would have made their own tools from timber – normally beech – into which a metal blade was then fitted.

**Round-face spokeshaves** have convex blades that are ideal for use on timber with a concave face. The blade is held in position by a cap iron, and the depth of the blade can be adjusted by loosening this cap and jiggling the blade into the required position. Alternatively, some spokeshaves have screws at the top two corners of the blade, which can be loosened and tightened for making precise adjustments.

**Flat-face spokeshaves** are the same as round-face versions, except that they have flat, narrow faces. This feature of the tool makes it suitable for skimming a convex curve.

A **half-round spokeshave** has a deep, concave blade and face, and is suitable for rounded tables and chair legs.

A **chamfer spokeshave** can be used to cut bevels up to 38mm (1½in) wide.

A **combination spokeshave** is dual-purpose, and has both a straight and half-rounded blade. It is useful on work with a range of surfaces, as it saves constantly changing blades as you move from one area to another.

## Rasps and files

Most commonly used by carvers for initial shaping, rasps and files also remove a lot of material. Rasps produce a fairly rough surface, which then needs to be smoothed with a file. The teeth on rasps range from coarse to quite smooth, and the tool is available in flat, round (rat tail) and, most usefully, half-round shapes.

**Files** are much finer than rasps and help to remove roughened timber left by the other tool. For a finer finish, they can be used with abrasive paper wrapped around them. **Riffler files** are designed for use in tight curves, while **needle files** are used for metalwork and are useful when adapting fittings such as hinges.

**'Surform' tools** are available in a range of plain or file types. The main difference lies in their carefully punched teeth, which enable timber shavings to pass through the metal. This means that the tool can move over the timber surface more quickly, because it is less inclined to get clogged. The most commonly used surform tools are the flat surform file and the round surform file.

## Adjusting the blade on a spokeshave

1  Remove the blade by undoing the locking screw on the cap iron. Sharpen the blade by grinding and honing, as required (see pages 72–3).

2  Carefully reposition the blade ground-side down and tighten the lead screw. If this screw is the sole means of adjustment, tighten the blade gradually and position the blade with your fingers until it protrudes at the correct depth. If the tool has adjustment screws, use these to achieve a more precise setting.

*Adjust the blade in the spokeshave to the desired projection.*

## Using a spokeshave

Effective shaping with a spokeshave can take time to master. It pays to practise on waste timber, before attempting a job on a piece of furniture. Keep the cutting edge of the blade sharp to ensure the best results, and remember to adjust the position of the blade to vary the depth of cut as required.

1  Secure the work in a vice. Hold the tool with both hands, so that your fingers curl over the front of the handles, and your thumbs rest at the back.

*Secure the work in a vice and hold the spokeshave with both hands.*

2  Rest the tool on the work and move it forwards and backwards, so that the blade cuts a shaving. Work in the direction of the grain, changing the position of the timber in the vice as you go, if necessary.

## Using rasps and files

There are frequently occasions when curves are so tight that edge tools are not suitable for the job. In these instances, it is best to use a file or rasp.

1  Fit a handle to the rasp or file. If possible, secure the work in a vice before you start. Use your spare hand to hold the timber securely, preferably with your fingertips near the area to be filed, to maximize the pressure.

2  Hold the rasp firmly with your dominant hand and apply forward pressure in order to cut away the timber.

*Cut away the timber with a rasp.*

3  After making a series of rough cuts with the rasp, use a timber file in order to remove some of the rough surface.

4  Then finish off the job with abrasive paper wrapped round a file or a piece of hardwood in order to achieve a more refined finish.

### Cleaning rasps and files

When rasps and files become clogged, use the wire bristles on a file cleaner – or file card – to loosen the shavings. Then remove the shavings with the coarse fibre brush on the other side of the file cleaner.

# DRILLING

*In woodwork and furniture making, you often need to make holes, either to use with special saws or to insert a range of screws, dowels and other fittings. It is important to be able to drill accurately to a specific depth and angle.*

## Hand tools

With the advent of the power drill, hand drills and braces are less commonly used today. However, they still have an important role to play in the woodworker's workshop.

A **bradawl** is a simple tool for marking pilot holes for small screws, or for creating the centre-mark for drilling.

A **gimlet** is similar to the bradawl, but it creates deeper holes by actually cutting into the timber.

### Hand drills

A **hand drill** is the simplest type of drilling tool. By operating the handle, a series of gear wheels rotates the chuck shaft. The drill bits, which are held in the chuck, are subsequently rotated. There are several types of drill bit that can be used in this tool and powered varieties to perform different functions.

## Drill bits

The following bits can be used in hand or powered drills. **Twist drills** come in a range of sizes. It can be difficult to drill precisely with these bits – they can easily move off course with the vibration of the tool. You could mark the drilling location with a bradawl, making a slight recess in the surface for the bit.

**Dowel bits** or centrepoint drills also come in a range of sizes

and have a point at the centre of the tip and two spurs. The centre tip can be placed exactly on the drill mark, and the two spurs help to prevent the bit from moving off course.

A **countersink bit** cuts a tapered recess around the main hole. This provides a useful home for the head of a screw, so that the top of the screw sits flush with the surface of the timber. This makes for a very clean and smooth finished look.

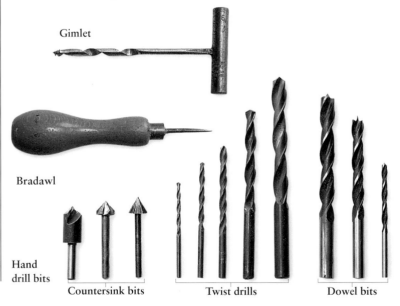

Gimlet

Bradawl

Hand drill bits

Countersink bits

Twist drills

Dowel bits

Hand drill

chuck

handle

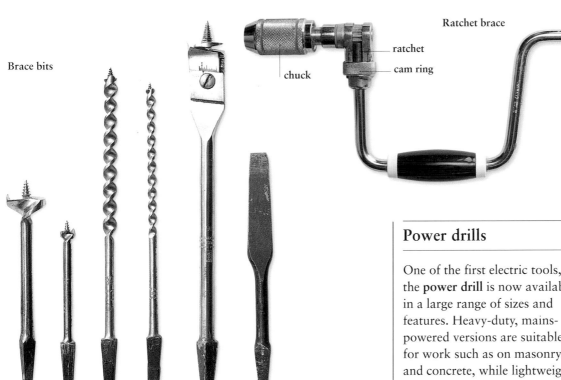

Brace bits

ratchet

chuck

cam ring

Ratchet brace

Centre bits    Auger bits    Expansion    Screwdriver
                              bit          bit

## Braces

A **brace** is also used to drill
holes, but the whole frame
of the tool is rotated in a
clockwise direction while
pressure is at the same time
applied to the rear, domed
handle. Most types of brace
have a ratchet mechanism, so
that the tool can be used in
restricted spaces. The chuck of a
brace has jaws that are designed
to house bits with square
shanks. However, some braces
can accept the same round-
shanked drill bits that are
used in power and hand drills.

## Brace bits

**Centre bits** come in a range
of sizes from 6–50mm ($\frac{1}{4}$–2in).
A single spur on one side of the
bit scores the edge of the hole.
Then the cutting edge on the
other side of the bit cuts into the
timber. A lead screw protruding
from the centre pulls the spur

and then the cutting edge into
the timber. This ensures that
a neat, crisp hole is made.

**Auger bits** are similar to centre
bits, but they cut deeper holes.
The long, spiral body behind the
cutting edge keeps the drill in
line and removes waste timber.

**Expansion bits** are similar to
centre bits, but have a cutter that
can be set to different diameters.
Available in two sizes, the total
cutting capacity ranges from
12mm ($\frac{1}{2}$in) to 75mm (3in).

**Countersink bits** work in the
same way as those for drills,
but they have square shanks to
fit in the brace chuck.

**Screwdriver bits** enable braces
to be used as a heavy-duty
screwdriver for long screws.
However, many people use
electric screwdrivers or light
power drills with screwdriver
fittings instead.

## Power drills

One of the first electric tools,
the **power drill** is now available
in a large range of sizes and
features. Heavy-duty, mains-
powered versions are suitable
for work such as on masonry
and concrete, while lightweight,
rechargeable types are ideal
for fine drilling, such as for
small screws.

Like hand drills, power drills
have a chuck that holds the
required bit. It is worth
remembering that the shank
of the bit corresponds with the
diameter of the hole that the bit
cuts. So large drills, which tend
to have a large chuck capacity –

### Safety first

- Wear safety glasses.
- Secure the work.
- Do not wear any loose clothing.
- Keep hands well away from drill bits.
- Tie back long hair securely.
- Always select the correct speed.
- Never use a tool to do a job for which it was not designed.
- Make sure that you use sharp drill bits.
- Never force the tool – let the bit do the work.

torque selector

keyless
chuck

trigger

forward/reverse
switch

battery pack

Cordless
power drill

97

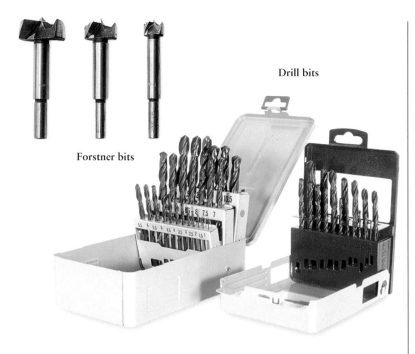

Forstner bits

Drill bits

up to 12mm (½in) – can take
larger bits, which means that
they are capable of drilling
larger holes. Smaller, lighter
drills have less chuck capacity
and are used for smaller holes.

Most drills come with a speed
selector. Some larger drills
have a hammer action, which
is useful when fixing battens
onto masonry walls.

## Power drill bits

There is a wide range of
drill bits available.

**Twist** and **centrepoint drill
bits** are the same as those
used for the hand drill although,
if they are to be used on
metal at any stage, it is worth
investing in high-speed steel
types. Large twist drills are
made with reduced shanks,
so they can fit in standard
power drill chucks.

**Spade bits** have long points
for positioning on the exact
centre of the hole mark. This is
especially helpful when you are

drilling at an angle to the face
surface as the point prevents the
drill from wandering.

**Forstner bits** are high-quality
drill bits that have a special
serrated ring around the main
point. These teeth help the bit to
stay on course, boring through
difficult areas and preventing
knots from deflecting the drill.

**Countersink bits** with reduced
shanks (again designed to fit
ordinary power drills) are also
available, as are drill-and-
countersink bits, which produce
both a hole and countersink in
one action.

**Drill-and-counterbore bits**
perform similar actions to the
drill-and-countersink bit, except
that they also produce a neat
counterbored hole, which can
be plugged with a piece of
timber, to conceal the screw
beneath. To cut the plug, use
a plug cutter, which will cut
a cylindrical piece of timber
exactly the right size for the
hole made by the drill-and-
counterbore bit.

## Pillar drill

Sometimes known as a drill
press, the **pillar drill** is a heavy-
duty machine tool and is very
useful in the workshop. In fact,
unless you are planning to carry
out a lot of site work, a pillar
drill is probably the next step
after a small power drill, rather
than investing in a large tool
and separate stand. Pillar drills
can be either bench or floor
mounted, and are ideal for
precise, repetitive drilling.

The tool has an adjustable table
to accommodate a range of sizes
of timber, and a feed lever that
works in much the same way as
the lever on a vertical drill stand
(see box, left). A depth gauge can
be set to determine the depth
of the hole, while a guard helps
to prevent any obstructions
or clothing from getting in
the way of the rotating chuck.
Remember never to wear loose
clothing while you are using
a piece of machinery.

Pillar drill

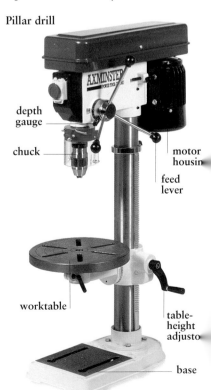

depth
gauge

chuck

motor
housin

feed
lever

worktable

table-
height
adjusto

base

## Using a hand drill

It is possible to use a hand drill from most positions. However, it is most common, and generally easier, to drill from a vertical position, so that you can apply a steady pressure to the rear handle.

1  Select the drill or bit you require. Open the jaws of the hand drill by holding the chuck with one hand and rotating the drive wheel anti-clockwise with the other. Or, some hand drill chucks are opened with a chuck key, just like power drills.

2  Insert the bit into the chuck and tighten the jaws, either by turning the drive handle clockwise or, if appropriate, tightening with the chuck key. Check that the bit is centred in the chuck jaws.

3  Mark the centre of the hole on the timber surface, preferably with crossed hairlines. Twist a bradawl on the exact centre of the mark, which will produce a starter hole.

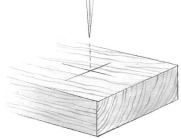

*Mark out the centre of the desired hole before you indent it with the bradawl.*

4  Put the tip of the drill on the starter hole. Bring the body of the drill to the correct angle – normally square with the face. Stand two try squares near the mark so that you can sight the drill bit to ensure accuracy.

*Rotate the hand drill's drive wheel.*

5  Hold the drill steady by applying a moderate amount of pressure to the rear handle. Begin to rotate the drive handle, so that the drill cuts into the surface. Continue rotating the handle while holding the drill steady and to the correct angle. You should not require a great deal of pressure or speed – experience will teach you how all the different timbers respond and how much pressure is required for each.

## Using a brace

1  Select the required bit for the job. Centre the cam ring so that the brace ratchet is locked in position. Then hold the chuck and rotate the frame clockwise, to open the jaws.

2  Insert the bit and tighten the jaws of the chuck by rotating the frame anti-clockwise. Ensure that the tapered shank of the bit is firmly in the chuck.

3  When you are drilling horizontally, place the work in a vice so that you are drilling at lower chest level.

4  To drill vertically, secure the work on the bench or in a vice. Hold the brace upright with one hand while you turn the brace with the other hand.

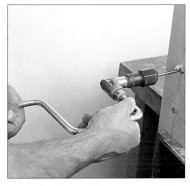

*Turn the frame of the brace steadily.*

5  Hold the brace steady. Most drills have a screw that pulls the bit into the work, so only the minimum amount of pressure is required. Turn the frame with your other hand, taking care to keep the tool level. Remember that the bits used in a brace are designed for slow and methodical cutting.

6  At the required depth, reverse the handle a couple of times to release the screw. Then gently pull the tool away from the hole, rotating the brace at the same time in order to clear the waste from the hole. If you are boring through holes, stop drilling as soon as the lead screw shows on the opposite side. Remove the brace and drill bit, as described, and then reverse the work to repeat the drilling from the other side.

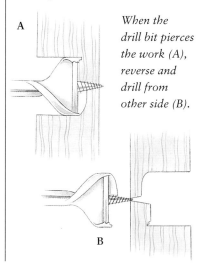

A

B

*When the drill bit pierces the work (A), reverse and drill from other side (B).*

**7** If there is not enough room to take a full sweep of the frame, set the cam ring on the ratchet. When the ratchet is set, it will turn the bit about one-quarter of a turn. Then reverse the handle direction and make another cut. This technique is useful when you are forced to work in confined spaces.

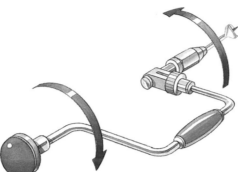

*Turn the ratchet brace with a quarter sweep to cut and then return.*

### Making a depth stop for a twist drill

Even though it is possible to buy metal depth stops for twist drills, it is very easy to make your own version. Take some square scraps of hardwood and drill a hole of the required size down the centre. Slip the timber over the drill bit, and mark the length of the hole required. Cut the timber on the mark. Slip the depth stop back on the drill and drill the hole until the stop touches the surface. You can keep several lengths of timber drilled to fit the drill sizes that you most commonly use so that you can cut suitable lengths when needed.

Now turn to pages 162–4 – the wine rack will be a good exercise to practise precise drilling.

*Homemade depth stops.*

## Using a power drill

Power drills are relatively easy to use – on timber there is less vibration than on materials such as concrete or masonry.

**1** Select the required bit and fit it into the chuck. This is usually done with a chuck key, in the same way as a hand drill, but some power drills have keyless chucks. Pull back the casing of the chuck, insert a bit with an appropriately grooved shank, to fit the type of drill, and release the chuck casing. The chuck will automatically grip the bit.

**2** Select the required speed on the drill. With some tools, the speed of the rotating chuck will depend on the amount of pressure applied to the trigger. Although knowledge of the desired speed comes with experience, it is generally best to have a fast setting for drilling holes in timber, and a slower speed for masonry.

**3** Hold the rear handle with your dominant hand and the secondary handle, if there is one, with the weaker hand. Stand comfortably with your body facing square to the work. Position the tip of the bit on the drill mark and pull the trigger.

*Position the drill bit and start to apply pressure to the trigger.*

**4** As the drill bit moves into the timber, keep the tool steady and at the required angle to the work.

**5** When you have achieved the depth of hole required, gently pull the tool away, with the bit still rotating, and release the trigger when the bit is clear of the work.

The power drill is used in a similar way when fitted with a screwdriver bit, although a slower speed is usually required to ensure accurate results. All power drills also have a reverse-action switch, so that the tool can be used both to tighten and loosen screws.

## Using the pillar drill

When using a pillar drill (see page 98), take extra care to hold the work securely. If possible, use G-cramps to hold it in position, and use a fence and end stop to drill identical holes in separate pieces of work.

**1** Select an appropriate bit and unlock the chuck of the drill with the chuck key. Insert the bit, tighten the chuck and be sure to remove the chuck key. It is extremely dangerous to leave the key in position when the machine is switched on.

**2** Lower the safety guard and switch the machine on. Holding the work securely, use the feed lever to lower the bit onto, and through, the timber. Keep your hands well clear.

**3** After you have achieved the required depth, use the lever to raise the bit. Once the bit is completely clear of the workpiece, you can turn off the machine.

# MAKING HALVING JOINTS

*Learning to make joints is a fundamental skill in woodwork, and marks the first step of proper construction. Halving joints are among the simplest of all the joints to make, although they still require accurate skills in measuring, marking, sawing and planing. They are used when two pieces of timber cross each other; the joint is made by removing half the thickness of the timber from each piece.*

## Types of halving joints

There are several types of halving joint. The most common that you might come across in your woodworking are described below.

**Cross halving joints** are used when two rails meet square to each other. It is usual for the vertical piece to look as though it continues through, but both halves are actually the same.

**Corner halving joints** are similar to cross halving joints, but the pieces meet at the corner, rather than in the main body of the rail, and may need additional reinforcement.

**Oblique halving joints** are made in a similar way to cross halving joints, but the cut-outs are set at an angle.

**'T' halving joints** are used when the end of a rail meets flush with the outside edge of another.

**Dovetail halving joints** are virtually the same as 'T' halving joints, but the pieces are cut to a specific dovetail shape – giving the joint additional strength.

Note that halving joints are not integral structural units and

so they will need to be secured either with adhesive or screws.

The illustrations show examples of halving joints where each joint is cut on the timber thickness. However you will find the joint is often cut the other way round for certain types of underframes – for example, on the small table project (see pages 178–81).

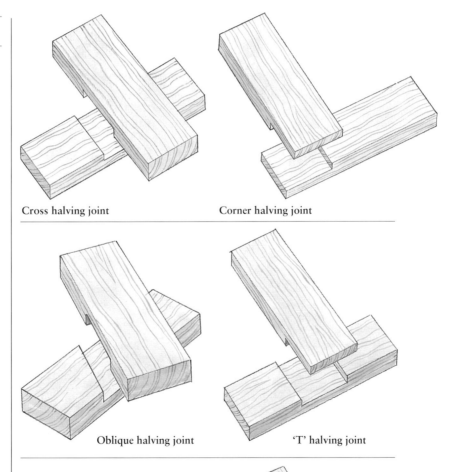

Cross halving joint

Corner halving joint

Oblique halving joint

'T' halving joint

Dovetail halving joint

**Making a cross halving joint**

**1** Take two pieces of timber of the same width and thickness and lay one across the other in the position of the finished joint.

**2** Use a try square and marking knife to mark the width of one piece on the face side of the other where the material will be removed, and square those lines half way down the edges. Repeat on the other piece. Note that the top half is removed from the first piece, while the bottom half is removed from the second.

*Mark the face sides.*

**3** Use a marking gauge, set to half the thickness of the timber, in order to scribe a line

in between the knife marks. Work from the face side of both pieces of timber.

*Gauge the edges.*

**4** Use a tenon saw to saw across the two shoulder lines down to the gauge line, working on the waste side of the lines.

**5** Make some extra saw cuts across the joint to make it easier to chisel out the waste.

*Make cuts across the grain to facilitate chiselling out waste.*

**6** Secure the piece in a vice or cramp. Pare away the waste across the grain until you have a flat surface. Chisel from both side edges to stop breakout and pare the shoulders of the joint to ensure a good fit.

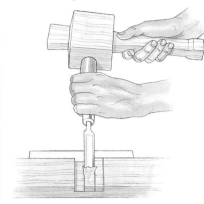

*Pare away the waste.*

**7** Repeat on the other piece. To ensure the joint is square and flush, dry test it before gluing the pieces and cramping them together.

*Dry test the halving joint.*

**Making corner or oblique halving joints**

A corner halving joint is made in the same way as a cross halving joint. However, all cuts can be made with a saw, so little chiselling should be required.

The photograph above right shows oblique corner halving joints. Exactly the same principles apply but the cross is angled rather than square.

*Dining table cross-rails made with a cross halving joint (see pages 218–22).*

*Oblique corner halving joints.*

## Making a 'T' halving joint

This joint is made in a similar way to the cross halving and corner halving joint.

**1** Put one timber piece in place on the other and mark its width. Mark the area to be cut out, including the depth.

**2** Measure and mark the end of the other butting piece, and use a marking gauge to mark the depth of cut on all three sides.

*Gauge and mark the depth of cut.*

**3** Saw away any excess from the lower cross piece, then use a chisel to cut the timber to depth.

**4** Secure the butting piece in a vice and saw down the gauged line, before you cut across the shoulder.

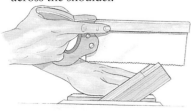

*Saw down the gauged line.*

## Making a dovetail halving joint

Although the principle behind this halving joint is similar to that of a 'T' halving joint, this joint requires very precise measuring and setting out. If possible, use a template for accurate results.

**1** Measure and mark out the butting piece, preferably using a template for the dovetail shape.

*Use a template to mark out the dovetail shape.*

**2** Cut out the dovetail with a saw.

**3** Trace the cut dovetail on the face side of the cross piece and square the lines down the edges. Gauge the depth of the joint. Use the dovetail as a template for drawing the area to be removed on the cross member.

*Draw around the dovetail shape.*

**4** Cut the halving across the angled lines with a tenon saw down to the gauge lines.

**5** Chisel away the material until the two pieces fit snugly.

*Trivet made with oblique halving joints (see pages 168–9).*

# MAKING MORTISE AND TENON JOINTS

*The mortise and tenon is generally a joint between a vertical piece, a stile or a leg,*

*and a horizontal piece, a rail. When glued, it makes a very strong structural unit.*

*The two components are usually the same thickness and both mortise and tenon*

*are one-third of that thickness. The tenon can travel right through the vertical*

*piece, a through joint, or be stopped within its width, a stopped joint.*

## Through mortise and tenon joints

Through joints are mainly used for decorative effect. The tenon on the end of the rail projects right through the stile or leg and shows on the outside. It can be wedged from the outside for extra strength.

## Wedged through mortise and tenon joints

Through joints can be strengthened by inserting wedges in the end of the tenon. This forces the tenon to splay and lock tight in the mortise.

## Loose-wedged through mortise and tenon joints

This is an old joint that is used on benches and tables. It can be assembled dry and therefore can be pulled apart and put back together – a knock-down capability.

## Stopped mortise and tenon joints

If a through mortise and tenon joint is not required, and this will be true in many

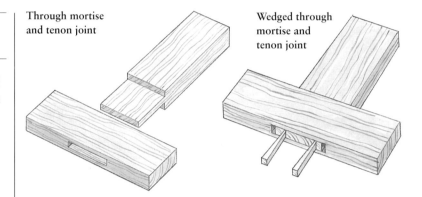

Through mortise and tenon joint

Wedged through mortise and tenon joint

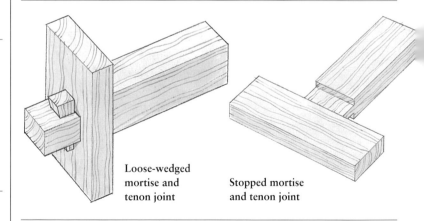

Loose-wedged mortise and tenon joint

Stopped mortise and tenon joint

frames, a stopped mortise and tenon joint can be used instead. In this type of joint, the tenon and mortise stop short of the outside face. This is the most common type of mortise and tenon joint. It is usually strong, but for extra strength it can be fox wedged – wedges can be inserted into the mortise and tenon joint before it is closed.

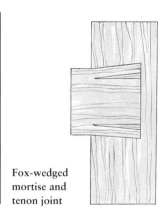

Fox-wedged mortise and tenon joint

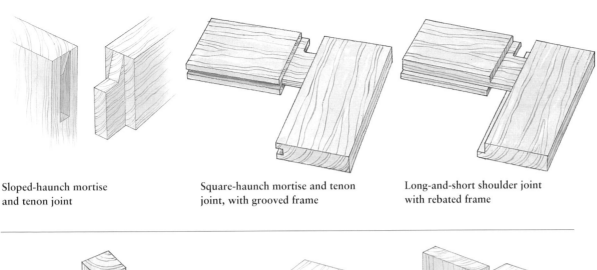

Sloped-haunch mortise
and tenon joint

Square-haunch mortise and tenon
joint, with grooved frame

Long-and-short shoulder joint
with rebated frame

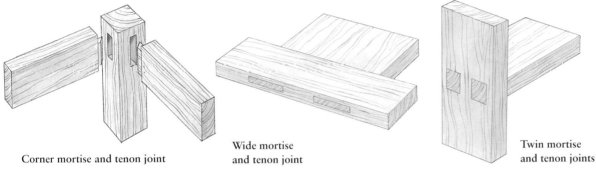

Corner mortise and tenon joint

Wide mortise
and tenon joint

Twin mortise
and tenon joints

## Sloped-haunch mortise and tenon joints

When the top of a stile has to be level with the outside face of a rail, the tenon will only usually be two-thirds the width of the rail. With a simple tenon, the rail could break away from the stile at the top. Therefore, to give the mortise and tenon as much contact as possible, an angled haunch is made to help keep the rail in line but this does not show on the top surface.

## Square-haunch mortise and tenon joints

This kind of joint is used where the components are either grooved or rebated. When making a frame with a groove on the internal edges, the groove is normally worked the whole way along each edge. Therefore the

haunch of the tenon must be square, thus filling the outside end of the joint and the groove.

## Long-and-short shoulder mortise and tenon joints

This joint is also used for grooved or rebated components. In traditional cabinet making the rebate is made before the tenon is cut. When making a frame with a rebate, one shoulder of the tenon needs to be long in order to reach across the rebate into the mortise and the other needs to be short to sit against the top of the rebate. In this situation it is possible to make a square top on the haunch.

## Corner mortise and tenon joints

When two rails join together at the top of a leg the mortises will intersect at the centre

point. Therefore the end of the tenons are cut at an angle so that they do not foul each other when the piece is assembled.

## Wide mortise and tenon joints

Sometimes in a frame a rail has to be quite wide and it will weaken the joint too much to have one wide tenon going into a wide mortise. Therefore, two tenons and two mortises are made so as to retain the strength in the stile or leg. This joint can be through as well as stopped.

## Twin mortise and tenon joints

On wide, thick components, the two mortises and tenons sit side by side rather than in vertical alignment as they are in the previous joint. This joint can be through as well as stopped.

# Making a through mortise and tenon joint

When making a mortise and tenon joint, it is best to start by making the tenon and then the mortise. Mark all the lines to be cut with a knife and gauge. Other marks can be made with a pencil.

### Marking the tenon

1 With the rail length slightly over size, mark the shoulders all round with a knife. Then mark the length of the tenon plus 3mm (1/8in) waste.

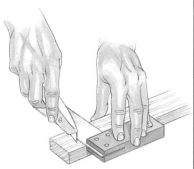

*Mark out the shoulders and length of the tenon.*

2 Set a mortise gauge to the exact width of a mortise chisel, which is close to one-third the thickness of the timber.

3 Gauging from the face sides, mark the thickness of the tenon from the shoulder lines towards the end of the rail, using a mortise gauge. Ensure that the mortise marks are in the centre of the rail.

*Mark the thickness of the tenon with a mortise gauge.*

4 Cut the tenon to length and mark across the end with the mortise gauge.

*Cut the tenon to length and mark out the end.*

5 If the tenon is to have a haunch or side shoulders, mark these on the face of the rail.

*Mark out the waste area of the tenon with a pencil.*

### Cutting the tenon

Place the work in the vice and make the following cuts with the tenon saw, ensuring that your saw is just on the waste side of the line.

1 With the tenon upright make some careful cuts across the end grain to a depth of about 3mm (1/8in).

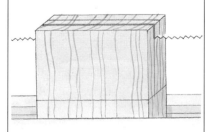

*Make a series of careful cuts across the end grain.*

2 Now reposition the rail and saw at a 45-degree angle from the first cut down the tenon, stopping short of the shoulder line.

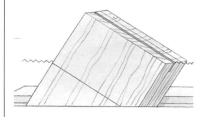

*Make the first cut and stop just short of the shoulder line.*

3 Turn the tenon around and saw down the other side. This will give you sawn lines across the top and down both sides. Secure the rail vertically in the vice and saw directly down to the shoulder line.

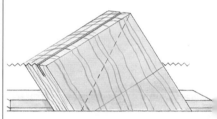

*Turn the tenon round and cut from the other side.*

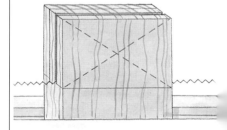

*Make the final cut and remove the waste from each side.*

4 When both sides of the tenon have been cut, lay it flat against a bench hook. Saw across the shoulder line with a tenon saw in order to remove the waste from each side of the tenon.

*The finished tenon.*

## Marking the mortise

1  Mark the position and width of the mortise all round. Use a pencil initially to mark all round the stile.

2  If the stile is the same thickness as the rail use the mortise gauge as already set to scribe the mortise on the face side.

3  If the stile is thicker than the rail, reset the mortise gauge so that it marks the mortise in the centre and mark on the joint face.

4  In this situation most tenons will have shoulders all the way round. The shape of the mortise will therefore need to account for this. With this in mind, mark the actual width of the mortise with a cut line on both the mating and outside surfaces of the piece of timber.

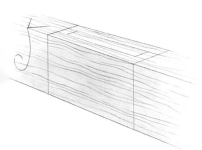

*Mark out the mortise, ready to be cut.*

### Cutting the mortise

1  To cut the mortise, start approximately 3mm (⅛in) from the cut lines at each end, which indicate the mortise's true width, and make a series of cuts in the timber using a mortise chisel to about 3mm (⅛in) deep.

*Make a series of cuts in the mortise using a chisel.*

2  Remove the waste from your first series of cuts.

3  Make several more cuts and remove the waste until you get approximately half to two-thirds of the way through the piece.

4  Turn the piece of timber over and start to cut from the other side.

5  Make a series of further cuts until the two parts meet in the middle.

6  Pare the faces within the mortise, if required.

7  Pare the ends of the mortises back to the cut line from both sides.

If you are making a stopped mortise rather than a through mortise, you will need to stop chiselling when you reach the required depth (see page 108).

*Bench constructed with mortise and tenon joints (see pages 257–65).*

## Choosing the best method

There is little to distinguish between different methods of cutting a mortise – it is a matter of preference. However, the methods using the mortise chisel are suitable if you only have a few mortises to cut. The drilling method has great advantages where you have a pillar drill or drill in a drill stand and have a lot of mortises to cut. Square mortise drill attachments are also available for pillar drills.

## Alternatives for cutting the mortise

There are alternative ways to cut a mortise.

Using only a mortise chisel, start from the centre of the mortise and take a series of cuts so that you make a 'V' in the centre of the mortise; then turn the chisel round and cut out the edges. Always leave the final cut to the end of the mortise until the rest has been cleared of waste.

*Cut a central 'V' in the mortise with a chisel.*

Alternatively, the bulk of the material can be removed from the mortise using a drill. It is best to use a pillar drill or drill in a stand. Set a guide on the drill table and drill a series of holes along the mortise; then use a mortise chisel at the ends, and a wider paring chisel to true up the inside faces of the mortise.

*Chisel away the waste from the mortise after drilling a series of holes.*

## Making a wedged through mortise and tenon joint

A wedged through mortise and tenon joint is made in a similar way to a through mortise and tenon joint. Note that the tenons are marked and cut over length so that the projection can be planed flush with the outside face after assembly. Adapt the basic method as follows.

1  Make saw cuts in the end of the tenon that are two-thirds the length of the tenon.

2  Slightly enlarge the mortise aperture from the outside face, by 3–5mm (1/8–3/16in) at each end, to about two-thirds the width.

3  Make the wedges. Fit the joint and glue and cramp it before driving the wedges into position. The cramps can be removed after the joint has been wedged if you prefer.

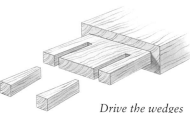

*Drive the wedges into the saw cuts in the tenon.*

## Making a loose-wedged through mortise and tenon joint

A loose-wedged mortise and tenon joint is made in the same way as a through mortise and tenon joint, but the proportion of the tenon has to allow for the removable wedge. Therefore, it needs to project out of the mortise some distance.

1  Make a hole in the tenon ensuring that its position will enable the wedge to tighten the joint. The outside edge of this

hole or mortise must be at the same bevel as the wedge.

2  Make the wedge and, when the joint is cramped, tap it into the joint. As the wedge is driven in, the tenon is pulled forward and secured in place.

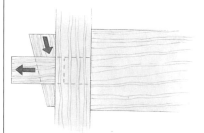

*Tap the loose wedge into the mortise and tenon joint.*

## Making a stopped mortise and tenon joint

All the steps are similar to the description for a through joint as detailed above except:

1  The tenon will be shorter than the width of the piece into which the mortise is cut.

2  The mortise will be cut only to a specific depth – that is, approximately two-thirds of the rail's width.

### Making a sloped-haunch mortise and tenon joint

A sloped-haunch mortise and tenon joint is commonly used in constructions such as frames, where the outside rail is level with the top of the stile and you do not want the haunch to show.

1  Cut the mortise to match the full length part of the tenon, two-thirds the width of the rail. Make the space for the haunch by making two saw cuts at an angle from the top edge of the stile into the mortise.

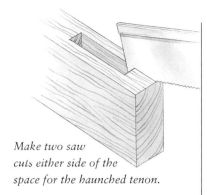

*Make two saw cuts either side of the space for the haunched tenon.*

**2** Pare away the waste timber from the mortise with a chisel.

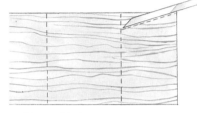

*Use a chisel to pare away the waste timber.*

**3** Cut a full tenon. Then saw the sloping haunch across from the outside edge to two-thirds the width. Finally cut along the tenon to remove the waste.

## Making a square-haunch mortise and tenon joint

When making a frame that has a groove on the internal face it is easiest to cut that groove right through from end to end; the square haunch is made so that it exactly fits the groove.

**1** Carefully mark out the square-haunch joint to allow for the groove. Remember that the mortise will be shorter than the width of the rail.

*Mark out the square-haunch mortise and tenon joint.*

**2** Cut the mortise as before.

**3** Mark and cut the square haunch on the tenon.

## Making a long-and-short shoulder mortise and tenon joint

Making a frame with a rebate on one face will require a tenon that has one shoulder shorter to fit on the top of the rebate. The longer shoulder fits into the mortise. The face of the tenon should line up with the face of the rebate because this makes for easier construction.

**1** Carefully mark out both the mortise and tenon of the long and short shoulder joint.

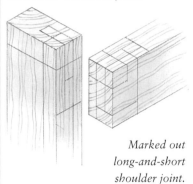

*Marked out long-and-short shoulder joint.*

**2** Cut the mortise as before.

**3** Cut the tenon with one long and one short shoulder to match the depth of the rebate.

## Making a corner mortise and tenon joint

A corner mortise and tenon joint is used when two rails meet a leg at the same level.

**1** When the mortises are cut, ensure they meet in the centre of the leg.

**2** When the tenons have been cut, make a 45-degree bevel on the end of each tenon, ensuring that they are cut the right way so that the mortise will be filled.

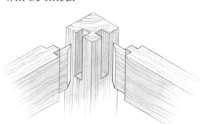

*Detail of the corner mortise and tenon joint.*

*Chair with stopped and through mortise and tenon joints (see pages 250–6).*

The small table on pages 178–81 was designed especially as an exercise in mortise and tenon joints. It is good practice and a lovely piece of furniture in its own right.

# MAKING HOUSING JOINTS

*Housing joints are grooves that are cut across the grain of the timber and are generally used when fixing intermediary shelves or dividers in cabinets. The through housing joint is the most common and easiest to make. The dovetail housing joint is more complex and requires more practice, but it is much stronger and more stable than the through joint.*

## Through housing joints

A **through housing joint** is simply a groove – or housing – that accepts the full thickness of the shelf or divider and shows on the front and the back edges.

## Stopped housing joints

The **stopped housing joint** is the same as the through housing joint, except that one end of it stops short and cannot be seen on the front edge of the side panel.

## Dovetail housing joints

In a **dovetail housing joint**, the end of the shelf is cut to a dovetail to run in the housing in the side panel.

Dovetail joints can show on the front but they are usually created as **stopped dovetail joints** – that is, cut short of the front edge so that the joint cannot be seen.

The dovetail can be on one side only – a **barefaced dovetail housing** – or on both sides.

When long housings are needed, a tapered dovetail housing joint is frequently

Through housing joint

Stopped housing joint

Through dovetail housing joint

Stopped dovetail housing joint

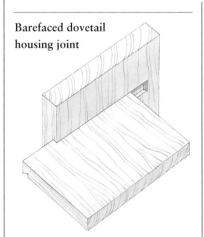

Barefaced dovetail housing joint

used so that the dovetail 'bites' in the last few millimetres or fractions of an inch.

## Cutting a stopped housing joint

**1** Start by marking out your guides on the inside face of the side to be housed. Use a marking knife to cut lines in order to indicate the desired position of the shelf – that is, the shoulders. Square these lines down the edge.

**2** Then, use a marking gauge to mark the depth of the housing – one-third the thickness is normal – and also the stopped part of the housing.

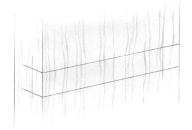

*Mark the position of the shoulders.*

**3** To cut the housing joint, chisel out a cut-out at the end of the stopped groove to the required depth. This will enable you to saw the groove from the rear.

*Chisel out the end to the required depth.*

*Saw the sides of the housing.*

**4** Chisel out the waste a little at a time across the grain down to the gauge line. Check the bottom for flatness.

**5** Now mark the end of the shelf using a marking gauge along the two faces and the front. Then you can gauge the waste at the stopped end.

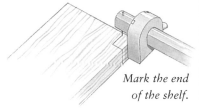

*Mark the end of the shelf.*

**6** Cut away the waste with a tenon saw and fit the joint. Adjust as required.

## Cutting a stopped, tapered dovetail housing joint

**1** Mark out the housing as for the previous joint.

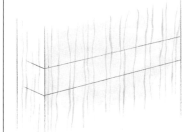

*Mark the shelf position in pencil.*

**2** Mark the dovetail on the edge with a sliding bevel. Mark the stopped end of the housing with a marking gauge. Mark the tapered and straight shoulders of the dovetail groove with a knife – a taper of about 3mm (⅛in) on the bottom; the top is usually square to the edge.

*Mark with a knife.*

**3** In order to be able to saw the joint, cut out a pocket at the end of the stopped groove to the required depth.

*Chop the front recess.*

**4** Saw the dovetail angle from the rear on the waste side of the shoulder lines. Place an extra saw cut in the centre to help remove the waste.

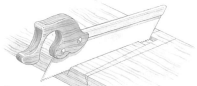

*Saw to the dovetail shape.*

**5** Now chisel out the waste by paring across the grain, taking care because the waste will be difficult to remove as it is wider than the top of the housing.

**6** Now mark shoulders for the dovetail on the shelf using a cutting gauge along the two faces. Use a pencil and square for the back edge.

**7** Gauge the stopped end. Then, mark the taper of the housing and, using the sliding bevel as set for the housing, mark the dovetail angles on the back edge of the shelf.

**8** Cut away the stopped part with a tenon saw. Then saw the shoulders and pare the dovetail angles across the grain.

**9** The shelf should now slide in smoothly from the back, making for a very sturdy and securely fitted joint.

*Slide the shelf into the housing.*

The small mirror and shelf on pages 174–7 is an ideal project to practise both housing joints and fretwork.

# MAKING DOVETAIL JOINTS

*The dovetail is considered to be the most beautiful of decorative joints. Fine craftworkers proudly use dovetail joints when making a piece of furniture to demonstrate the highest levels of their craftwork. So, in this case the joints should definitely be seen and the most common type is a through dovetail, possibly positioned on the corner of a cabinet or box.*

## Through dovetail joints

The **through dovetail joint** is the simplest of the dovetail joints, but still requires careful marking out and cutting. It is a traditional joint used for joining the ends of solid-timber pieces often on cabinets and other box constructions. The pins and the tails show on the outside faces.

## Single-lap dovetail joints

The **single-lap dovetail joint** is a common joint in cabinet making. It is mostly used for connecting drawer sides to a thicker drawer front – cases in which the dovetail joint is required for strength, but must not interfere with the finish of the piece. With the single-lap, the dovetails are visible on the sides, but the front piece stays complete and clean-looking.

## Double-lap and secret-mitre dovetail joints

Although great satisfaction can be derived from making double-lap and secret-mitre dovetails, the craftwork will never be seen unless it is a demonstration joint that will be taken apart.

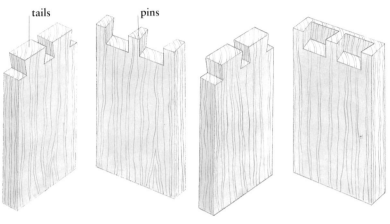

tails    pins

Through dovetail joint    Single-lap dovetail joint

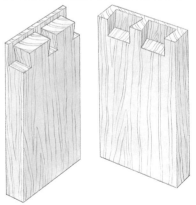
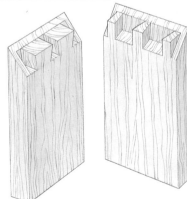

Double-lap dovetail joint    Secret-mitre dovetail joint

The growing use of routers, to make tongue and groove joints, and of the biscuit jointer, makes these joints an interesting, but not very practical option.

The **double-lap dovetail joint** is used on cabinets or boxes where you do not want the joint to be seen. You will only see a thin strip of end grain on one lap – either the tail or pin member.

The **secret-mitre dovetail joint** is often used in very fine woodworking and requires extremely careful marking out and cutting. In this instance, the dovetail joint is completely enclosed and will never be visible from the outside.

### Pins or tails first?

Some craftworkers prefer to cut tails first, but it is easier when making a double-lap dovetail or a secret-mitre dovetail to cut the pins and mark from them to the tail side. This description is for the latter method, but the step-by-step instructions for the small casket project (see pages 182–5) describe making the tail first and then marking the pin.

## Dovetail angles

The angle of the dovetail should not have too much slope; otherwise it will be weakened by short grain. Not enough slope will reduce the potential strength of the joint. Experience has shown that in hardwood the angle should be 1:8 and in softwood 1:6.

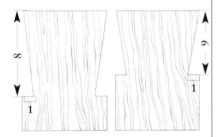

*Too much slope.    Too little slope.*

*Hardwood angle.    Softwood angle.*

## Making a through dovetail joint

There are different approaches to dovetailing. The main options are to mark and cut to the exact length of the dovetail as described here or to mark the length, but add an extra 2mm (¹⁄₁₆in) waste to be cleaned off.

1  Mark the lengths of the timber pieces, including the dovetail. Cut to length and carefully plane the ends straight and square on both halves of the joint.

2  Set the gauge to the thickness of the timber and mark out the shoulder lines on both of the pieces.

*Gauge the shoulder line.*

3  With a pencil, set out the pins on one piece to the required spacing and number. To do this, mark the full width of the first pin parallel to the edge (b). Divide the remaining width of timber into equal divisions (c).

4  Transfer these marks to the top edge and set out the wider ends of the pins (d). Set a sliding bevel to the required pitch (1:6 or 1:8) or use a dovetail template and mark the bevelled sides of the pins, back to the narrower ends, where the tails will fit (e). Make sure you mark the bevel on the end pin marked out in step 3 and that all the bevels slope the correct way.

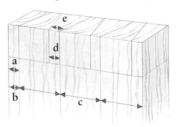

*Set out a dovetail joint – the pins must have bevelled lines either side of original squared back line.*

5  When you are satisfied, mark the pins on the end of the timber with a knife.

6  Using a knife and square, mark the pin sides down to the shoulder line. With a pencil, mark the areas to be removed.

*Mark the waste areas carefully, ready to saw.*

7  With a fine dovetail saw, saw down the waste side of the cut lines. Be sure to stop before you reach the shoulder line.

*Saw carefully down the marked out lines.*

8  Using a coping saw, remove most of the waste between the pins.

9  Pare right down to the shoulder line using a sharp chisel. After some practice, you will be able to pare from one side only, but when you are starting out, you may find it easier to pare from the shoulder lines on both faces.

10  Mark the tails from the pins. Lay the timber that will have the tails on the bench. Hold the pins upright in the correct position between the shoulder line and edge of the timber. Mark the tails using a knife or a scriber.

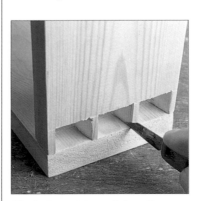

*Mark the positions of the tails by drawing around the pins with a knife or scriber.*

**11** Square the lines across the ends of each joint and use a pencil to mark out the waste (the pin areas).

*Square the lines across the ends of the joints.*

**12** Cut the tails carefully on the waste side of the cut mark.

**13** Remove the waste and pare between the tails as before.

## Making a single-lap dovetail joint

Since the dovetail in this joint is stopped short of the front face of the timber, you must chisel as well as saw to remove the waste.

**1** First, gauge the thickness of the side – the tail piece – on the inside face and edge. Then, you can mark out the dovetail pins using a sliding bevel or a dovetail template and a steel square.

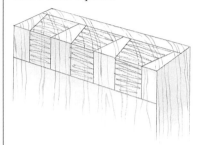

*Mark out the pins with due care and accuracy.*

**2** Next, place the timber in the vice and secure in place. Saw down the dovetail angle and the square line. Remember to make sure that you are sawing on the waste side of the cut line.

**3** Make some saw cuts in the waste area to relieve the timber and to make the process of chiselling easier.

*Saw out some narrow cuts, ready for paring.*

**4** Pare the waste at an angle from shoulder to shoulder, and then pare away the remaining waste in order to produce the dovetail socket.

**5** Mark the position of the tails from the pins, holding the pins upright between the shoulder line and edge of the timber. Then, cut the tails carefully on the waste side of your mark.

The small box on pages 182–5 is a good way for you to practise your dovetail joints.

*The simple through dovetail joint can be an attractive feature on wooden boxes – and, when cut to a bevelled edge as on this box (see pages 182–5), is also an impressive illustration of quality craftsmanship.*

# USING ABRASIVES

*You may produce a satisfactory surface with a plane or scraper but, in most cases, before you apply a finish, you will need to smooth with abrasive papers – sheets of paper with a variety of abrasive materials glued to the face to give a cutting surface.*

## Abrasive papers

There are different abrasive papers available, usually named from the type of abrasive grit that is used.

**Glasspaper** is used on softwoods but not usually in fine cabinet making.

**Garnet paper** is generally a reddish-brown colour with hard particles that form sharp cutting edges. It is a good general-quality abrasive.

**Aluminium-oxide paper** is harder than garnet paper, and is widely used as the abrasive sheet for power sanders.

**Silicon-carbide paper** is generally used for finishing metals or for smoothing paint surfaces between coats. It is usually lubricated with water and therefore called wet-and-dry paper. For woodwork a silicon-carbide paper dusted with zinc-oxide powder is used, with the powder acting as a lubricant. This gives a very good finish between coats when using lacquers and polishes.

## Grades of abrasive papers

You should always work from the coarser to the finer grades, the idea being that the next finer grade will remove the scratches caused by its rougher

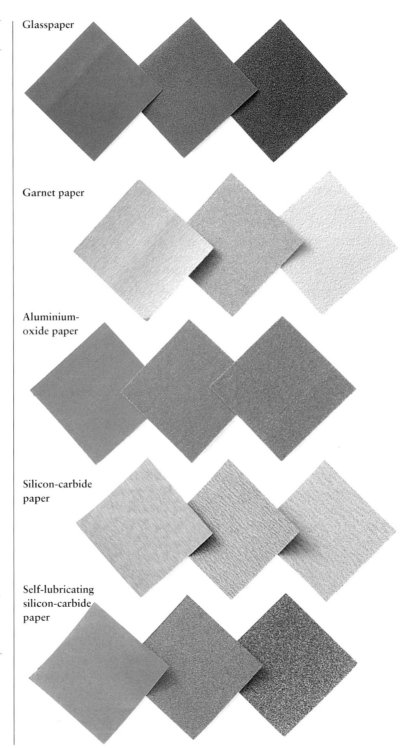

Glasspaper

Garnet paper

Aluminium-oxide paper

Silicon-carbide paper

Self-lubricating silicon-carbide paper

## De-nibbing

The coarser abrasive papers are used for smoothing the surface. The finer grades are used after a finish has been applied to remove any slight runs or blemishes in the finished surface. This is known in the trade as de-nibbing.

## Using wire wool

A small pad of very fine wire wool can be used after applying a finish, to obtain a final smooth surface or to apply a coat of wax polish for a surface that is attractive to touch. Dip the wire wool in the wax and apply with the grain. Finish with a soft cloth.

# SCRAPING

*On some timbers the grain will make it difficult to achieve a good finish with a plane and the final surface finishing will need to be carried out with a scraper. A scraper will take very fine shavings from difficult surfaces.*

## Scraping tools

The basic **cabinet scraper** is a thin rectangular sheet of tempered steel. It is very useful for finishing surfaces of irregular or interlocked grain where the cut of a plane is not fine enough.

Continued use of the scraper may cause your thumbs to become sore. If you have a lot of scraping to do, use a **scraper plane**. This is a cast metal tool with a double handle that holds a scraper blade in the right position and at the correct angle. While a cabinet scraper is sharpened on four edges, the blade for the scraper plane is generally sharpened on only one edge of the two long faces.

A **hook scraper** is a versatile tool that can be used instead of a scraper plane and will also remove paint or varnish.

Another useful tool is the **burnisher**. This is made from hardened steel with a round, oval or triangular section. It is used to form a burr on a scraper.

## Sharpening a scraper

The long edges of the scraper have to be sharpened to produce a burr that will remove small amounts of timber when pushed across the surface.

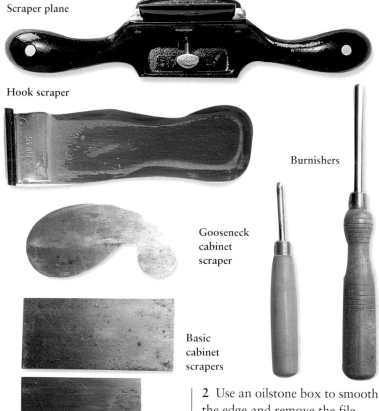

Scraper plane

Hook scraper

Burnishers

Gooseneck cabinet scraper

Basic cabinet scrapers

**1** Ensure that the edges of the scraper are square by drawing a file along the edge.

**2** Use an oilstone box to smooth the edge and remove the file mark. Simply place the edge of the scraper between the top and bottom parts of the oilstone box and move the scraper backwards and forwards a number of times.

*Square the edge of the scraper using a file.*

*Smooth the edge of the scraper in an oilstone box.*

**3** True the sides of the scraper on the stone to produce a perfectly square edge.

*True the sides of the scraper on the side of the oilstone box.*

**4** You now need to create a burr on the edge of the scraper. To do this, run a burnisher or a small gauge along the flat edge at an angle in order to create the burr.

*Create a burr on the edge of the scraper with a burnisher.*

**5** You will probably have to practise this technique a number of times in order to produce a satisfactory edge on the scraper.

**6** When using the tool, you will frequently have to reraise this cutting burr, so use the burnisher in order to flatten the edge of the scraper. Re-turn the edge over the face before starting the sharpening process again from the start.

*Burnish the edge of the scraper.*

*Re-turn the edge of the scraper.*

## Using a scraper

**1** Hold the scraper in two hands with the fingers positioned as shown. Bend the scraper slightly and, keeping it at an angle, carefully take thin shavings from the timber surface. The angle will depend on the burr and timber surface.

*Hold the scraper with both hands.*

**2** Cabinet scrapers usually have four edges on which burrs have been created, but if you are scraping a very hard timber with difficult grain you will have to resharpen your cabinet scraper quite frequently.

## Using a scraper plane

**1** First, take the blade out of the scraper plane so that you can sharpen it. Now, carefully work a burr on the edges of the blade, as described above.

*Work a burr onto the blade of the scraper plane.*

**2** When you are happy with the burr that you have produced, set the blade back into the scraper plane. Make sure that you allow the scraper to protrude just a little above the surface.

**3** Holding the two handles of the scaper plane, carefully scrape the tool over the timber surface until you achieve the desired finish.

*Carefully scrape the plane across the surface.*

**4** You will probably find that you have to sharpen the blade of your scraper plane frequently.

## Hammers and nails

Most cabinet making uses well-cut glued joints. However, a selection of hammers is useful for some joints and for building mock-ups.

The **cross-pein hammer** is a useful general hammer. It is good for tapping assemblies together or apart, will insert nails and larger pins and the pein end will start off small nails and pins. Hold the hammer at the end of the handle and ensure that its face hits the top of the pin vertically.

The **pin hammer** can be used for light work – to drive small nails, panel pins or veneer pins.

*Use a pin hammer to drive in a small pin, held in place with some paper.*

The **claw hammer** is normally used by carpenters and woodworkers because it performs two functions. The round flat head is used to drive in nails while the claw at the back is used to remove nails when necessary. Always use a piece of waste timber under the head when removing nails to protect the surface of the work.

**Pincers** are also used to remove nails and pins before they have been driven home; again protect the surface of the work when using pincers.

A **nail punch** is used to drive pins under the surface of the work, enabling the small hole to be filled.

*Hammer a small pin using a nail punch so that the timber is not damaged.*

## Pins and nails

Nails are seldom used in fine cabinet making except perhaps when making moulds and jigs. However, small pins are often used – either veneer pins or panel pins. Their heads are punched below the timber surface so the hole is filled.

Claw hammer

Pin hammer

Cross-pein hammer

Pincer

Club hammer

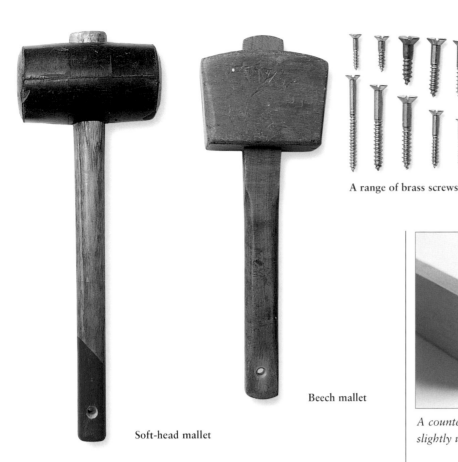

Soft-head mallet

Beech mallet

A range of brass screws      A range of metal screws

*A countersunk screw sits flush or slightly under the timber surface.*

## Mallets

A **beech mallet** – or carpenter's mallet – is used with firmer and mortise chisels to protect their wooden handles and during some assembly operations.

The **soft-head mallet** is used for light work and the **club hammer** for heavier assembly work.

## Screws

Screws are essential to woodworking and you will find a good range available. Screws come in different metals, with steel and brass being the most commonly used for fine woodwork. The conventional screw has a head, a shank and a thread.

head

shank

thread

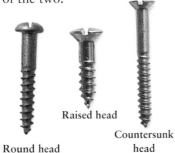

Round head

Raised head

Countersunk head

The growth in the use of particle and fibre boards has seen the introduction of the twin-thread screw where a double thread grips the material and there is no shank between the thread and head.

Three types of screw head are normally available, the most useful for cabinet making being the **countersunk head**, which fits flush or slightly under the timber surface, allowing the hole to be filled and completely disguised. The **round head** sits proud of the surface and the **raised head** is a combination of the two.

The slots in the top of the screw heads also vary. Simple **slot** screws have one groove for the screwdriver. **Cross-head** screws have a cross pattern, sometimes with an extra set of shallower indents between the four points of the cross. These provide greater grip and less chance of damaging the screw head when using a screwdriver.

Slot      Cross-head

The traditional slot head uses an ordinary screwdriver blade, while the cross-head is generally of two types – the Posidriv and the Phillips – both of which use cross-headed screwdrivers. Avoid using a Phillips head screwdriver with a Posidriv screw, and vice versa, as otherwise the recess in the head can be damaged and extracting the screw, if necessary, will also be difficult.

### Using brass screws

When you are using brass screws you should always first insert a steel screw of the same size and gauge in order to cut the thread. Remove this and insert the brass screw. It is often useful to apply a lubricant such as candlewax or petroleum jelly to the brass screw to ease it in.

### Drilling pilot holes

When making fine furniture, always drill pilot holes prior to inserting screws. First drill the clearance hole that will accept the shank. This must be right through the material that is to be held down. Next drill a pilot hole to guide the thread shank as the thread cuts into the bottom piece. When using countersunk screws countersink the top surface.

Never overtighten screws, particularly twin-thread screws, because their heads tend to break off more easily with this type of screw than they do with the regular slotted timber screw.

Modern cross-head screws are often referred to as chipboard screws. They have a sharp point and a thin thread that makes them easier to drive into manufactured boards.

Screws are bought according to their length and gauge (shank diameter). The gauge is expressed as a number from 0 to 20 – 0 is the smallest and 20 the largest.

## Screwdrivers

The tip of a screwdriver should fit the screw slot exactly. This avoids damage to either the work or the screw head. You will find a range of screwdrivers useful.

The **cabinet screwdriver** is used with traditional slot-head screws, and a range is needed for different sizes of screw.

The **ratchet** and **spiral ratchet screwdrivers** are useful tools when a number of screws have to be inserted.

**Cross-head screwdrivers** are specifically for use with cross-head screws.

The **stub screwdriver** or **stubby screwdriver** is useful when space is limited, and the **cranked screwdriver** when there is very little space at all.

The cabinet and ratchet screwdrivers have largely been replaced by the cordless drill/driver (see page 97). For screwdriving, choose a drill with a two-speed gearbox so the speed can be controlled. You can buy sets of differently sized screwdriver heads and a quick-change holder that is fitted in the chuck.

## Fittings

Poorly made or unattractive fittings can ruin the appearance of your craftwork. Always plan ahead and choose fittings that will enhance the appearance of your work.

## Hinges

Many hinges are available, and the most common are described here.

The **butt hinge** is the traditional cabinet maker's hinge. Those with wide leaves are suitable for larger pieces of furniture, such as cupboards, while those with smaller hinges are more suited to small cabinets and boxes.

A **piano hinge** is a long hinge, which is made in continuous lengths and then cut to size. It is used where an especially strong fitting is needed.

The **cylinder hinge** is used for doors, such as concertina doors, which need to open to a full 180 degrees.

The **soss hinge** is similar to the cylinder hinge, but is used for

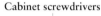

Cabinet screwdrivers

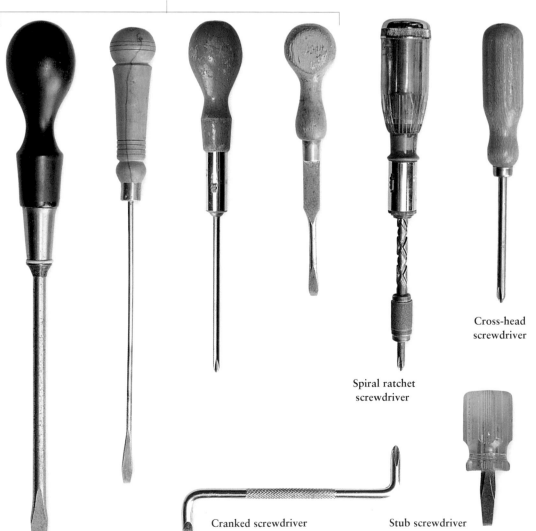

Cross-head screwdriver

Spiral ratchet screwdriver

Cranked screwdriver

Stub screwdriver

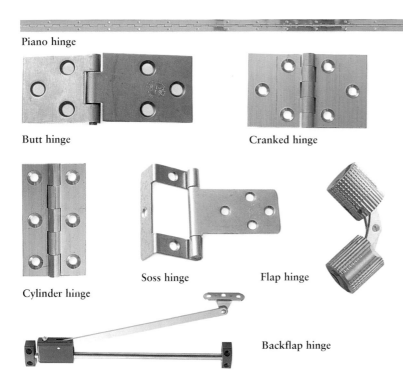

Piano hinge

Butt hinge

Cranked hinge

Cylinder hinge

Soss hinge

Flap hinge

Backflap hinge

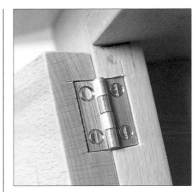

*The fitted butt hinge.*

very heavy doors. It is invisible when the door is closed.

The **cranked hinge** is normally used for finer work with lay-on doors. The door can swing through an arc of 180 degrees, allowing clear access to the cupboard.

The **flap hinge** is an adjustable hinge where the flap lies flush when open.

The **backflap hinge** has wide leaves recessed into the timber, and is used for attaching writing bureau door flaps. The hinged door 'falls' down to provide a desk work surface.

**Fitting a butt hinge**

When fitting hinges, precise marking, cutting and screw positioning is essential.

1 Set two marking gauges from the centre of the hinge pin – the first to the outer edge of the leaf to gauge its width and the second to the face of the hinge to gauge its thickness.

*Chisel out the recess for a butt hinge.*

2 Mark the length of the hinge with a square and knife in position on the door or flap, and then gauge the width and thickness of the recess.

3 Chisel out the recess, keeping inside the set-out lines, by first tapping the chisel 3mm (⅛in) within the squared lines. Hold the chisel at a 45-degree angle and lightly tap it to raise the grain. Pare across the recess from the depth-gauge line, guiding the chisel by hand and levelling up the bottom of the recess. Test the hinge to make sure that it fits and adjust as required.

4 Using the hinge as a guide, mark the centre of the screw holes with a bradawl. Remove the hinge and drill pilot holes for the screws. If using brass screws, insert steel screws first as guides to prevent damage to the softer brass. Then remove the guide screws, and place the hinge in position using the brass screws.

5 Fit the other leaf of the hinge using the same technique.

*Hinges can be used to make falls (see pages 268–73).*

125

### Escutcheons

*Escutcheon is a heraldic term to denote either a whole coat of arms or the field on which the arms are painted. The term is used in cabinet making to describe the carved armorial shields that are sometimes used as a central feature on the pediments of large pieces of case furniture. It also refers to the ornamental metal plate and pivoted metal cover that surrounds a keyhole. When a key is inserted in a lock it very rarely locates on its pin at once without striking the drawer front first – the escutcheon protects the drawer from damage. This type of escutcheon was used on cupboard doors as well as on desk and drawer fronts. They are often found in brass, which was first used from about 1650. By 1770 escutcheons began to vary in size and often formed part of larger designs found on the overall piece. For example, late 18th-century backplates had Neoclassical motifs embossed on them and the escutcheons were often made to match. The one shown here is a simple brass example.*

Fall lock

Cabinet lock

Sliding-door locks

## Locks and catches

A variety of locks can be fitted to furniture and boxes.

The traditional **cabinet lock** is normally used to secure cupboards and drawers. The **fall**, or **fall-flap lock**, is a cylinder lock that is designed to fit flush with the inside surface of a fold-down bureau. The key can only be removed when the flap is shut.

The **sliding-door lock** is another type of cylinder lock that can be used to lock over-lapping sliding doors.

*Specialist ironmongers may also produce individual fixtures.*

A variety of catches are also available, including the magnetic catch, the ball catch and the magnetic touch latch.

## Stays

Stays are designed to support a fall-flap in a horizontal position, and take the strain off the hinge. The simplest fall-flap stay is the **joint stay**. The sliding stay is a better-quality version, which slides on a bar fixed to the inside of the cabinet. The friction stay controls the movement of the flap so that it moves smoothly under its own weight.

Joint stay

## Knock-down fittings

It is often convenient to be able to disassemble large pieces of furniture for transportation. The industry has developed a range of fittings in order that furniture can be sent flat-pack. You will probably not have

access to a wide range of these but the following might be available in your local hardware store.

It is better to use **machine screws** than wood screws since with frequent assembly and disassembly wood screw threads and holes can become slack. The machine screw has a metal thread – like a bolt – and different lengths, gauges and thread size can be found. However, some type of insert such as a screw socket needs to be placed in the wood component to act as a nut. It has a thread in the centre that accepts the machine screw, but on the outside has a screw that can be driven. This is a neat fitting as the insert is never seen.

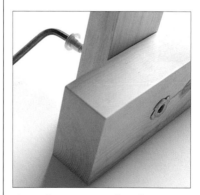

*A machine screw and socket.*

The **tee-nut** is used in material where there is not enough depth for a screw socket to be used. It is often used when fixing upholstered seats to chair frames. The nut is a disc with a central threaded socket. The socket accepts a machine screw and four prongs that bite into the surface. This keeps it in position when it is inserted into a clearance hole on the side that will not be seen.

A **barrel nut** is used when connecting a rail to an upright – for example, when fitting rails between a bed head and footboards. It is a cylinder, which has a thread drilled and tapped perpendicular to the barrel direction. To fit, drill a longitudinal hole for the bolt, and a cross-hole in the rail for the barrel nut. Insert the barrel nut, align the thread and tighten the bolt. You can also use bolts with nuts and washers if you cut a square mortise or recess to accept them. Another extremely useful approach is to use metal studding – lengths of threaded rod – that can be cut to the necessary lengths to suit the size of the job in hand.

*A barrel nut and screw.*

**Saw sets** can be used for connecting cabinets together and are a development of the saw sets that are used to hold saw blades in saw handles.

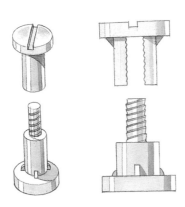

*A saw set*

## Handles

Even though many woodworkers prefer to make their own handles as part of the overall design, there are very many proprietary handles available in all shapes, styles, materials and colours.

Proprietary handles include **traditional door** or **drawer knobs,** which are available in timber, metal or ceramic. These are usually fixed from behind, where a screw passes through the cabinet front into the knob. **D-shaped handles** are a modern-style handle, which are fitted in the same way and available in metal, plastic or wood.

**Cabinet handles** are available in a variety of forms, including the swan neck. This type of handle is suspended from two pivots – one at each end of the handle.

*Period handles are still available.*

**Drawer-pull handles** are very strong handles, and are often used for large or heavy drawers.

For smaller drawers, the **drop handle** is common. Both the drop handle and the drawer-pull handle are fitted from the front.

The **flush handle,** as its name suggests, fits flush with the surface. Used for drawers, it is fixed with countersunk screws.

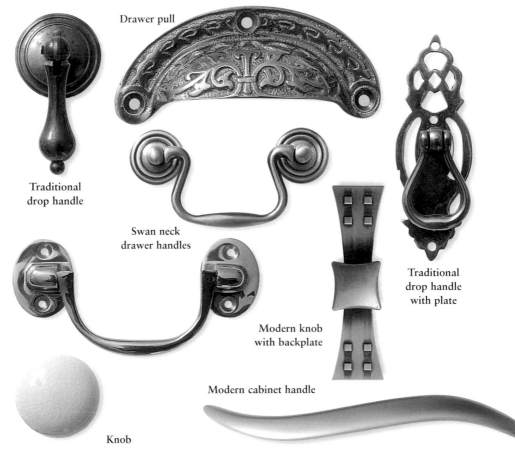

Drawer pull

Traditional drop handle

Swan neck drawer handles

Knob

Modern knob with backplate

Modern cabinet handle

Traditional drop handle with plate

# USING ADHESIVES

*Adhesives were traditionally derived from natural substances and could suffer degradation if exposed to moisture or heat. During the last century, however, a vast range of adhesives was developed for industrial applications and these became available to the woodworker. Adhesives that are totally moisture- and heat-resistant are now available.*

### Early adhesives

Early adhesives or glues were often made from animal skins and bone. A **double container glue pot** was used. The inside container held the glue and the outside held the water, which, when boiled, softened the adhesive. It would usually come in slab or cake form, which first needed to be softened in water, and then brought to the right temperature and viscosity in the double container. Later, adhesive was available in the form of fine granules or **pearls**. These glues are seldom used today and generally only in the restoration trade or when laying veneers by hand. They have little resistance to heat and solvents.

## Types of adhesives

The first popular synthetic adhesive developed was based on urea-formaldehyde (UF). Another very popular adhesive is polyvinyl-acetate (PVA). UF and PVA have become the main-stay for cabinet makers, although special adhesives are available for specific purposes.

### Urea-formaldehyde

**Urea-formaldehyde** (UF) usually comes as a powder that has to be mixed with water before use. It is essential to ensure that the correct balance of water and powder is used and that it is well mixed in order to remove all lumps. The curing takes place by moisture evaporation and chemical reaction. This adhesive can be supplied as two liquids – one being a separate catalyst or hardener. The two liquids are applied to the two different mating faces of a joint, with curing taking place by chemical reaction.

### Polyvinyl-acetate

**Polyvinyl-acetate** (PVA) is available as a white liquid and, when applied to a joint, sets by water evaporation. Initially it had poor water and mechanical

Double container glue pot

Pearl glue

Urea-formaldehyde

PVA

Epoxy-resin adhesive

Contact adhesive

Cynoacrylate

resistance, being limited to interior applications. It was not deemed suitable for laminating purposes. Now, however, there have been many developments and PVA can achieve high standards of moisture and mechanical resistance.

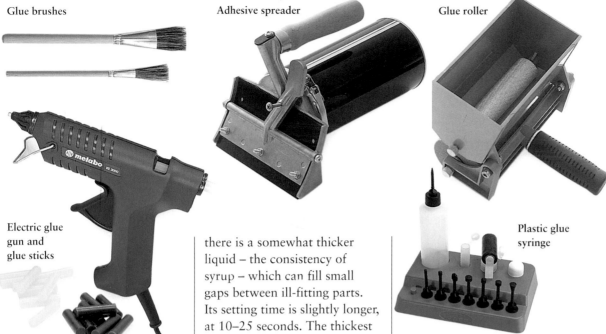

Glue brushes

Adhesive spreader

Glue roller

Electric glue
gun and
glue sticks

Plastic glue
syringe

### Epoxy-resin adhesives

**Epoxy-resin adhesives** are useful
for joining different materials
together, but are less satisfactory
for general woodwork. They are
ideal for external work, although
they are very expensive.

### Contact adhesives

**Contact adhesives** are generally
solvent based and are applied
to both surfaces, left until
tacky and then brought
together under pressure. They
are often used for applying
decorative plastic laminates to
manufactured board or when
gluing fabric. It is not advisable,
however, to use such adhesives
for laying veneer because the
latex rubber base allows too
much movement to occur.

### Cynoacrylates

**Cynoacrylates** are instant glues
and are available in different
consistencies. The thinnest
variety is like water and is used
for parts that fit together snugly.
It cures in 5–10 seconds. Then

there is a somewhat thicker
liquid – the consistency of
syrup – which can fill small
gaps between ill-fitting parts.
Its setting time is slightly longer,
at 10–25 seconds. The thickest
of the glues is almost treacle-
like and has the best gap-filling
ability. Its slow cure rate
(30–50 seconds) means that
you can realign components
after you have assembled them.
You can, however, use an
accelerator spray with the
glue so that it cures instantly.

### Hot-melt adhesive

**Hot-melt adhesive** is available
in cylindrical sticks, which
can then be applied using a
convenient hot-melt adhesive
gun. The gun is electrically
heated, and the adhesive sets
within seconds, making it ideal
for constructing mock-ups.

## Applying adhesives

Adhesives can be applied
with a **brush**, **flat stick** or
**roller**. A **plastic glue syringe**
is useful when trying to
reach inaccessible joints. When
applying UF or PVA, a **hand-
held adhesive spreader** can
save time and help to ensure
a thin, even spread of adhesive.
An **electric glue gun** is an

extremely useful applicator
to use for large jobs. Used
with solid glue sticks, it melts
the adhesive and forces it
out through the nozzle in
a liquid form.

## Using adhesives

Choose the adhesive that
will best suit the assembly
process, considering factors
such as drying time, moisture
resistance and strength.

Apply adhesive to flat surfaces
using a brush, spreader or
roller. Apply the adhesive to
joints using a brush or a stick.

Almost all assemblies will
need cramping to fix the pieces
together securely. Pressure
will need to be maintained
until the adhesive has cured
completely. The curing time
of the different adhesives varies
from product to product so
be sure to check the packaging.
It is worth remembering that
heat will accelerate the curing
of most adhesives.

### Expert tip

When assembling work
adhesive will invariably
squeeze out of the joint
when finally cramped.
If adhesive is left in
place until it has cured,
the surface of the work
is bound to be damaged
by its removal. You
could remove the excess
when the adhesive is
still wet, using a cloth
and water to remove all
traces. Or, wait until the
adhesive has cured to a
'rubbery' state, when it
can be removed easily
by scraping across the
surface with a chisel.
It will still need to
be wiped down with a
damp cloth to remove
all traces of the
adhesive. Do not drown
the work with too much
adhesive or water as
this can stain timber,
especially hardwoods.

# WOOD FINISHING

*Wood finishing is sometimes viewed as the final but brief operation of a*

*woodwork project. However, it actually needs to be carefully considered at*

*the outset in order to decide on the most appropriate finishing method and*

*when it is best to apply it. Make sure that you leave enough time for finishing*

*and prepare and plan thoroughly before you start any project.*

Even though finishing is generally the final process that you will undertake in any woodworking project it can often be useful – and sometimes essential – to prefinish your timber components before assembly. This is so that the

finish can be applied to all the nooks and crannies that cannot be reached after assembly.

Finishing technology has developed to satisfy two criteria for when the object is in use – practicality and appearance.

Tack cloth

Shellac sticks

Filling knives          Paintbrush          Solvent-based stopper          Water-based stopper

Wax sticks          Plastic wood filler          Fine surface filler

Use may often dictate the finishing strategy – for example, the amount of physical or environmental wear that the piece will have to resist. Will it be used indoors or outdoors, or will it be subjected to continuous wear?

There are a wide range of finishes available today: natural clear, synthetic-coloured as well as some unusual surface finishes. Before you apply finish though, it is important to prepare the timber surface as necessary.

## Fillers

You will often have to fill small cracks and holes in order to prepare the timber for finishing. There are a range of filling materials available.

A **filling knife** is used to apply a filler. A filling knife is a thin, flexible piece of stainless steel fixed to a handle. It is used to work the putty or filler into the defect within the surface of the work before sanding and applying a finish.

Small cracks and holes can be filled with a 'stopper' as near as possible to the timber's colour. You can also use preparations based on shellac. **Shellac sticks** come in timber-like colours and are ideal for repairing small cracks or knotholes.

**Wax sticks** are made from carnauba wax and mixed with resin and colouring pigments. Wax sticks are normally used for repairing small hairline cracks in the timber surface. Remember that you should only use wax sticks when you intend to use a wax finish on the work (see pages 132–3).

**Wood filler** is made from natural and/or synthetic materials, and is normally used to fill timber defects such as splits and knotholes. It can be readily sanded down to provide a smooth surface for a polish. It is available in a variety of colours to match almost any timber, and can also be mixed with lighter or darker filler or paint pigments for a perfect colour match. Most filler for cabinet work is water-based although spirit types, which dry more quickly, are also available.

**Grain fillers** are much the same as wood fillers, except that they are more watery. Grain fillers are rubbed into the surface with a cloth, left to dry and then fine sanded. Even though powder grain fillers are available, it is preferable to use successive coats of lacquer cut down between each application.

When using softwoods the resin in the timber can bleed, especially from knotholes. **Knotting** is a shellac-based sealer that prevents resin bleed.

**Knotting**

## Preparing the surface

Decisions made as to the practicality and appearance of wood finishes are closely linked and the brief history of finishes (see box right) will help explain the reasons for some of our choices over the centuries.

1  Before applying any finish, ensure that the surface is well prepared by planing, scraping and using abrasive papers.

*Plane before applying finish.*

2  Ensure that the surface is free of dust or other particles by wiping it with a tack cloth.

3  In some situations you may need to fill the grain, or any other defects, with a filler. Place the filler between the filling knife and the defect. Apply pressure with the knife while dragging it across the surface. This forces the filler into the defect. As with any putty or filler, slightly overfill the defect. When dry, sand back to a flush finish.

If you are using a softwood that has knots you may need to use knotting at this stage.

*Timber partially filled with filler.*

**A brief history of finishing**

During the earliest times there were few finishing options available – those that were around were natural and often based on waxes or oils.

As society developed, quality furniture finishes became more important as furniture became a mark of status. Finishes enhanced the grain and colour of timber as well as serving a protective function. This was especially the case with the introduction of timbers such as walnut and mahogany, the use of veneers and inlay, and the appearance of specialist finishes such as gilding. It was during this time that French polish, based on shellac, became the main finish for most types of indoor furniture. Fashion, however, caused other systems to be introduced. The popularity of Japanese and Chinese furniture led to the use of opaque coloured lacquer as well as painted as well as inlaid decoration. Society furniture was usually given a high gloss finish and French polishers became expert at achieving this. Vernacular furniture did not always follow fashion and often oils and waxes were used.

In the twentieth century synthetic materials were developed that could be applied more rapidly and were more resistant to the elements and general wear and tear. These were originally based on cellulose, a natural substance, but chemical developments enabled the use of synthetic resins based on melamine, polyester and polyurethane, among others.

### Ebonizing

*This is the European process of staining and polishing wood to give a surface finish that resembles ebony. It was particularly popular in the 18th and 19th centuries and was influenced by the craze for all things Eastern. Edward Godwin, for example, had an intense interest in Japanese art and used ebonized wood to create a lot of his designs. In fact, he pioneered what came to be known as Anglo-Japanese furniture. In the late 19th century Japanese mania was at its height within furniture design – European shapes were retained but Japanese details added, and ebonized wood was used a lot to create the furniture. Philip Speakman Webb was another 19th-century designer and the picture below shows an example of his work in ebonized wood. Ebonized furniture very quickly became an accepted part of the Victorian interior. English furniture makers had also been heavily influenced by France, which had ébénistes – specialized carvers who worked mainly in ebony. The English makers, however, relied heavily on ebonized oak and mahogany in their designs but borrowed techniques and ideas from the French.*

## Natural clear finishes

When quality timbers are used nowadays, there is generally no need to change the colour, only to bring out the natural qualities of the timber species. It is worth remembering that on exposure to light the colour of most will usually tend to darken anyway. For this reason, the clearest finish possible is often the most desirable.

### French polish

French polish is made out of shellac, a natural substance made from beetles that is dissolved in industrial alcohol. It has been used for many years and used to be the furniture maker's standard finish during the nineteenth and early twentieth centuries. It can be finished to a very high gloss but unfortunately is vulnerable to both water and alcohol. There are various types of French polish available today.

**Button polish** is the highest grade of French polish and is a golden-brown colour.

**Garnet polish** is a dark red/brown and is used on timbers that are made to look like mahogany.

**White polish** is made from bleached shellac and is used for pale-coloured timbers.

**Transparent polish** is used where minimum colour change is required on light timbers such as ash and sycamore.

**Coloured polish** contains a spirit-based stain and is used in order to modify the colour of the timber.

## Oils

Oils soak right into the timber, giving a beautiful rich finish that enhances the grain rather than simply coating the surface. When applying oil finishes, it is best to thin the first coat to encourage penetration into the timber, and then follow this with several coats to build up a good finish. This is better than simply flooding on a thick coat. Oil is the most easily repaired of all wood finishes. Simply sand down and re-oil. A range of oils is available today.

**Linseed oil** can be raw or boiled. Raw oil takes a long time to dry, boiled less so. Since drying has to be done naturally, the resulting finish is not as hard as with other oils. Its performance can be improved by adding dryers, such as gold size or terrabin.

*French polish on maple.*

*Button polish on beech.*

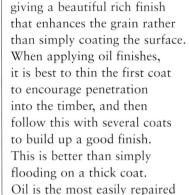
*Tung oil on teak.*

*Tung oil on maple.*

*Limed wax on oak.*

*Brown Boot Tan wax on teak.*

**Danish and teak oils** already have dryers added. Different formulations will give very good results in terms of penetration and hardness.

**Tung oil** is from the tung tree, and is also known as Chinese oil. It is very durable and is also heat and alcohol resistant.

## Waxes

Wax polish is made from beeswax or carnauba wax in turpentine. Each of these waxes can be used alone but it is generally better to seal the grain with a thin lacquer or with white shellac before building up wax coats. Wax is often used as a final finish on top of other materials. A very fine wire wool is used to apply a soft wax, giving a semi-matt surface. The surface is then buffed-up with a soft cloth. With so many ready-made preparations available, waxes are no longer so popular.

## Applying French polish, oils and waxes

Some of these finishes are combustible and prone to self-ignite, so after you have applied the finish, be sure to open out the cloth or rubber and leave it outside to dry completely.

### Application by rubber
French polish is applied with a soft pad, known as a rubber.

Other finishes such as oils can also be applied in the same way.

1  Make the rubber from a square of white linen cloth with a ball of wadding or cotton wool placed on the cloth. Fold the cloth over the wadding or cotton wool, and then turn in the edges. The rubber is then held in the palm of the hand.

2  The wadding centre can be charged with shellac, oils or some of the other finishes.

3  Dip the rubber in the finish, letting it soak up a reasonable amount of the finish but it should not be dripping wet.

*Apply polish with a rubber.*

### Application by cloth
A cloth is usually used for applying waxes and oil. Cotton is best for this process.

1  When applying oil soak the cloth thoroughly in a finish of your choice.

2  Rub the cloth over the timber surface with even strokes.

*Fold the cloth over the wadding to make a rubber.*

*Apply oil with a cloth.*

It is very important when you have finished with the cloth to open it out and leave it outside until it has dried, as otherwise it can self-ignite.

### Application with wire wool
This method is used for applying wax.

Wire wool

1  Wax can initially be applied with a pad of very fine wire wool, rubbing in the general direction of the grain.

*Apply wax with wire wool.*

2  Subsequent burnishing is made with a cotton/lint-free cloth formed into a pad. This is then used to rub the wax to a dull shine.

133

## Spraying wood finishes

Setting up spray equipment in a proper working environment is expensive. It is essential that the area is clean, that there is adequate extraction for the noxious chemicals and that lighting is suitably flameproof. Unless you already have experience in spraying or want to turn your hobby into something more, it is preferable to use the other techniques described here.

# Synthetic clear and coloured finishes

With the rapid developments that have taken place in the manufacturing processes in recent years, there is now a wide range of different types of synthetic finish available: stains, resins, lacquers and paints. Each is suitable for a particular purpose and so be sure to choose carefully.

## Stains

Staining was traditionally done to modify the colour of timber when the original did not suit the maker's requirements. More recently, makers have chosen timbers for their specific virtues, but also a smaller range of other colours has been developed. They add an overall finish that will colour the timber but still show the grain. These stains are available in water-, spirit- and oil-based forms. Water-based stains have been formulated to give results as near as possible to traditional products, without using dangerous substances. The table below shows the variety of effects that you can achieve by applying the same stains to three different base woods.

## Lacquers (varnishes)

Lacquers, or varnishes as they are sometimes called, also have a long history, but are not so favoured today. They create a fairly hard, resistant surface and can be used in clear form over another surface or as a flat, opaque colour that disguises the grain. They are available in gloss, semi-gloss and matt finishes and can be water- or solvent-based. Water-based lacquers have the same benefits as water-based stains.

## Paints

Interesting effects can also be produced with paint either completely disguising the grain, or with a broken finish, allowing some hint of the timber to show through. Traditional paints have been oil-based but water-based and more recently plastic-based paints have become very familiar, and all come in huge ranges of colours. When completely dry, finish the effect with wax for a soft finish or a clear lacquer for a harder-wearing finish.

## Applying lacquers, stains and paints

These finishes are often applied by brush, although stroking a stain on with a cloth is also effective. Taking the care to achieve an even finish is always a main priority.

*Pine spirit stain on beech.*

*Canadian Cedar spirit stain on beech.*

*Burmese Teak spirit stain on beech.*

*Pine spirit stain on oak.*

*Canadian Cedar spirit stain on oak.*

*Burmese Teak spirit stain on oak.*

## Application by brush

1 Take a scrap piece of the same wood as that used in the project that you are working on and apply your chosen stain to check if it gives a suitable result. You can create a deeper colour by applying more coats.

*Test a strip of timber with varying degrees of stain.*

2 When you are happy with your test piece you can then proceed with your project.

3 Apply the finish with straight strokes of the brush along the grain and let the film settle naturally. When using paint you need to brush initially in different directions, finishing off with light strokes in one direction. This should be with the grain if the piece is solid timber. If you are painting up to an edge always brush outwards.

*Apply the finish with a brush.*

4 Wipe off any excess with a cotton cloth. Lightly take the brush across the grain again to avoid leaving any cloth marks.

5 When it is dry, rub down with self-lubricating silicon-carbide paper.

6 Remove any sanding dust and apply subsequent coats of finish as needed.

7 When you have achieved the colour that you want, a clear finish can be applied.

## Unusual surface finishes

If you are seeking an interesting finish for your work, a variety of options are available, including fuming, blasting, scrubbing and scorching.

### Fuming oak

Oak and other timbers that contain a proportion of tannin can be fumed effectively when exposed to ammonia, which makes the timber darken. Take an airtight container into which the project can be placed after final finishing. Place some saucers of strong ammonia in the compartment with the project and seal it. After a time the oak will change colour to an attractive grey. When the desired colour is obtained, remove the ammonia and apply a transparent finish. Take the utmost care when using ammonia because the fumes are very toxic. Always wear a face mask and goggles.

### Sand blasting

Sand blasting is an industrial method of cleaning components prior to other finishing treatments. When timber is sand blasted the softer grain is removed and the hard grain remains. It is then usual to apply a transparent finish. This process should be carried out by a specialist.

### Scrubbing

Until recently timber work surfaces in kitchens used to be scrubbed for cleaning purposes. The resulting finish was a light bleached timber surface. As with sand blasting, this is because the soft grain was worn away. For the right piece of woodwork this can be a very interesting effect.

### Scorching

Scorching is not normally a method that is utilized on fine furniture because this finishing technique uses a blowtorch in order to burn the surface of the timber. The resulting charred material is then carefully wire brushed away. Subsequent finishing with a lacquer or an oil gives an unusual finished effect, particularly when used on softwood species of timber.

**Unusual surface finishes**

Fumed finish

Sand blasted finish

Scrubbed finish

Scorched finish

**6** Use a veneer hammer to press the veneer down; squeeze any air and excess moisture from under it. Use zig-zag strokes and always work from the centre to the outer edges.

*Press the veneer into place with a veneer hammer.*

**7** If the adhesive begins to cure, place a damp cloth over the veneer and use an old iron set to a low heat to soften the adhesive. Press down with the hammer again.

*Soften the adhesive using a cloth and iron.*

**8** Check for blisters under the veneer, by tapping the surface with a fingernail. You will hear if there are any areas that have not adhered correctly.

**9** If you are applying extra veneer pieces, such as a border, prepare the new veneers for application.

**10** Working from the centre to the edges, lay the new pieces of veneer overlapping the original.

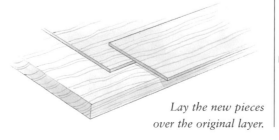

*Lay the new pieces over the original layer.*

**11** Using a sharp veneer knife and a metal straightedge, cut along the required line.

*Cut the veneer with a veneer knife.*

**12** Soften the adhesive with the cloth and iron, remove the waste pieces and press down with the veneer hammer using zig-zag strokes.

**13** Continue to lay the veneer to complete the desired pattern.

## Caul or press veneering

A caul is a press that applies pressure to the groundwork and veneer. It is made from two sheets of manufactured board at least 25mm (1in) thick, which should be slightly larger than the piece of work to be veneered. For small areas it is possible to use G-cramps on the caul as long as their throats are deep enough to give some pressure near the centre. For larger areas, however, you need to make cramping strips or bearers that have a slight curve in the centre to span across the caul. As cramping force is applied, maximum pressure is initially concentrated on the centre, while subsequent pressure spreads to the outside.

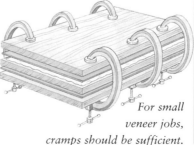

*For small veneer jobs, cramps should be sufficient.*

### Making the caul

The caul is quite easy to make.

**1** Having decided upon the size of the component you want to veneer, cut the two thick sheets of manufactured board, which need to be approximately 50mm (2in) larger than the work.

**2** Make some bearers that will apply pressure to the two boards. In order to ensure that the initial pressure is at the centre of the boards and progresses towards the edges as the cramps are tightened, make a slight curve on one face.

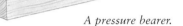

*A pressure bearer.*

**3** Prepare two sheets of polythene to place between the work and the boards to prevent the veneer sticking to the caul face.

### Pressing veneer in a caul

**1** Prepare the package that is to be pressed. There will be the element to be veneered, normally called the groundwork, a face veneer on the show side and a backing veneer on the other face, all sandwiched between two sheets of polythene. Also, a paper pad or rubber sheet can act as a softening pad, and sometimes an aluminium sheet that is able to be heated can be inserted to help the adhesive cure.

*Prepare the veneer package.*

*The layers of veneer in a caul press.*

2  The two boards of the caul are then placed on the top and bottom of this package.

3  To ensure pressure is applied in the centre, place the bearers in position with the curved faces in contact with the caul. Using G-cramps, apply initial pressure.

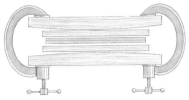

*Apply the initial pressure.*

4  When the cramps are tightened, the pressure applied by the shaped bearers will start from the centre and will spread to the outside on further tightening.

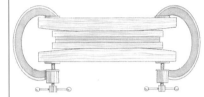

*Tighten the cramps to apply the final pressure.*

5  If the caul is to be used frequently to press similar sized veneered work, then it is advisable to use threaded rods, nuts and washers in place of cramps.

*The arrangement of threaded rods, nuts and washers on the caul.*

6  When the adhesive has completely cured, the veneer package can be carefully removed from the caul.

*A chessboard, veneered using the caul method (see pages 165–7).*

## Stringing

*When veneers were first used they were usually banded to make a decorative border and the veneer just ran to the edge of a piece of furniture. But by about 1780 it had become fashionable to inlay furniture with boxwood and ebony stringing, which strengthened the edges of a piece with very tough, durable timber. Stringing, therefore, is basically made up of thin square strips of coloured, patterned woods, which range from tiny lines only as thick as paper up to about 3mm (⅛in). Stringing had been used earlier, on its own, in Tudor and Elizabethan furniture purely as decoration, but is most often used in combination with veneer banding. The wire-like, linear stringing becomes the framework to the borders or marquetry panels on veneered furniture. The commonest designs found on stringing are rectilinear (as shown below) or radiating and they are usually made from satinwood, boxwood, purplewood or ebony.*

# CARVING

*Carving is a specialized craft, often used to produce items that are carved in the round. These may represent animals, people or a variety of other objects. In relief carving, a pattern is applied to a panel or an edge – a simple form for the beginner.*

## Carving tools

A wide range of carving tools is available to the specialist who will have many unusual ones for particular jobs. The furniture maker can generally manage with a small number of carving tools. The carver will also have a variety of different types of holding tools, especially where the work being undertaken is of a sculptural nature.

Here we look at simple forms of carving, rather than more sculptural work. The focus is on how decoration can be applied using chip carving, where a pattern is cut into the work. Carving chisels, carving gouges and special knives are generally used for this.

Carving chisels and gouges are usually bevelled on both sides so that the timber can be cut at a variety of angles. The cutting profile of each tool is different – ranging from a straight chisel for cutting straight lines through to special fluting, parting and veining tools. There are also a number of blade shapes to make special operations easier, including **straight, curved, spoon-bent, back-bent, skew** or **fish-tailed blades**.

A **carver's mallet** is needed for driving chisels and gouges when cutting across the grain or when working difficult pieces.

### Cutting curves

When making curved cuts, work the gouge by hand. Straight cuts can be helped by using a carver's mallet.

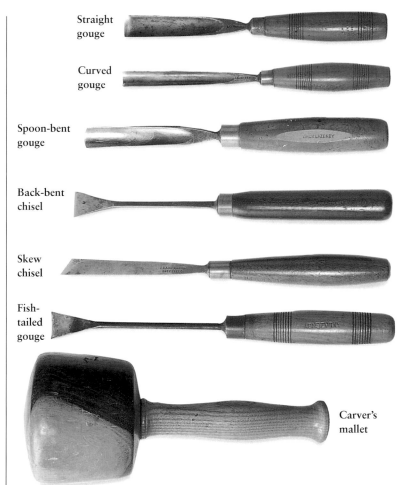

Straight gouge

Curved gouge

Spoon-bent gouge

Back-bent chisel

Skew chisel

Fish-tailed gouge

Carver's mallet

**Carver's punches** are made of steel and used to produce a wide variety of patterns and textures. Look for them in second-hand tool stores.

## Tool sharpening

It is particularly vital that carving tools are very sharp. Sharpening is covered in an earlier section (pages 72–3), but for carving tools a set of **shaped slipstones** is essential.

## Sharpening a (carving) chisel

The honing angle should be the same as the ground bevel.

**1** Place the bevel on an oilstone, lowering the handle as you pull backwards and lifting it as you push forwards. This will result in a rounded bevel.

**2** Repeat until the bevel is smooth and rounded, and a fine burr is made on the cutting edge.

**Shaped slipstones**

**Flat slipstones**

*Make a fine burr on the cutting edge.*

3 Remove the burr from the cutting edge and polish with a leather strop.

### Sharpening a (carving) gouge

1 Hone the outside of the gouge on a flat slipstone and work the inside with a slipstone that fits the curved shape.

*Work the inside of the gouge using a slipstone.*

2 Finish sharpening by polishing the carving gouge using a leather strop.

*Polish the gouge with a leather strop.*

## Chip carving

Decide the pattern that you want to carve to add interest to your work.

1 Begin by marking out the design of your choice onto the surface of the timber using a pencil. If you draw it out first on a piece of paper it can then be transferred using carbon paper. Alternatively, you may find it easier to use a stencil to mark out your pattern directly onto the timber.

2 Next, cut the pattern with a cutting knife and rule or combination square. Select the best shaped chisel for the cut you want to make. Start to remove the waste; you may want to start the cutting by using a mallet to drive the chisel, but final cuts should be made with hand pressure only.

*Cut the pattern with a knife.*

3 Continue and complete the pattern as required. It is best to work with the grain.

*Work with the grain as you carve.*

## Texturing

Use carver's punches to create interesting patterns or textured effects. Decide the effect that you want to achieve on the work. Carefully position the punch and tap with a hammer. Carving is a tricky skill that may take some time to perfect.

## Using the tools

When you are cutting, set the tool rest just below the centre of the work. Check that the work will clear the rest completely as it turns. Then, place the blade on the rest, hold the tool at an angle and start the cut. The tool should then be positioned in the direction of the movement, which will induce a slicing action. At the same time, roll the blade in the direction of the movement as you work.

*Place the blade on the rest.*

*Hold the tool at an angle and start the cut.*

*Position the blade in the direction of the movement.*

## Sanding

The safest way to sand while the lathe is in operation is to hold a piece of abrasive paper with one hand underneath the work. However, make sure that your hand does not actually make contact with the piece of work. You can apply pressure to the free end of the abrasive sheet by using your other hand.

*Use an extractor when sanding while the lathe is in operation.*

## Turning between centres

1  Prepare the material by marking the centre of both ends with diagonals and centre punch the crossed lines. It can be an advantage to plane square timber to an octagon before you begin turning – this will reduce the amount of work you will need to do on the lathe.

2  Tap the drive centre firmly into one end of the work.

*Tap the drive centre into the work.*

3  Place it into position in the headstock and bring the tailstock to the other end of the work, locating the revolving centre on the centre mark.

4  Make sure that you lock the machine into position.

5  Cut to the required diameter with a roughing gouge, then smooth with a chisel. Finish by using abrasive paper to smooth and then apply a suitable finish.

*Use a roughing gouge to cut to shape.*

6  Mark the object's length. Then, use a parting tool to cut a deep slot in the work. Leave a small spindle at the centre of the workpiece at each end.

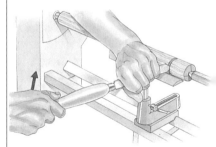

*Use a parting tool to cut a slot.*

7  Remove the object from the lathe and cut with a saw. In addition to producing straightforward cylinders, many different patterns can be cut.

## Turning on a faceplate

On larger lathes the faceplate may be fitted to the opposite side of the headstock or, in some cases, the headstock itself may revolve to give greater access for bowl turning.

1  If you have a bandsaw, cut the disc of timber to the size you require, plus 5mm (¼in).

2  Mount the faceplate onto the centre of the work. Screw it directly or glue a thick piece of spare timber to the work with a sheet of paper between the two to facilitate easier removal when turning is finished, and screw the spare piece through the back to the faceplate.

3  If you are turning a bowl, mount the faceplate on the inside; turn the outside shape and the spare timber to the same diameter as the faceplate.

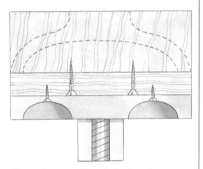

*Turn the outside of the bowl.*

4  Turn this outside face first. Remove the bowl from the spare timber and faceplate.

5  Turn a small recess on the spare timber face, the same size as the base that you have already cut, and remove it from the faceplate.

*Turning on a face plate.*

7  Fit the turned side to the spare timber recess with screws; replace it on the faceplate and turn the inside.

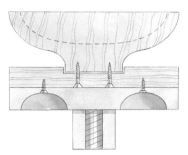

*Turn the inside of the bowl.*

8  If you are using a baulk where the grain crosses the disc, work from the outside inwards – otherwise the work can split.

9  If you have timber that presents end grain, work from the inside out.

Faceplate turning requires practice. To start turning, you should turn between centres until you gain experience.

*A turned plantstand (see pages 208–11).*

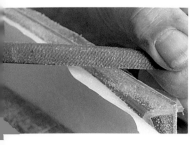

# USING METALS AND PLASTICS

*Non-timber materials are now common in the furniture industry. You will also find materials like sheet plastics and metal sections such as studding and steel bars and tubes useful in your own projects.*

## Tools for metals

The most likely process that you will undertake with metal is cutting. For cutting thick metal, both tubes and rods, you will need a **hacksaw**. You will also require a scriber – a sharp steel point in a holder – to mark out the line to be cut.

**Metal shears** or **snips** can be used for cutting thinner pieces of metal. There are left and right handed, straight and offset, and large and tight curved shears available for almost any shaped cut required.

**Metalworking files** are used for metal finishing and there is a range of grades from coarse to fine. There is also a wide range of shapes, including flat, half-round and round in different sizes.

For very fine metalwork a set of **needle files** is useful.

## Tools for plastics

The main types of plastics that you will come across are **acrylics** and **polycarbonates**. These have the advantage of being able to be worked with most woodworking tools.

## Preparing to work with metals

It is not recommended that you work metals in your woodworking vice or on your bench. You need a separate metalworking vice, which will be mounted on a block of timber that is held in your woodworking vice. Cut and fit a sheet of ply over the work area; swarf and filings laying on or embedded in the work area can ruin later woodwork. Some metals are much easier to work than others – aluminium

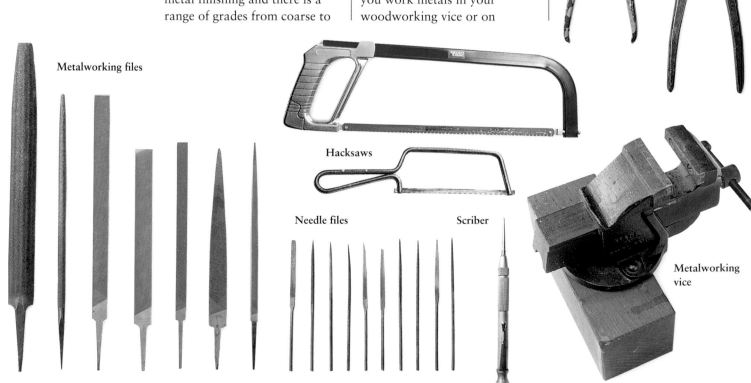

Metal shears/ snips

Metalworking files

Hacksaws

Needle files

Scriber

Metalworking vice

is soft and bends and works easily, brass is harder but can still be worked and bent, while steel can be much more difficult.

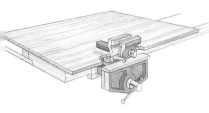

*A workbench cover for metalwork.*

## Sawing a metal bar, rod or tube

Use a hacksaw for cutting a metal bar, rod or tube with any substantial thickness.

1 Mark the line to be cut with a scriber. Take care not to mark or damage any finish on the metal.

2 Cut with firm strokes; hacksawing will take much longer than sawing timber.

*Cut the metal tube with a hacksaw.*

3 When the cut is almost finished, support the waste.

## Cutting sheet metal

If you are using sheet metal that is not too thick it can be cut with metal shears or snips, used in a similar way to scissors.

1 Mark out the shape to be cut.

2 Cut to the line. The sheet will bend as it is cut and you will probably have to beat the sheet flat with a hammer on a rigid surface if it curls up too much. However, if you use the correct shears this should not be too much of a problem.

## Finishing and filing

The cut edge will nearly always need some finishing with metalworking files and/or needle files.

1 Set the work in the vice.

2 Holding the file firmly at both ends, use it to remove material in a forward motion. With a little practice you will be able to file accurately to a line. Always ensure the handle is on the file.

*File across the metal tube.*

## Joining metals

It is quite difficult to join metals with most adhesives, and the two main methods are heat and physical fixings. Very high levels of heat are needed to melt and fuse most metals together. Unless you happen to have an engineering background or facilities, you

will most likely need to have this type of work undertaken by a metal workshop.

Physical fixings are more easily used, and can range from screws to bolts and nuts for structures to rivets for sheet materials. Screws can be self-tapping and/or self-drilling.

## Using plastics

Plastics, other than adhesives and finishes, are less likely to be used even though often it may be better to use transparent clear plastics than glass. Plastics are generally easy to work. Some plastics can be joined with solvent adhesives, and modest heat can be used to soften local areas so that sheet can be bent. After sawing plastics, smooth the sawn edges first with a fine metalworking file and then with wet-and-dry paper.

*Filing a plastic edge.*

*Sanding a plastic edge.*

147

# THE PROJECTS

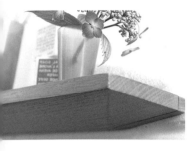

# Small shelf  Basic

*This small shelf has no apparent supports, which helps to give it a compact, attractive appearance. Provided it is fixed to a substantial wall, the shelf is perfectly safe and should be able to take the weight of normal household items. However, do not place very heavy articles on it, or extend the shelf width, as this will reduce its strength.*

## Tools

Jack plane

Drill and 12mm (½in) and countersink bits

Tenon saw

Smoothing plane

Screwdrivers

### Measuring tools

For all projects, a rule or tape measure is needed for setting out. A try square is needed to square any set-outs across an edge or face.

### MATERIALS

| Part | Materials and dimensions | No. |
|------|--------------------------|-----|
| | Hardwood | |
| Shelf | 750 x 128 x 38mm (28 x 5 x 1½in) | 1 |

**Other materials:** one 300 x 12mm (12 x ½in) diameter dowel; four 50mm (2in) 10 gauge countersunk screws; adhesive (PVA recommended); wax; finish.

**1** Plane all of the surfaces of the timber to the correct overall length, width and thickness with a jack plane. Ignore the bevels for the moment – you will not complete these until steps 8, 9 and 10. Using a try square and rule, measure and mark a line 16mm (⅝in) in from one of the long edges of the piece. This is the line where the timber will later be cut into two pieces to make the shelf and its support fixing (rear strip). Following the measurements given on the

drawing below, mark out on the back edge of the timber the position of the three support dowels and the four wall-fixing holes in the centre.

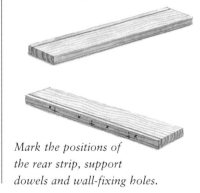

*Mark the positions of the rear strip, support dowels and wall-fixing holes.*

### Skills required for project

Measuring and marking *pages 64–7*

Basic sawing *pages 68–71*

Planing *pages 74–81*

Drilling *pages 96–100*

Using adhesives *pages 128–9*

Wood finishing *pages 130–5*

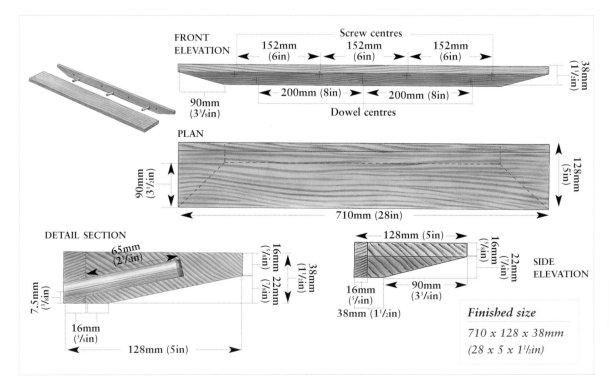

FRONT ELEVATION

Screw centres
152mm (6in) — 152mm (6in) — 152mm (6in)

200mm (8in) — 200mm (8in)
Dowel centres

38mm (1½in)

90mm (3⅜in)

PLAN

90mm (3½in)

128mm (5in)

710mm (28in)

DETAIL SECTION

65mm (2½in)

7.5mm (³⁄₁₆in)

16mm (⅝in)

16mm (⅝in)

22mm (⅞in)

38mm (1½in)

16mm (⅝in)

128mm (5in)

128mm (5in)

16mm (⅝in)

22mm (⅞in)

16mm (⅝in)

90mm (3⅜in)

16mm (⅝in)

38mm (1½in)

SIDE ELEVATION

*Finished size*

*710 x 128 x 38mm (28 x 5 x 1½in)*

**2** Use a 12mm (½in) drill bit to drill four holes through the timber for the support dowels. Drill at an angle of 15 degrees so that once the dowels are in place, they do not protrude through the bevelled face of the shelf. These holes should be 80mm (3¼in) deep so that when the board is sawn into two pieces they will be deep enough to accommodate the dowels. Next, drill the wall-fixing screw holes in the rear of the board to a depth of 16mm (⅝in). Make sure that the holes are square with the face side.

*Drill the dowel holes at a 15-degree angle and then the screw holes.*

**3** Next, cramp the timber to a bench and use a large tenon saw to cut down the marked line to separate the rear strip from the front section. Work carefully so that you remove the minimum amount of material. Then plane the two new faces so that they fit precisely together.

**4** Finish the screw holes by countersinking them on the joining face.

*Cut to separate the two sections and countersink the screw holes.*

**5** Cut three dowels. Chamfer one end of each dowel piece. On the opposite end, cut 10mm (⅜in) along its length

with the tenon saw. Insert the dowel into the front half of the shelf, applying some wax to the holes and the dowel so that they can be separated again easily.

*Wax the dowel and insert into the shelf.*

**6** From waste material cut wedges that are approximately 20mm (¾in) long and 6mm (¼in) thick to match the diameter of the dowel.

*Cut wedges to match the size of the dowels.*

**7** Next, bring the two sections together to wedge the dowels into position. Apply adhesive to the dowel holes in the rear strip. Push the rear strip panel onto the dowels and secure with adhesive. Drive the wedges in from the back to spread the dowel ends. Once dry, clean off the face of the timber flush.

*Push the rear part onto the dowels, ready to be wedged in firmly.*

**8** Mark out the bevel with a pencil on the bottom of the shelf, 90mm (3⅜in) in from the ends and front edge. Again, on the ends and front edge make a pencil line 16mm (⅝in) down from the top of the shelf.

**9** Hold the timber vertical in a vice with the bevel face towards you. Using a sharp, finely set jack plane – with the

shelf and support strip together – shape both ends. Hold the plane so that it cuts at a slight angle to prevent any breakout.

*Plane a bevel on the front section.*

**10** Turn the timber horizontal on the bench and use a bench stop to hold the work; plane the bevel along the length of the shelf.

*Plane a bevel onto the bottom and sides of the shelf.*

**11** Sand and finish the shelf. Separate the parts and fix the rear to the wall using countersunk head screws. Finish by placing the shelf back on the dowels.

*Fix the rear strip to the wall and position the shelf on the dowels.*

# Letter rack  Basic

*This simple project should enhance your sawing ability, particularly your fine-sawing skills. The slats are held in place on the battens with dovetail joints, so you will need a dovetail saw as well as a curve-cutting coping saw.*

## MATERIALS

| Part | Materials and dimensions | No. |
|------|--------------------------|-----|
| | Hardwood | |
| Slats | 750 x 210 x 12mm (30 x 8½ x ½ in) to make seven | 1 |
| Battens | 350 x 50 x 20mm (14 x 3 x 1in) to make two | |

**Other materials:** fourteen 40mm (1½in) 6 gauge countersunk screws; finish.

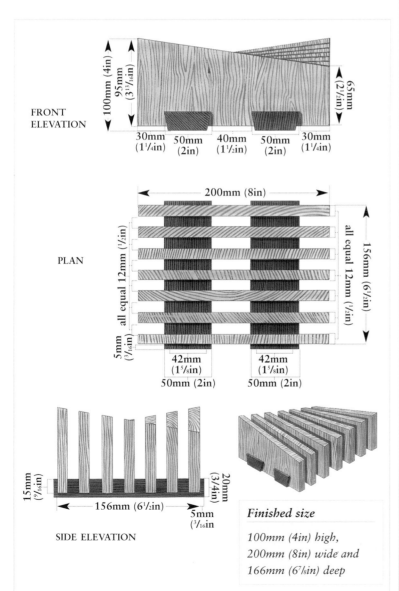

FRONT ELEVATION

100mm (4in) / 95mm (3¹³/₁₆in) / 65mm (2½in)

30mm (1¼in) / 50mm (2in) / 40mm (1½in) / 50mm (2in) / 30mm (1¼in)

PLAN

200mm (8in)

all equal 12mm (½in) / 156mm (6½in) / all equal 12mm (½in)

5mm (³/₁₆in)

42mm (1⅝in) / 42mm (1⅝in)

50mm (2in) / 50mm (2in)

SIDE ELEVATION

15mm (⁹/₁₆in) / 156mm (6½in) / 20mm (3/4in) / 5mm (³/₁₆in)

### Finished size

*100mm (4in) high, 200mm (8in) wide and 166mm (6⁷/₈in) deep*

**1** First, measure, mark and cut the seven vertical slats (100mm/4in high x 200mm/8in wide). Make sure that the grain direction is vertical. Plane the face side, face edge, width and thickness.

*Prepare the timber slats, ensuring that the grain direction is vertical.*

**2** Carefully plane the bottom edges to ensure they are square, checking with a try square. You will not cut the top edges to shape until step 10.

**3** Plane the two supporting battens, face side, face edge, width and thickness. Mark the dovetail angles by gauging a pencil line along the bottom face 4mm (⅛in) in from each edge and then across the face edge to the top corner. Hold the batten in a vice and plane the bevels on each edge.

*Make the dovetail angles on the two supporting battens.*

## Tools

Smoothing plane

Sliding bevel

Drill and 4.5mm (³/₁₆in), 3mm (⅛in) and countersink bits

Marking knife

Dovetail saw

Coping saw

25mm (1in) paring chisel

Straightedge

Screwdriver

### Skills required for project

Measuring and marking *pages 64–7*

Planing *pages 74–81*

Fine sawing *pages 82–5*

Drilling *pages 96–100*

Making dovetail joints *pages 112–14*

Wood finishing *pages 130–5*

4 Set up a sliding bevel to measure the angle of the dovetail on the batten. You will then be able to repeat this angle in step 6 to make sure that the slats are cut to exactly the right shape.

*Use a sliding bevel to work out the angle of the dovetail battens.*

5 On the battens mark where the slats will be positioned at 12mm (½in) intervals (see the drawing on page 153) and, for each slat, drill a 4.5mm (³⁄₁₆in) clearance hole for the screws. Countersink the screw holes on the bottom of the rack. All the slats will be held in the centre of the dovetails.

6 Take the slats and use a marking knife to mark precisely the positions of the dovetails that will accept the supporting battens. From the bottom of each slat, measure up 15mm (⅝in) and square a pencil line right around the timber. Use the measurements on the drawing on page 153 to mark out the position and width of the dovetails on the slats. Set a sliding bevel to the angle of the

*Mark the dovetails on the slats.*

the dovetail on the battens that you measured in step 4. Use this and a marking knife to mark the dovetail angles. Gauge a line between these to represent the top cut-line of the dovetails.

7 Cut down the shoulder lines carefully with a dovetail saw, and remove the waste from the centre with a coping saw. Pare to the top cut-line with a 25mm (1in) paring chisel, ensuring a square cut is maintained. Cut one dovetail at a time, checking that each fits the batten well.

*Use a paring chisel to pare out the waste from the dovetail joints.*

8 Try all the slats dry on the battens to check that they are square with the battens.

9 Next, drill a 3mm (⅛in) pilot hole from the existing clearance hole into the slats; insert and fix the screws in place.

*Fix the slats and battens together with screws.*

10 Now that the slats are held firmly, mark the angles on the top surfaces.

Measure up 95mm (3¹³⁄₁₆in) on the two diagonally opposite corners of the end slats. Then mark 65mm (2½in) up on the other two diagonally opposite corners. To find the heights of all the middle slats, lay a straightedge along the outside of the rack and join up the 65mm (2½in) mark at one end with the 95mm (3¹³⁄₁₆in) mark at the opposite end. Mark with a marking knife. Number the bottom of each slat in sequence.

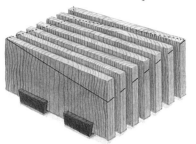

*Use a straightedge to mark out the heights of the middle slats.*

11 Remove the screws and, having marked the positions of all the slats, slide them off the battens.

12 Cut the angles on the top surfaces of the slats. Saw carefully as the surface does not have a right-angled edge but twists from side to side. Hold in a cramp, saw end angles a short way and then follow the line along the face to the centre on both sides. These will act as guides for planing.

13 Plane and sand these top edges. Then sand all the faces and apply a finish to all components before assembly.

14 Now slide the slats, one by one, onto the battens and align with your marks. Reinsert the screws.

15 Apply another coat of finish to the areas that you can still reach if desired.

# Animal shapes   | Basic |

*A basis of all work is cutting precisely to a line, and then chiselling – or paring – vertically or horizontally. This project gives the opportunity to practise chiselling skills and, since the design is so simple, achieve a very crisp result.*

## Tools

Smoothing plane

Marking knife

Marking gauge

Tenon saw

Bevel-edge paring chisel

Drill and drill bit

Dovetail saw

### MATERIALS

| Part | Materials and dimensions | No. |
|------|--------------------------|-----|
| All pieces | Hardwood length and width to suit the scale of the animals chosen (220mm x 200mm/8¾ x 8in used here) x 25mm (1in) thick. | |

**Other materials:** abrasive paper; finish.

**1** Use the drawing below in order to choose the scale at which to make the animals.

The size of the grid can be changed to suit your own individual requirements –

if you want to make the animals twice as big, then simply double the size of the grid that you use.

**2** When you have chosen your scale, true the timber with a smoothing plane by working systematically all around. Then you are ready to mark the grid on the timber with a pencil.

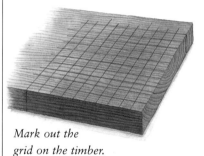

*Mark out the grid on the timber.*

**3** Draw the animal shapes onto the grid with a pencil. Then mark the outside edges and details of the animal shapes across the grain with a knife and along the grain with a gauge. Also mark centres for the eye positions and cut lines for the slot detail.

**Maximum size**

*170mm (6¾in) long and 100mm (4in) high*

Each square represents 10mm (³⁄₈in).

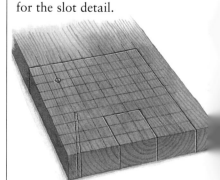

*Mark out the animal shapes in the grid, including centres for the eyes.*

**Skills required for project**

Measuring and marking *pages 64–7*

Planing *pages 74–81*

Fine sawing *pages 82–5*

Chiselling *pages 86–9*

Drilling *pages 96–100*

Using abrasives *pages 115–17*

Wood finishing *pages 130–5*

**4** Cut out the rectangle that contains each animal using a tenon saw. Where there are square or rectangular portions to be removed from the main block, cut them out, sawing to the waste side of the line.

*Saw away the bulk of the waste.*

**5** Carefully pare to the cut lines, vertically paring the end grain and either horizontally or vertically paring the long grain.

*Use vertical strokes to pare back to the marked line carefully.*

**6** Now drill out the holes for the animals' eyes and cut the thin slots with a fine dovetail saw.

**7** If your planing, sawing and paring have been done well, then you may not wish to use abrasive paper on the faces and edges of each piece, but the sharp arrises on all corners will need removing at this stage.

**8** If the animals are to be handled by children, then do not apply a finish. As an alternative, you could use a vegetable-based oil.

# Early development of furniture

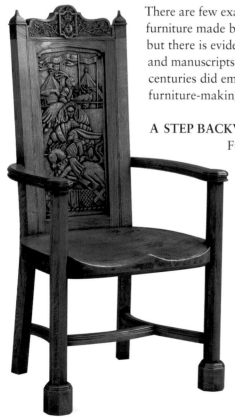

*A Catherine of Aragon-style chair, designed by Stewart Linford furniture.*

There are few examples left today of furniture made before the 16th century but there is evidence in carvings, pottery and manuscripts that much earlier centuries did employ well-developed furniture-making techniques.

### A STEP BACKWARDS

Furniture making is an ancient tradition, with its roots going right back to early civilizations. In Ancient Egypt there was a tradition of burying furniture in tombs. Throughout the first and second dynasties skills were being developed, including the use of mortise and tenon, dovetail and mitre joints. The furniture was mostly crude three-legged stools or armless chairs, and tables were almost unknown. Although through stone carvings and frescoes it can be seen that beds, stools, throne chairs and boxes were common. Everything was made to be transportable and decoration was derived from religious symbols.

Our knowledge of early Greek furniture is mainly taken from painted pottery, but we know they adapted techniques from both Egypt and the Orient. In turn, Greek civilization heavily influenced the Romans and in both cultures the principal piece of furniture was the couch. It was the Romans who first developed cupboards, and wall paintings from Pompeii show plain, undecorated wooden tables, benches and cupboards with panelled doors.

When the Roman Empire collapsed during the 4th and 5th centuries, Europe sank into the Dark Ages during which time very little furniture was used. What was in existence was far inferior to the quality of furniture in Greek and Roman times.

During the 14th and 15th centuries there was a shift in furniture making. Previously, it had mainly been monks who worked on furniture but now lay people began to learn the skills involved. There were many developments in Europe during this time – various cupboards and desks evolved and crude dovetailing and mortise and tenon joints, secured by pegging, were employed. Furniture remained transportable because if a nobleman owned more than one dwelling he usually still only had one set of furniture that needed to be carried with him. Throughout this period, and into the 16th and 17th centuries, all furniture was scarce and mainly belonged to nobility and the wealthy. Chairs symbolized authority – even a large household may have owned

OPPOSITE LEFT *Mortise and tenon joints were first used in Ancient Egypt, as seen in this stool.* ◆ OPPOSITE CENTRE *An oak court cupboard from the mid-17th century.* ◆ OPPOSITE RIGHT *An oak refectory table, made in 1540, with carved angel figures on both sides of each upright.* ◆ ABOVE LEFT *A late 17th-century oak settle with turned baluster back.* ◆ ABOVE CENTRE *A Jacobean oak bench with turned legs and carved detail.* ◆ ABOVE RIGHT *A Jacobean oak settle with an arcaded design on the back panels.*

just three; one for the lord, one for his wife and the other for visitors. The peasant households of Europe, even as late as the 18th century, had only rather crude, roughly constructed basic pieces of furniture.

## A NEW VISION
In Italy in the 15th century there was huge growth within the powerful bourgeoisie and this created a new demand for strong, fine furniture. Furniture makers looked to Greece and Rome to draw inspiration from the ancient civilizations. Other countries in Europe were influenced by this new mood. French furniture had been made of oak, which was difficult to carve, but the influence of Italy turned them towards walnut, which allowed carvers to create elaborate carved heads and strapwork. When Francis I returned for France after captivity in Italy in 1525, he employed several Italian craftsmen and French furniture of the 16th century became remarkably graceful. For example, chairs became lighter, with heavy panelled sides and bases replaced by carved and turned arms and supports, and legs joined by stretchers.

*With a caned seat and back, this chair was made in c1670 out of beech and walnut.*

Italy also influenced Germany and the Low Countries. Germany blended classical architectural motifs with animal masks and grotesques. The north of Germany, however, had no direct experience with Italy and there was a marked difference there – heavy oak furniture was still preferred while in the south softwood was being used.

England was not affected by the Italian Renaissance until about 1525. It was much more conservative, remaining Gothic and heavy in style. But Henry VIII made efforts to bring Britain up-to-date and employed Italian and German furniture makers. Classical motifs began to appear and craftsmen developed framed-panel joinery – furniture that is made up of tenon-jointed rails and stiles. There was also a technical breakthrough in the 1540s, when the true mitre was developed. Most furniture in Britain continued to be heavy and made of oak, but richer homes began to favour walnut and other native hardwoods. Turned decoration was introduced, such as balusters, and Britain started to catch up with the rest of Europe. However, it was not until the reign of Charles I, which marked a new era of artistic patronage, that things began to take off, with the range of furniture expanding and armchairs with scrolled wooden arms making an appearance.

# Wine rack  Basic

*This simple, stylish wine rack requires accurate drilling work. You can achieve good results slowly with hand tools but, if you are making a large rack, then it will be easier to use a pillar drill or power drill. The steps below describe a method where each hole is individually marked. For a larger rack, it would be easier to use a jig to drill the holes in the correct position without needing to mark each piece.*

## Tools

Tenon saw

Marking gauge

Drill and 10mm (⅜in) dowelling bit

Smoothing plane

### MATERIALS

| Part | Materials and dimensions | No. |
|---|---|---|
| | **Hardwood** | |
| Slats | 30mm (1³/₁₆in) square – the total length needed depends on how many bottles you wish to store; for a four-bottle rack you need nine slats, 190mm (7½in) long | 1 |

**Other materials:** 10mm (⅜in) diameter dowel – for a four-bottle rack you will need 24 lengths each 94mm (3¾in) long; abrasive paper; adhesive; finish.

**1** First, decide how many bottles you want to store in your wine rack. Then use a tenon saw to cut the required number of timber pieces, each measuring 30mm (1³/₁₆in) square and 190mm (7½in) long. To make the four-bottle rack shown here, you will need nine slats.

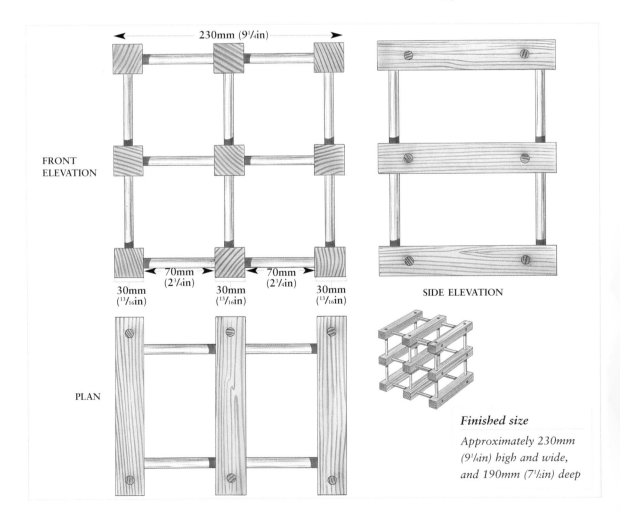

230mm (9¼in)

FRONT ELEVATION

70mm (2¾in)    70mm (2¾in)

30mm (¹³/₁₆in)    30mm (¹³/₁₆in)    30mm (¹³/₁₆in)

SIDE ELEVATION

PLAN

### Skills required for project

Measuring and marking *pages 64–7*

Planing *pages 74–81*

Fine sawing *pages 82–5*

Drilling *pages 96–100*

Using abrasives *pages 115–17*

Assembling projects *pages 120–7*

Using adhesives *pages 128–9*

Wood finishing *pages 130–5*

### *Finished size*

*Approximately 230mm (9¼in) high and wide, and 190mm (7½in) deep*

a mitre square, carefully mark mitres on the ends of the lippings so that they fit exactly in the corners.

2 You can either join these lippings to the board with loose tongues or simply glue them to the edges. If using tongues and grooves, work 6 x 6mm (¼ x ¼in) grooves with a router prior to cutting the mitres.

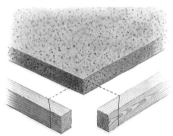

*Apply lippings to the board, mitring the edges to allow for the corners.*

3 If using adhesives, glue the lippings in place. Hold with sash cramps as required.

4 When the adhesive has cured, with a smoothing plane very carefully plane the excess lipping flush to the surface of the board on both sides.

*Plane the lippings so that they are flush with the board.*

5 Key the top and bottom of the board with a toothing plane. As veneers can exert a pull on the face of a board, put a backing veneer on the underside.

6 Select the veneers for the underside. Carefully cut the light and dark veneers for the top face into precise 40mm (1½in) wide strips. Join nine of these strips in alternating colours with veneer tape.

7 Now carefully cut another nine 40mm (1½in) wide strips at right angles to the first set so that you are left with strips of alternating light and dark squares.

*Cut nine more strips at right angles to the first set.*

8 Next, shift every other strip up by one square so that you end up with a chequered effect. Fix in position with veneer tape.

*Move every other strip up by one square to create a chessboard effect.*

9 Lay this matrix in the centre of the board and trim the excess squares off the end so that you end up with a chessboard of eight squares by eight squares. Lay the four border strips in position with veneer tape, overlapping and trimming the mitred corners as necessary with a veneer knife.

10 Ensure that as well as face and backing veneers you have two polythene sheets about the same size. Spread adhesive onto the undersurface of the board and place the backing veneer in position.

11 Apply more adhesive to the top surface of the backing board and place the top veneer assembly in position.

*The top veneer assembly kit consists of polythene sheet, caul, backing veneer, core board and top veneer.*

12 Lay a sheet of polythene on the bottom of the caul and lay the package of backing veneer, core board and top veneer on it. Lay another polythene sheet on top of this and place the top caul in place.

*Cramp the assembly together.*

13 Apply even pressure to the cramping bearers all the way round.

14 When the adhesive has cured, remove the veneered board from the caul and trim all the edges.

15 Carefully remove the veneer tape, sand all the surfaces and apply the required finish to the board.

# Triangular trivet    Basic

*A trivet is a small frame that can be put beneath a hot platter or dish to protect the table or kitchen surface. This is a relatively straightforward project, which is put together with oblique halving joints.*

## Tools

Smoothing plane

Sliding bevel

30/60-degree set square or protractor

Marking gauge

Marking knife

Tenon or dovetail saw

25mm (1in) bevel edge chisel

G-cramps

### MATERIALS

| Part | Materials and dimensions | No. |
|------|--------------------------|-----|
|      | Hardwood                 |     |
| Side | 610 x 32 x 20mm (24 x 1¼ x ¾in) | 3 |

**Other materials:** adhesive; abrasive paper; finish.

**1** Prepare the timber by planing it until it is rectangular in shape. Measure and cut the three side pieces of the trivet to length, using the drawing below as a guide. Apply face-side and edge marks.

**2** Set a sliding bevel to 60 degrees, with a protractor or set square.

*Set the bevel to a 60-degree angle and mark with a pencil.*

**3** Firstly, mark the piece of wood that will be sawn off the end of each piece of timber (A) – measure from one corner up to the opposite edge at a 60-degree angle. Carefully saw off these sections.

**4** Next, mark the shoulder – the piece of wood that will be sawn part way through each end to make the halving joint (B). Mark a line 32mm (1¼in) in from one end at a 60-degree angle across the face side, parallel with the end that you cut in step 3. Turn the piece over and mark the shoulder at the opposite end in the same way. Check that the distance between the shoulders is 93mm (3¾in). Use a try square to square these lines across the edges. Gauge a centre line from the shoulder lines out and around the end of each piece and back to the first shoulder line. Repeat until all the pieces of timber are marked up.

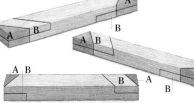

*Marking out shoulder lines.*

**5** Go over the shoulder marks with a marking knife, then carefully saw part way down the shoulder lines until you reach the centre line. Be sure to saw across the grain.

## Skills required for project

Measuring and marking *pages 64–7*

Planing *pages 74–81*

Fine sawing *pages 82–5*

Chiselling *pages 86–9*

Making halving joints *pages 101–3*

Using abrasives *pages 115–17*

Assembling projects *pages 120–7*

Using adhesives *pages 128–9*

Wood finishing *pages 130–5*

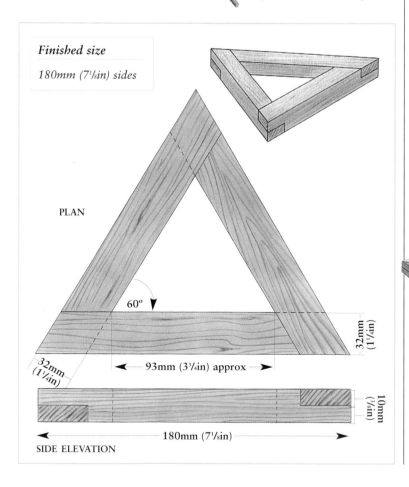

**Finished size**

180mm (7⅛in) sides

PLAN

60°

32mm (1¼in)

32mm (1¼in)

← 93mm (3¾in) approx →

10mm (⅜in)

← 180mm (7⅛in) →

SIDE ELEVATION

*Saw the shoulder lines across the grain.*

**6** Hold one of the pieces of timber in a vice so that the shoulder line is vertical. Saw down the gauged centre line on the waste side of the shoulder. It should be possible to saw accurately to the line but, if you are new to woodworking, you may have to trim the faces of the joints with a chisel. Repeat to achieve shaped ends on all the pieces of timber.

*Saw down the centre lines on the shoulders.*

**7** Lay the three components of the trivet together and check that the joints are tight. Adjust as required.

*Check the fit and adjust if necessary.*

**8** Apply adhesive to the joint faces and cramp together with G-cramps.

**9** When the adhesive has cured, shoot the outside edges with a plane.

**10** Use abrasive paper to sand the trivet and apply the finish of your choice.

# Carved mirror frame   Basic

*The construction of this piece is very simple and the carving on the face is*

*particularly effective. Here the frame has been used to house a mirror but*

*you could adapt it to fit a picture or a photograph.*

## Tools

Smoothing plane

Router with 12mm ($\frac{1}{2}$in) straight cutter

Mortise gauge

Tenon saw

Mortise chisel

Carving tools

Carver's mallet

Cramps

Drill and 4mm ($\frac{1}{8}$in) and 2mm ($\frac{1}{16}$in) bits

### Skills required for project

Measuring and marking *pages 64–7*

Basic sawing *pages 68–71*

Planing *pages 74–81*

Chiselling *pages 86–9*

Grooving *pages 90–3*

Drilling *pages 96–100*

Making mortise and tenon joints *pages 104–9*

Using abrasives *pages 115–17*

Using adhesives *pages 128–9*

Wood finishing *pages 130–5*

Carving *pages 140–1*

## MATERIALS

| Part | Materials and dimensions | No. |
|------|--------------------------|-----|
|      | Hardwood                 |     |
| Uprights | 575 x 50 x 25mm (23 x 2 x 1in) | 2 |
| Horizontals | 325 x 50 x 25mm (12¾ x 2 x 1in) | 2 |

**Other materials:** one 470 x 320mm (18½ x 12⅝in) mirror; one 470 x 320mm (18½ x 12⅝in) sheet of 6mm (¼in) plywood and hardwood strips removed when making internal rebates for use as retaining strips (if you rout rebates you will need more material for strips); adhesive; abrasive paper; finish; 20mm (¾in) 6 gauge countersunk screws.

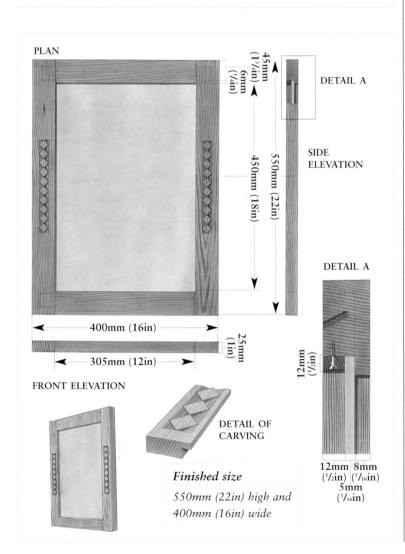

PLAN

DETAIL A

SIDE ELEVATION

45mm (1¾in)

6mm (¼in)

550mm (22in)

450mm (18in)

DETAIL A

12mm (½in)

400mm (16in)

305mm (12in)

25mm (1in)

FRONT ELEVATION

DETAIL OF CARVING

**Finished size**

550mm (22in) high and 400mm (16in) wide

12mm (½in)   8mm (⁵/₁₆in)

5mm (³/₁₆in)

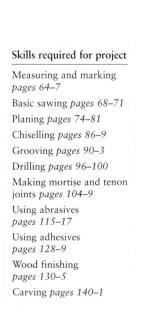

1 First, prepare the timber for the basic frame. Plane the two uprights and two horizontals face side and face edge. Apply marks and plane the width and thickness to 50 x 25mm (2 x 1in). The finished horizontals will be 374mm (14¾in) long (the internal size of the frame plus the two tenons) and the finished uprights will be 550mm (22in) long. Cut these pieces to length.

2 Use a router to cut the rebates on the back edge of the internal faces 12mm (½in) wide and 17mm (⅝in) deep.

3 Mark the long-and-short-shouldered mortise and tenons to suit the rebate size in their respective positions. Mark the tenon with the mortise gauge 8mm (⁵/₁₆in) wide. Grip the horizontals vertical in a vice and cut down to the set-out shoulder lines with a tenon saw. Lay them on a bench against a bench hook and cut the shoulder. Place each horizontal vertical in the vice again and cut 10mm (⅜in) off the outside edge of each tenon. Remove waste by cutting across the long shoulder line.

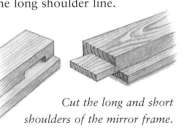

*Cut the long and short shoulders of the mirror frame.*

4 The mortise lines up with the rebate on one face. Hold each upright on the edge and chisel out the mortise for each – 25mm (1in) deep to suit the stopped tenons. First pare away the waste within the mortise to the required depth, and then pare back to each shoulder. Check each joint for fit and adjust as required.

5 Mark out the shapes of your pattern. Using the relevant carving tool, make cuts to the required pattern. You can practise on some waste timber.

*Use a chisel and mallet to practise carving on a piece of waste timber.*

6 When the carving is complete, assemble the frame with adhesive and cramp the joints. Ensure that the frame is square and free of wind.

7 When the adhesive has cured, prepare the frame for finishing and apply the required finish.

8 Make the four retaining strips to fit in the rebate. Place the mirror or picture in the frame. Lay a couple of sheets of paper over the back to protect it, then a sheet of plywood. Drill holes for the screws through into the rebate and screw the four strips in place. An angled hole can be drilled at the top of the frame for wall mounting.

# Small mirror and shelf  Basic

*This simple mirror and shelf, ideal for a bathroom wall, will enable you to put several key skills into practice. You will need to make a dovetail housing joint to attach the shelf to the frame, use an electric router to remove the timber to fit the mirror in place and use a fretsaw to produce the fine fretwork detailing along the top and bottom of the frame.*

### Tools

Marking gauge

Smoothing plane

Marking knife

Tenon saw

Sliding bevel

Paring chisel

Straightedge

Cutting gauge

Electric router or Forstner drill bit and hand router

Fretsaw

Drill

### Skills required for project

Measuring and marking *pages 64–7*

Planing *pages 74–81*

Fine sawing *pages 82–5*

Making housing joints *pages 110–11*

Using abrasives *pages 115–17*

Using adhesives *pages 128–9*

Wood finishing *pages 130–5*

## MATERIALS

| Part | Materials and dimensions | No. |
|---|---|---|
| Frame and shelf | Hardwood to make both the back board and the shelf: 550 x 210 x 20mm (22 x 8 x ¾in) | 1 |

**Other materials:** one 205 x 140mm (8⅛ x 5½in) mirror; adhesive (PVA); silicon; double-sided tape or mastic to fit glass; abrasive paper; finish.

**1** Prepare the timber face side and face edge. Use a marking gauge and then a smoothing plane to plane to a width of 200mm (8in) and a thickness of 20mm (¾in).

**2** First, mark the finished lengths of the two components – 400mm (16in) for the backboard and 112mm (4½in) for the shelf. Square all round with a marking knife. Set out the position for the dovetail housing 50mm (2in) from the bottom of the backboard. Use a pencil to square the top and bottom of the shelf across the backboard. Square the other lines on the board with a pencil: gauge a line 30mm (1¼in) in from each edge to represent the ends of the fretwork and the recess for the mirror, as shown in the drawing on the right.

**3** Cut the backboard and shelf with a tenon saw and carefully plane the end grain true to the finished length.

**4** Square the two set-out lines for the shelf across each edge of the backboard. Use a marking gauge to gauge a depth of 10mm (⅜in) between these squared lines. Set a sliding bevel to a pitch of 1:4 and mark the dovetail on the edge from the gauge line (see detail Bb on drawing opposite).

*Set a sliding bevel to pitch of 1:4 and mark the dovetail housing on the edge of the back board.*

**5** Use a marking knife to square the shoulder lines where the bevel line meets the face. Cramp the piece flat on the bench and cut on the waste side of the line with a tenon saw to the gauge line. Place another saw cut in the centre, stopping short of the gauge line.

*Use a tenon saw to cut away the dovetail housing.*

**6** Use a paring chisel in order to remove the waste from both sides; work carefully to the gauge lines. Place a straightedge along the bottom to ensure it is perfectly flat.

**7** Next, set out the dovetail on the shelf across each face with a cutting gauge set to 10mm (⅜in), the depth of the housing. Using a pencil, square these lines down each edge of the shelf. Then reset the sliding bevel to the correct pitch and mark the angle of the dovetail from the corner back to the squared line.

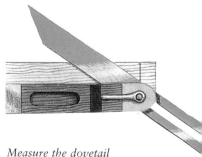

*Measure the dovetail on the edge of the shelf.*

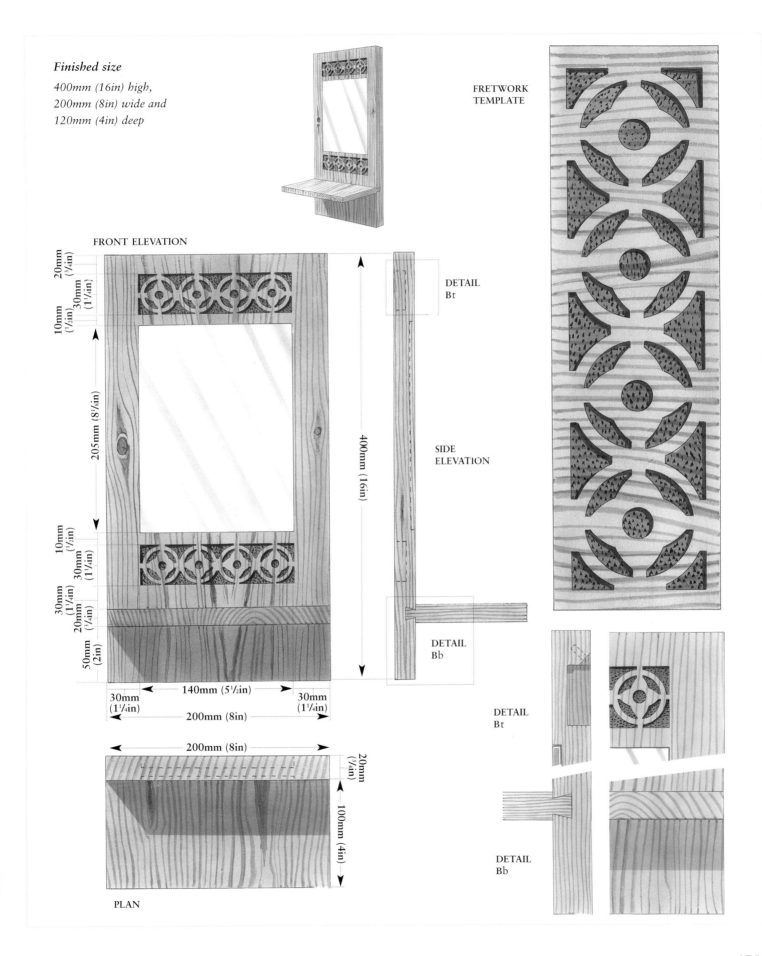

*Finished size*

400mm (16in) high,
200mm (8in) wide and
120mm (4in) deep

FRETWORK
TEMPLATE

FRONT ELEVATION

20mm (¾in)

30mm (1¼in)

10mm (½in)

205mm (8⅛in)

10mm (½in)

30mm (1¼in)

30mm (1¼in)

20mm (¾in)

50mm (2in)

30mm (1¼in)

140mm (5½in)

30mm (1¼in)

200mm (8in)

400mm (16in)

DETAIL
Bt

SIDE
ELEVATION

DETAIL
Bb

200mm (8in)

20mm (¾in)

100mm (4in)

PLAN

DETAIL
Bt

DETAIL
Bb

## Fretwork

*Fretwork is made from thin wood that has been cut with a very fine saw, called a fretsaw, to form patterns – usually interlocking geometric designs. These are used decoratively on furniture: they are sometimes left open, or applied to a background or can be backed with a different material, such as silk, which shows through the holes. Fretwork was used widely on bookcases, cabinets, commodes, table tops and chair backs and the term often refers specifically to the mid-18th century Chinese-style of furniture. At this time there was a craze for Oriental designs and chinoiserie (a general term for Chinese decorative work such as motifs or carvings) was applied to a range of furniture. Fretted galleries were added to tables, pagoda-like fretted tops put on cabinets and fretwork chair backs were designed.*

**8** Square the lines all around the shelf edge. Hold the shelf flat on the bench and cut each shoulder on the waste side of the cut line to the required depth. Pare away the waste with a sharp paring chisel, working from each side across the grain.

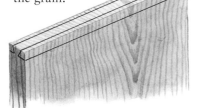

*Square the dovetail lines all round the shelf edge and cut to size.*

**9** On the backboard make gauge marks along the grain and knife cuts across the grain to the precise dimensions of the mirror. It is always better to obtain the mirror first and make the recess to fit it, because you cannot always rely on obtaining glass that is cut precisely to size.

**10** Now cut away the recess, which will house the mirror. The best tool to use for this is an electric router. Set the router to the correct depth and the fence to enable the tool to cut to the gauge lines. Take a cut from each edge, stopping short of the total length. Leaving the depth setting the same, adjust the fence so that a series of cuts from each side will remove the bulk of the material. When this has been completed, pare to the top and bottom cut lines. If you do not have an electric router, you can remove the bulk of material with a flat-bottomed bit such as a Forstner, setting the depth in a drill press and making a series of holes in the waste area. Use a hand router to remove the remaining waste and carefully pare squarely to the four edges.

*Use a Forstner drill bit to cut the recess for the mirror.*

**11** The thickness of the board is designed to give a stable piece and still allow for jointing. Some material will need to be removed from the back where the fretwork details will be cut, thus giving a thickness of about 8mm (5/16in). Remove this as described in step 10.

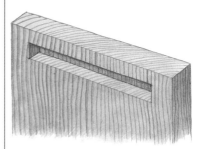

*Reduce the thickness of the area where you will do the fretwork.*

**12** Use the template (see drawing on page 175) to mark out the fretwork detail carefully on the prepared area of the mirror frame. Make knife lines and drill holes to accept the fretsaw blade in each of the areas to be removed. This can be easily achieved by tracing the pattern with carbon paper. Alternatively, photocopy the design and glue it down in the required location. The latter is by far the best method to use because the glued-down paper will hold the surface firmly and help prevent chipping.

**13** If you have not used a fretsaw before, practise on a spare piece of timber and, when confident, cut the patterns. Take your time and follow the lines exactly.

*Cut the pattern with a fretsaw.*

**14** To hang the mirror up, make a chamfer and drill a hole at an angle in the centre of the top fretwork recess on the back. This can then be located on a screw or pin in the wall.

*Fix a screw at an angle on the wall and position the mirror over screw.*

**15** Sand all the timber components, taking care to remove all set-out marks. Glue the shelf in place on the backboard with PVA adhesive. Apply the required finish of your choice.

**16** Glue the mirror in position by placing three or four lumps of mastic on it, or use silicon or double-sided tape.

# Small table   Basic

*This small table was designed by Rupert Williamson, one of the top UK designers/makers of the late twentieth century. It was specifically designed as an initial exercise for students of fine woodworking. It is a simple and classic piece but requires precise work to complete well, particularly when making the legs octagonal in shape and the mitred top frame.*

### Tools

Smoothing plane

Combination square

6mm (¼in) mortise chisel

Mortise gauge

G-cramp

Box square

Tenon saw, or if you have machinery, radial-arm saw or saw bench

Six small sash cramps

Drill and 4.5mm (³/₁₆in) 8mm (⁵/₁₆in) and 3mm (⅛in) bits

Mitre square

Marking knife

Hand plane or mitre shooting board

Screwdriver

### Skills required for project

Measuring and marking *pages 64–7*

Basic sawing *pages 68–71*

Planing *pages 74–81*

Fine sawing *pages 82–5*

Drilling *pages 96–100*

Making mortise and tenon joints *pages 104–9*

Using abrasives *pages 115–17*

Assembling projects *pages 120–7*

Using adhesives *pages 128–9*

Wood finishing *pages 130–5*

| MATERIALS | | |
|---|---|---|
| Part | Materials and dimensions | No. |
| | Hardwood | |
| Legs | 510 x 30mm x 30mm (20 x 1¼in x 1¼in) | 4 |
| Top rails | 270 x 45 x 16mm (10⅝ x 1¾ x ⅝in) | 4 |
| Cross-rails | 340 x 30 x 16mm (13½ x 1¼ x ⅝in) | 2 |
| Top frame | 375 x 75 x 20mm (15 x 3 x ¾in) | 4 |

**Other materials:** the top can be plate glass, stone, tile, slate, metal or cork – 6mm (¼in) thick, 220 x 220mm (9 x 9in); four 30mm (1¼in) 6 gauge countersunk screws; adhesive (PVA); abrasive paper; finish.

**1** Begin by planing all the components face side and face edge to the correct width and thickness, as shown in the drawing opposite.

### Making the underframe

**2** Keeping each leg square for the moment, mark a pencil line around each to indicate the length of the leg. Also mark the sloped-haunched mortises for the top rails at the top of each leg. Each is 33mm (1⁵/₁₆in) long and there are two in each leg, at 90 degrees to each other. Use the mortise gauge to set the width – 6mm (¼in) – between the shoulder lines. On the end of each leg, set out the octagonal shape (see page 246).

**3** With a combination square or rule used as a pencil gauge, draw a line along each edge of the leg to indicate the amount to be removed from each corner to create the octagonal shape.

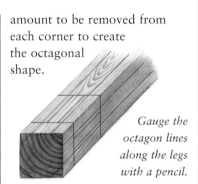

*Gauge the octagon lines along the legs with a pencil.*

**4** Cut the sloped-haunch mortises with a 6mm (¼in) mortise chisel. The mortises will meet in the middle of the wood as this is a corner joint.

*Use a chisel to cut the mortises.*

**5** Plane each leg precisely to an octagon by holding each one in a vice and planing to a 45-degree angle at each pencil line.

**6** Mark the position of the mortises on the diagonal faces for the cross-rails. These are on the face between the two mortises that you cut in step 4. Measure and mark up from the bottom 150mm (6in), and then a further 30mm (1¼in). These mark where the top and bottom of the cross-rails will sit. Square a line 3mm (⅛in) in from each of the lines to represent the shoulder lines of the mortise. Use a box square and pencil to produce these squared shoulder lines (see box on page 180). Set a mortise gauge to leave a gap of 6mm (¼in) between the pins and mark the mortise in the centre between the shoulder lines. Leave the gauge set at this position.

**7** Secure the legs on the bench with a G-cramp and cut the mortises to a depth of 20mm (¾in).

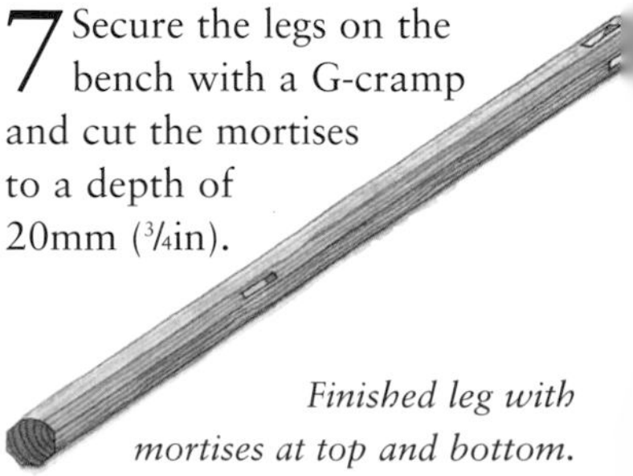

*Finished leg with mortises at top and bottom.*

From this stage, it is best to give each joint a number or letter and ensure that this is also marked on the corresponding ends of the six rails. When fitting, always check that the markings match.

**8** Next, mark and cut the four top rails to length – 190mm (7½in) plus tenons (265mm/10¼in) – and mark the tenons with their haunches: 20mm (¾in) each.

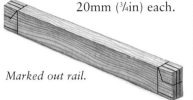

*Marked out rail.*

**9** Using a tenon saw, cut the tenons, including the mitred end where they will meet inside the leg.

*Legs and rails in the various stages of marking out and cutting.*

**10** This is the best time to drill the countersunk holes that will enable you to screw the underframe to the top frame. There should be one hole per rail. From the underside of the rail drill a hole that will accept the screw head, and then a clearance hole right through.

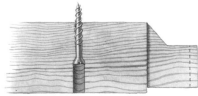

*Drill the screw holes into the rails.*

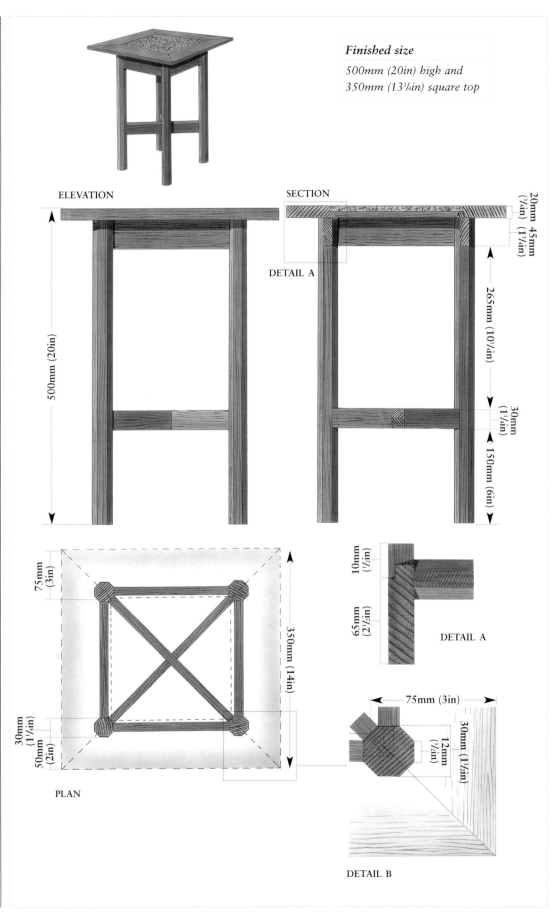

*Finished size*

*500mm (20in) high and 350mm (13¾in) square top*

ELEVATION

SECTION

DETAIL A

500mm (20in)

20mm (¾in)
45mm (1¾in)

265mm (10¼in)

30mm (1¼in)

150mm (6in)

PLAN

75mm (3in)

350mm (14in)

30mm (1¼in)
50mm (2in)

10mm (½in)

65mm (2½in)

DETAIL A

75mm (3in)

30mm (1¼in)

12mm (½in)

DETAIL B

179

**11** Fit these four rails into the four legs, ensuring that the joints are a good fit; you may use a little pressure with the sash cramps at this stage. Do not use any adhesive, and ensure that the assembly is perfectly square.

**12** Next, mark and cut the two bottom cross-rails to length. Mark the shoulders and check that the preassembled frame is square by laying one cross-rail over the top diagonally. Square a line up onto the face of the rail to correspond with the face of the leg. Square these lines around the rail. Use the mortise gauge to set out a 6mm (¼in) tenon in the centre with 3mm (⅛in) shoulders top and bottom.

*Check that the preassembled frame is completely square.*

**13** Cut these tenons, checking that the shoulder length is the true diagonal length. Disassemble the top rails and legs, and fit the cross-rail tenons into the mortises. Repeat with the other joint at the centres of the cross-rails. Cut this joint and fit.

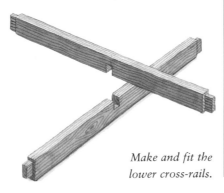

*Make and fit the lower cross-rails.*

**14** You should now be able to assemble the whole underframe dry.

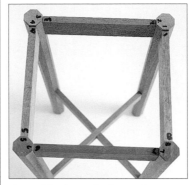

*Assemble the underframe dry.*

**Making the top frame**

**15** Prepare the timber for the top frame by planing to size – 75 x 20mm (3 x ¾in). Place all four pieces together – on edge, face edge up and flush on one end. Mark the inside edge 75mm (3in) in from the flush end. Measure along 200mm (8in) from this and square a second line across the edge with a marking knife. Lay each piece flat and mark the mitres out on the face side with a mitre square.

*Mark the top frame components.*

**16** Cut the mitres; you may use a tenon saw or, if you have machinery, a radial-arm saw or saw bench. To ensure that the mitres fit exactly you will probably have to plane them, using either a hand plane with the timber held in the vice or a mitre shooting board.

**17** Mark and work a rebate (10mm/½in wide and 6mm/¼in deep) on the inside edges of the top frame to suit the material chosen for the top.

**18** Try the joints together dry, checking that the mitres meet and that the frame is square. Adjust with the plane.

**19** A joint will be needed to hold each mitre, and this can be a tongue set in a groove or dowels.

*For the mitred corners, use either tongue and groove or dowels.*

**20** Try the assembly dry. If the joints are correct, disassemble and apply adhesive to each joint and cramp, again ensuring that the frame is square and free of wind.

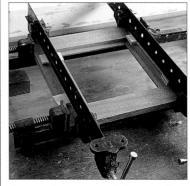

*Cramp the top frame joints together.*

**21** The table looks more delicate if the underside of the mitred top frame has a long bevel planed on it, visually reducing the thickness of the edge. Ensuring that the top surface is flat and smooth, plane the four outside edges and then work the long bevel.

**22** Before assembly, ensure that all the components are smooth. You may have achieved this when planing but may want to sand it again.

## Assembly and finish

**23** Assemble the sash cramps. Apply adhesive to the joints and cramp the underframe. When the adhesive has cured, check the top frame and underframe, and apply finish.

*Cramp the underframe together.*

**24** The underframe can now be fitted to the top using the pocketed screws between the top rails and the top frame. Drill the clearance hole 4.5mm (³⁄₁₆in) through the top rails, 30mm (1¼in) in from each end. Then counterbore from the underneath about half way through the rail with the 8mm (⁵⁄₁₆in) bit. Hold the top in position with an even overhang on all four sides, and drill through the holes into the bottom face of the top with the 3mm (⅛in) bit for a pilot hole. Fix in place with the screws.

**25** One of the many options for the panel in the top frame is a glass panel located in the rebate around the inside top edge. To ensure that the glass fits, cut a piece of scrap ply or thick cardboard that fits the space exactly, and give this to your glazier to use as a template. Alternatively, you can think up your own decorative panel using other materials such as tiles, stone, slate, metal or cork.

**12** Hold each piece in a vice and cut the mitre at each corner with a dovetail saw. Partially assemble the box, by putting each joint together about half way.

*Partially assemble the box sides.*

**13** Check that the top and bottom edges of the box are exactly level at each corner; adjust with a smoothing plane if necessary. This is important to ensure that the grooves for the top and bottom coincide perfectly when the box is fully assembled.

**14** Next, mark and plane to size the top and bottom of the box – 380mm (15in) long and 230mm (9in) wide. You will need to cut a groove into all the edges of the top and bottom pieces using a plough plane or router. Set the groove 3mm (⅛in) in from each face, 3mm (⅛in) wide and 8mm (⅜in) deep. Hold the work on edge in a vice and run the cutter along the top edge from the face side on the end grain, and then along the grain. Next, cut grooves at the top and bottom of each of the inside faces of the four side pieces.

**15** Clean up the inside surfaces of all the pieces and apply the required finish to all six inside surfaces. Since it is necessary for the top and

bottom to be able to move slightly in the grooves, rub a little wax onto them.

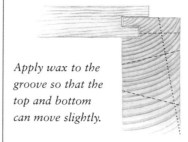

*Apply wax to the groove so that the top and bottom can move slightly.*

**16** Assemble the box by applying adhesive to the dovetail joints. Tap two short sides onto one long side. Slide in the top and bottom and fit the last long side and cramp the joints with sash or G-cramps.

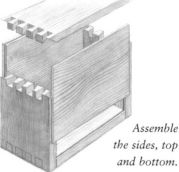

*Assemble the sides, top and bottom.*

**17** Next, separate the top and bottom of the box. When the adhesive has cured, run a groove around the middle of the box. Hold it on edge and use a marking gauge to score a line 50mm (2in) in from each face, leaving a space of 6mm (¼in) between these lines. Use a tenon saw to start a cut at each corner – saw about 20mm (¾in) along both sides between these gauge lines. Do not separate the two parts yet.

*Score a line around the box to mark the top and bottom pieces.*

**18** To give the tapered shape, pencil gauge a line around the top and bottom 8mm (⅜in) from each face side. Hold the box on edge in a vice and use a smoothing plane to produce the taper, planing in from each end so as not to break out any end grain. At this stage the outside of the box can be cleaned up and a first coat of finish applied.

**19** Complete the separation of the top and bottom with your tenon saw and then carefully plane the two mating surfaces.

**20** Around the inside of the box a thin lining sits 2mm (³⁄₃₂in) proud of, or higher than, the edges. Plane the timber to 45mm (1¾in) wide and mark it to length to match the inside face of the sides. Square the lines across the outside face of each piece of lining with a marking knife. Set out mitres on each edge and return them back across the inside face. Remember to ensure the mitres face the correct way.

**21** Hold the lining pieces on edge against a bench hook and cut the mitres with a tenon saw. Check each piece for fit inside the box and adjust by planing. Round over the top edge of each piece with abrasive paper. Apply a little adhesive and position each one.

**22** Fit hinges and a lock of your choice. Fit the hinges slightly away from the edge of the box so that the box lid will only open to a chosen angle. Apply a finish of your choice.

# All-purpose workbench Intermediate

*A sound and sturdy workbench is essential in order to achieve the best possible results in your woodworking. As such it is advisable to make this workbench one of your first major projects. The joints are basic mortise and tenon joints, held secure with dowels and bolts. A well-constructed workbench will serve as a good investment for the future.*

## Tools

Jack plane

Straightedge

Marking gauge

Hand saw

Mortise gauge

G-cramps

Power drill and 3mm (⅛in), 4.5mm (³⁄₁₆in), 6mm (¼in), 10mm (⅜in), 20mm (¾in) and countersink bits

10mm (⅜in) and 20mm (¾in) mortise chisel

32mm (1¼in) firmer or paring chisel

Tenon saw

Sash cramps

Sanding block

Screwdriver

Spanner

Electric router with 12mm (½in) straight cutter

### Skills required for project

Measuring and marking *pages 64–7*

Basic sawing *pages 68–71*

Planing *pages 74–81*

Fine sawing *pages 82–5*

Chiselling *pages 86–9*

Grooving *pages 90–3*

Drilling *pages 96–100*

Making mortise and tenon joints *pages 104–9*

Making housing joints *pages 110–11*

Using abrasives *pages 115–17*

Assembling projects *pages 120–7*

Using adhesives *pages 128–9*

Wood finishing *pages 130–5*

### MATERIALS

| Part | Materials and dimensions | No. |
|---|---|---|
| | **Solid timber:** softwood can be used for the underframe, but hardwood is needed for the backboard and the worktop. | |
| Underframe | | |
| Legs | 900 x 75 x 65mm (35⅝ x 3 x 2½in) | 4 |
| Cross-rails | 600 x 75 x 65mm (24 x 3 x 2½in) | 4 |
| Front/back rails | 1320 x 75 x 32mm (52 x 3 x 1¼in) | 2 |
| Backboard | 1500 x 200 x 32mm (60 x 8 x 1¼in) | 1 |
| Worktop | 1500 x 300mm (60 x 12in) | 1 |
| | **Plywood** | |
| Tool well | 1500 x 320 x 12mm (60 x 12⅝ x ½in) | 1 |

**Other materials:** eight 125 x 10mm (5 x ⅜in) bolts/nuts/washers; ten 25mm (1in) 8 gauge countersunk screws; four 50mm (2in) 8 gauge countersunk screws; four 75 x 10mm (3 x ⅜in) coach screws with washers; woodworker's vice; adhesive (PVA); abrasive paper (120-grit); finish (oil).

**1** Prepare the timber by cutting and planing all components to size. Apply face and side marks. Timber that is already planed is available to buy.

### Making the underframe

**2** The first parts of the bench to be made are the two end frames, which consist of the front and back legs and two cross-rails each. These are held together with wedged mortise and tenon joints.

**3** Begin by measuring up 100mm (4in) from the bottom of one leg and square a line around the timber in order to represent the top of the cross-rails. Mark a second line on the face edge 75mm (3in) down from this point and square as before. A mortise will be set out between these lines with a 10mm (⅜in) shoulder.

**4** To make the shoulder, measure in 10mm (⅜in) from the marked out lines and square around all faces of the leg. Set a mortise gauge to scribe a 20mm (¾in) wide mortise between the shoulder lines.

**5** Set out a second mortise of the same dimensions for the top cross-rail on the same face. The top edge of the rails will be level with the top of the legs. Mark the other three legs.

**6** Hold each leg in turn face up on a firm flat surface with a G-cramp. Use a power drill with a 20mm (¾in) bit, and drill out the mortise, removing the bulk of the waste. Take care to drill in the centre of the mortise and keep the drill straight. Drill approximately half way from both sides. Clean out the waste with the 20mm (¾in) mortise chisel, by cutting back to the shoulder lines from the centre of the mortise. Pare the sides with a 32mm (1¼in) firmer or paring chisel. Work from both sides of the leg, cutting a little at a time back to the set-out lines.

**7** To cut the tenons, mark the shoulders by squaring a line around the four cross-rails 75mm (3in) in from both ends. Using the already set mortise gauge, gauge the tenons towards each end, down and back to the shoulder line.

**8** Hold each in turn firmly on edge in a vice or on a saw stool and cut the tenons using a tenon saw. Clean up the face of the tenons with a sharp chisel. Remove 10mm (⅜in) off each edge of the tenons to reduce its width to match the mortises. Check for fit and adjust as required.

9 The mortise and tenon joints are secured with wedges. Place a saw cut for the wedge along the tenons 10mm (³/₈in) from each edge, and approximately two-thirds the length of the tenons. You can either make the wedges out of the waste from the tenon (as shown here) or cut them from another waste piece of timber.

*Mark out the wedges that will be cut from each edge and make a saw cut into which they will be secured.*

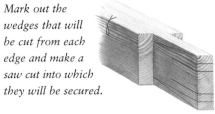

*Finished size*

*1500mm (60in) long, 965mm (38in) high and 635mm (25in) wide*

SECTIONAL
SIDE ELEVATION

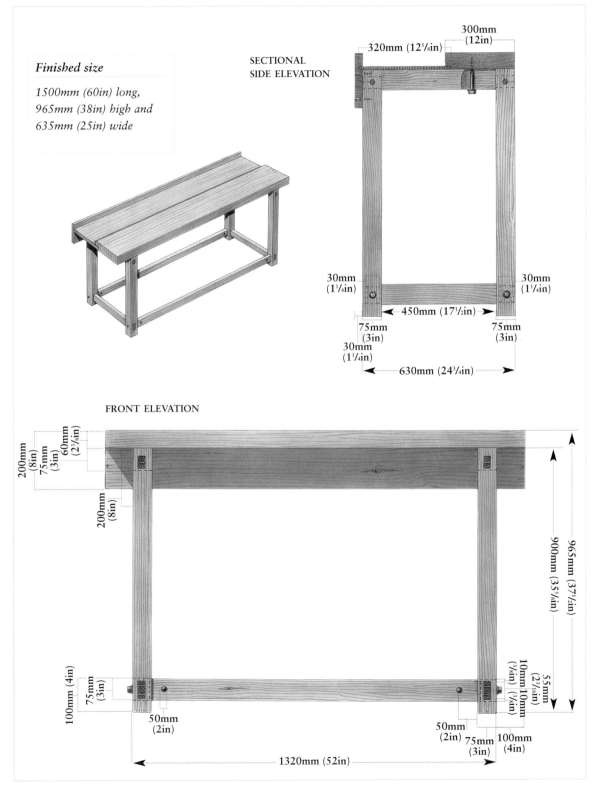

300mm (12in)

320mm (12⁵/₈in)

30mm (1¼in)

30mm (1¼in)

450mm (17½in)

75mm (3in)

75mm (3in)

30mm (1¼in)

630mm (24³/₄in)

FRONT ELEVATION

60mm (2³/₈in)

200mm (8in)

75mm (3in)

200mm (8in)

965mm (37½in)

900mm (35⁵/₈in)

55mm (2³/₁₆in)

10mm (³/₈in)

10mm (³/₈in)

100mm (4in)

75mm (3in)

50mm (2in)

50mm (2in)

75mm (3in)

100mm (4in)

1320mm (52in)

**10** Dry fit each end frame. If satisfactory, they may now be glued up with PVA. Do not use an adhesive that is brittle when set because the joint will be subjected to a lot of vibration. Apply the adhesive to the tenons and place in their respective mortises.

*Fit each end frame together.*

**11** Place one of the frames in a pair of sash cramps and apply a light pressure. Check that the rails are parallel and the whole frame is square and not in wind. Adjust the job as needed so that the frame is true. Tighten the cramps and recheck. Lay a straightedge along the rail across each leg to ensure the joint is flat. The sash cramps may need to be adjusted to correct any faults. Repeat with the other frame.

**12** Once the adhesive is dry, clean up the faces with the plane, and 120-grit abrasive paper and sanding block. Cut any excess length off at the top to finish flush with the rail.

**Making the front and back cross-rails**

**13** Next, you will need to mark out and cut the mortises for the front and back cross-rails, which will join the two end frames together. These have a stopped mortise and tenon joint that is secured by a nut and bolt. Set these out as

before on the face side of the legs using the measurements on the drawing on page 189. The mortise only needs to be chiselled out 10mm (³⁄₈in) wide and 10mm (³⁄₈in) deep. Cut the 75 x 32mm (3 x 1¼in) rails 1320mm (52in) long, and set out the stopped tenons on each end 10mm (³⁄₈in) long. Fit each into the corresponding mortise and adjust as required.

**14** Drill a 10mm (³⁄₈in) hole right through the leg from the outside to correspond with the centre of the mortise just cut. Hold the rail in its mortise and place the drill back in the hole. Start the drill to make the location on the end of the rail. Remove the rail and drill the hole in the end 70mm (2³⁄₄in) deep.

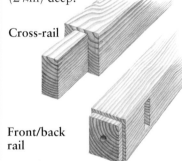

**Cross-rail**

**Front/back rail**

*Cut the tenons in the cross-rails and the front and back rails.*

**15** Lay the rail flat and set out a mortise 50mm (2in) in from the shoulder, 10mm (³⁄₈in) wide and approximately 20mm (¾in) high to allow for fitting the nut. Chisel this deep enough so that the bolt will align correctly with the thread of the nut.

**16** Fix each rail in place by putting the nut and a washer into the mortise. Position the rail and insert the bolt with the washer through the leg into the end of the rail. Tighten with a spanner and check to make sure it is square.

*Fix the lower rails to the end frames with a nut and bolt.*

**Making the backboard**

**17** Next, make the backboard, which is 200 x 32mm (8 x 1¼in) and set at the same height as the front work surface. Set up a router to cut a 12mm (½in) wide groove 8mm (⁵⁄₁₆in) deep and down 48mm (1⁷⁄₈in) from the top edge. Secure the board on a flat surface and run the groove.

**18** Fit the backboard to the back of the underframe. Cut the backboard to 1500mm (60in) long and set out a housing joint 100mm (4in) in from each end to attach to the back legs. Square these lines from the groove down and across the bottom edge. Gauge the housing 8mm (⁵⁄₁₆in) deep between the lines. Cut the housing with a tenon saw, or with the router, which should already be set at the correct depth.

*Components of back of bench.*

### A simple bench stop

On some traditional benches a rectangular strip of timber is located in a mortise in the worktop in a position where it runs against a leg. It is held in place with a wing nut that runs in a groove so that it can be both adjusted and held in place. An alternative and simpler system is to make the stop so that it is a tight fit in a hole – square, rectangular or round. They are adjusted simply by tapping them to the required height.

**19** Place the backboard in position. It will be fixed to the back legs with two 50mm (2in) 8 gauge countersunk wood screws at each end. Keep the groove clear of the top frame to enable the ply well to slip in easily. Drill 4.5mm (³/₁₆in) clearance holes through the backboard and use a 6mm (¼in) pilot hole into the leg. Countersink the outside for the screw heads. Secure with screws.

### Making the worktop

**20** Next, make and fix the worktop and tool well to the bench. First, cut a rebate in the back bottom edge of the worktop, into which the tool well will slot. Set the router to cut a rebate 12mm (½in) wide and 12mm (½in) deep. Square a line around each end of the worktop and cut with a hand saw to 1500mm (60in) long.

**21** Cut the plywood for the tool well 320mm (12⅝in) wide and 1500mm (60in) long with a hand saw. Straighten the edges with a plane. Test the ply and worktop for fit. Turn the worktop over and fix the ply into the rebate with 25mm (1in) 8 gauge countersunk screws about 150mm (6in) apart.

**22** Drill two 10mm (³/₈in) holes through each top cross-rail to enable coach screws to be used to hold the worktop down. Position the worktop on the top of the underframe, with the tool well in the groove in the backboard. Drill a 6mm (¼in) pilot hole through the cross-rail into the bottom of the work surface. Fix in place from underneath with 75 x 10mm (3 x ³/₈in) coach screws.

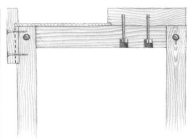

*Secure the worktop in place with coach screws.*

**23** You should now be left with a strong, rigid workbench. Ensure that the working surface is perfectly straight and flat, planing if necessary. Sand the surface in order to remove any sharp corners and apply several coats of oil to finish.

### Fitting a vice

**24** Unscrew and remove the main work surface again and fit the vice. Calculate the final position of the vice so that the cheek will be in line with the front of the worktop. Make bearers for the vice casting to sit on, which are thick enough so that the casting does not show on the surface. Drill holes for coach bolts to go through, into the underside of the worktop. Replace the worktop and fix the vice cheek on the bench side so that it is in line with the front of the bench. Fix the outer vice cheek to the front of the vice.

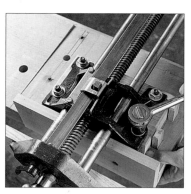

*Fix the vice in position.*

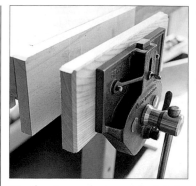

*Fix the vice so the inner cheek is in line with the front of the worktop.*

**25** The jaws of the vice can also be used to cramp material while you work on it.

*Cramp materials while you work.*

**26** Fit bench stops to your worktop, against which wood can be planed. Proprietary metal ones are available or you could make your own wooden version (see box left). Another method is a rectangular timber cam fitted to the end of the bench that can be turned against the steel pin.

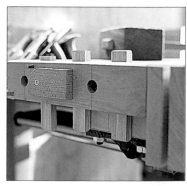

*Timber cam bench stops.*

# Garden pergola  $\boxed{\textit{Intermediate}}$

*The design of this pergola is such that it can be added to at any time, by building extra bays or horizontal elements. The wood is supported above ground level, removing the likelihood of timber degradation and thus ensuring a long life.*

## MATERIALS

| Part | Materials and dimensions | No. |
|------|--------------------------|-----|
| | Sawn or planed treated softwood, or exterior hardwood – to make one bay of four uprights | |
| Uprights | 2100 x 50 x 50mm (83 x 2 x 2in) | 16 |
| Cross-pieces | 800 x 150 x 40mm (32 x 6 x 1½in) | 4 |
| Horizontal beams | 180 x 150 x 40mm (7 x 6 x 1½in) | 4 |

**Other materials:** sixty-four 75mm (3in) 10 gauge galvanized countersunk screws; four 200 x 10mm (8 x ⅜in) steel threaded/studdings; sixteen nuts and washers; four 100 x 100 x 3mm (4 x 4 x ⅛in) steel plates; adhesive (exterior-grade); finish (exterior-grade). Note: use galvanized metal and fixings.

## Making the timber components

**1** Mark out the length of the four uprights for each leg and square a line around the timber. Mark the positions of the joining cross-pieces 20mm (¾in) up from the bottom and 300mm (12in) down from the top.

**2** Each upright requires four cross-pieces, 150 x 40mm (6 x 1½in) in section.

## Tools

| |
|---|
| Marking gauge |
| G-cramp |
| Coping saw |
| Power saw |
| Hand saw |
| 30mm (1³/₁₆in) firmer chisel |
| Drill and 4.5mm (³/₁₆in) and 10mm (⅜in) bits |
| Hacksaw |
| Smoothing plane |
| Screwdriver |
| Spanner |

### Skills required for project

Measuring and marking *pages 64–7*

Basic sawing *pages 68–71*

Planing *pages 74–81*

Fine sawing *pages 82–5*

Drilling *pages 96–100*

Making halving joints *pages 101–3*

Using abrasives *pages 115–17*

Assembling projects *pages 120–7*

Using adhesives *pages 128–9*

Wood finishing *pages 130–5*

Using metals and plastics *pages 146–7*

*Finished size*

*1980mm (6ft 6in) high and approximately 812mm (32in) square*

**DETAIL PLAN**

20mm (¾in)

165mm (6½in)

**ELEVATION**

40mm (1½in)

50mm (2in)  50mm (2in)  100mm (4in)

50mm (2in)

150mm (6in)

150mm (6in)  150mm (6in)

150mm (6in)

200mm (8in)

2000mm (6ft 6in)

150mm (6in)

20mm (¾in)

Set out four lengths of 180mm (7in) on the 800mm (32in) timber lengths and then a series of cross halving joints in the centre of each piece – 70mm (2¾in) in from each end and 40mm (1½in) wide. Use a knife and try square in order to transfer the set-out round onto both faces of all four cross-pieces. Use a marking gauge to mark the depth 75mm (3in) from one edge.

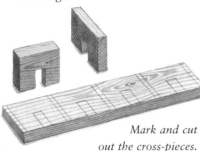

*Mark and cut out the cross-pieces.*

**3** Place the timber in a vice with the marked housings on top. Saw down the waste side of the cut lines as far as the centre gauged line. Remove the waste with a coping saw. Finish the joint by paring down to the gauged line with a 30mm (1³/₁₆in) firmer chisel.

**4** Cut all cross-pieces to the required length – 180mm (7in) – with the power saw. Check that each pair fits snugly to form a finished cross-piece. Adjust as required.

**5** Use exterior-grade adhesive to assemble the halving joints to form the finished cross-pieces. Apply the adhesive in each halving joint and press the two halves together until the tops are flush. Check that each cross-piece is square and leave to cure.

**6** Drill a 10mm (³/₈in) hole through the centre of the bottom cross-piece.

**Making the metal leg bases**

**7** Cut a 3mm (¹/₈in) thick galvanized steel plate 100 x 100mm (4 x 4in) with a hacksaw. Your supplier may be able to cut these to size.

**8** Drill a hole to accept the threaded studding in the centre. Mark the diagonals on the face of the plate and use a centre punch to create a small dent in the surface for the drill. When drilling through steel, first drill a pilot hole. This will help the larger drill bit stay in place and will also keep it straight.

**9** Secure the work in a vice on a pillar drill. Use a sharp bit at a low speed and, if available, use cutting fluid to lubricate the drill. Coat all surfaces of the metal with a preservative before assembly to prevent rusting.

**10** Fix the steel plate in position with washers and nuts about 50mm (2in) from the bottom of the studding. Place another nut followed by a washer on the long end of the studding, approximately 160mm (6⁵/₁₆in) down. Insert the studding through the bottom of the cross-piece. Fix in place with a washer, followed by a nut on the top. Ensure that all nuts are pulled up tight so that they will not become loose.

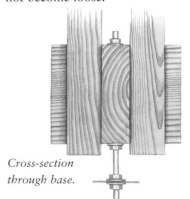

*Cross-section through base.*

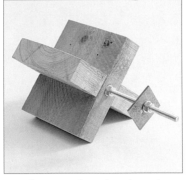

*Fix the nut and washer through the base cross-pieces.*

**Assembling the legs**

**11** Before assembling the pergola, remove all sharp edges with a smoothing plane. To make each leg of the pergola, lay one pair of uprights on the saw stools face down. Place two cross-pieces in the correct position using the marks that you set out in step 1: the studding of the bottom cross-piece should be on the 20mm (³/₄in) set-out line and the top cross-piece on the 300mm (12in) set-out line. Place the other pair of uprights on top and push them firmly into the corner of the cross.

**12** To fix the timber components together, drill two 4.5mm (³/₁₆in) holes through each upright and fix with the galvanized countersunk screws. You may also choose to add some adhesive to the joint before assembly. Repeat this process at the top cross.

**13** Turn the half-constructed leg over and fix the other uprights to the cross-pieces in the same manner. Repeat steps 11, 12 and 13 in order to assemble the other three legs.

*Screw the four uprights into the cross-pieces to make each leg.*

**14** Next, decide on the length of the horizontal beams. Check with your local building authority as to any regulations specifying span or section sizes. Allow for a 200mm (8in) overhang past each leg and cut them to length. Finish off with bevels cut on the top edges.

*The horizontal beams overhang the uprights and have bevelled edges.*

**15** Lay the beams flat on the saw stools and sight along the timber to locate any bowing. If bowing is evident, place the bowed edge as the top edge. Mark and cut the bevel on the top edge with a power saw. Apply a finish as required.

**16** Finally, install the uprights by drilling additional holes in the baseplate for bolting down or setting them into a concrete footing.

# Feature table  Intermediate

*This is an interesting and unusual feature table that is constructed from solid timber. It shows the wood to excellent effect and, with its glass top, gives an open visual space, which creates a useful display area. Its simple and effective appearance requires the marking out and cutting of extremely fine dovetail housing joints.*

### Tools

Smoothing plane

Straightedge

Winding sticks

Steel square

Power saw

Marking gauge

G-cramps

Hand saw

13mm (½in) and 30mm (1³⁄₁₆ in) chisels

Marking knife

Tenon saw

Router

Mitre square

Drill and 3 mm (⅛in), 4.5mm (³⁄₁₆in) and countersink bits

Screwdriver

**Skills required for project**

Measuring and marking *pages 64–7*

Basic sawing *pages 68–71*

Planing *pages 74–81*

Fine sawing *pages 82–5*

Chiselling *pages 86–9*

Grooving *pages 90–3*

Making dovetail joints *pages 112–14*

Using abrasives *pages 115–17*

Assembling projects *pages 120–7*

Using adhesives *pages 128–9*

Wood finishing *pages 130–5*

### MATERIALS

| Part | Materials and dimensions | No. |
|---|---|---|
| | **Any stable hardwood** – elm was used here | |
| Structural shelf | 900 x 400 x 25mm (36 x 26 x 1in) | 1 |
| Legs | 450 x 330 x 30mm (18 x 13 x 1¼in) | 4 |

**Other materials:** one 1000 x 500 x 8 or 10mm (40 x 20 x ⁵⁄₁₆ or ⅜in) toughened glass top with polished edges; eight furniture glides; eight self-adhesive clear plastic buffers; four 50mm (2in) 8 gauge countersunk screws; adhesive; abrasive paper (150-grit); finish.

**1** Prepare the timber for the shelf and legs, which must be dry and stable. If you are unable to find boards wide enough, you may need to join strips together, ensuring that the grain direction is as near quarter-sawn as possible (see box top right).

**2** Plane the timber's face side, face edge, width and thickness. Test with a straightedge, winding sticks and try square. Plane all pieces true as required. Apply face-side and face-edge marks.

## Making the legs

**3** First, make the table legs. To determine the height of the legs, use a pencil and steel square to square two lines across the legs 450mm (18in) apart on the face edge. Hold the material firmly in place

on a pair of saw stools and cut each leg to length using a power saw.

**4** Next, mark out the slots in the legs into which the shelf will fit. Square a line across the face of one leg 225mm (10in) up from the bottom and then a further 25mm (1in) up to take the thickness of the shelf. Repeat on the other legs.

**5** The shelf is held in place in dovetail housings, with 5mm (³⁄₁₆in) high dovetails. Set out two more lines on the legs 5mm (³⁄₁₆in) in from the two lines already marked out in step 4. Square all lines around the edge back to the other face.

**6** Next, square a line 95mm (3¾in) from the inside edge to mark out the wood that will be removed from the bottom inside corner of the legs.

The waste timber is represented by the shaded area in the diagram below.

*Mark out the legs. The shaded area shows the waste timber and the double lines the dovetail joint.*

**7** Now, remove the waste timber from each leg – lay them flat on a pair of saw stools and hold firm with a G-cramp. Use a tenon saw to remove the waste from the corners.

**8** Next, cut the waste away from the slots, remembering to leave 5mm (³⁄₁₆in) at the top and bottom to make the dovetail joint marked out in step 5. Use the tenon saw and then a 13mm (½in) chisel to remove the waste.

**9** To cut the dovetails, score a line with a marking knife on the existing set-out lines on each leg. The dovetail pitch must match the router cutter you are going to use to cut the housing in the shelf. Hold the leg firm on a flat surface and cut down on the waste side of the line the required depth with

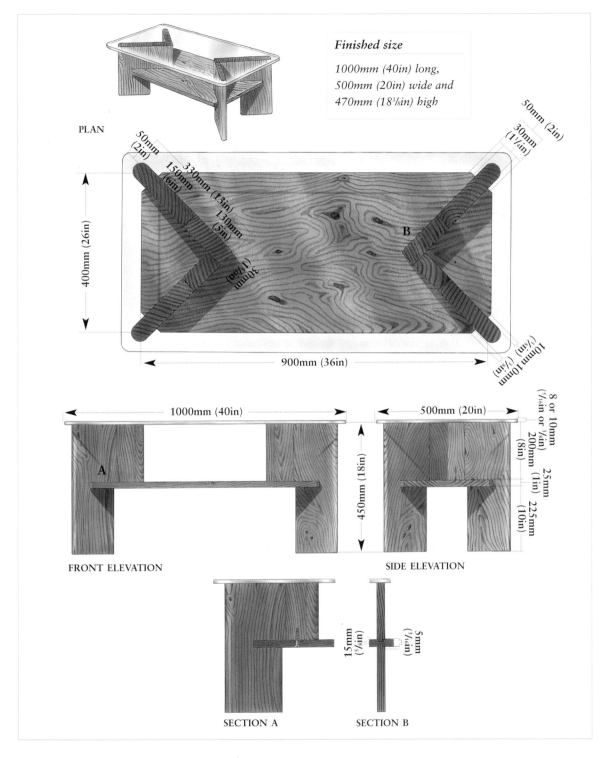

**PLAN**

*Finished size*

*1000mm (40in) long,
500mm (20in) wide and
470mm (18³/₈in) high*

50mm (2in)

50mm (2in)

30mm (1¼in)

150mm (6in)

330mm (13in)

130mm (5in)

30mm (1¼in)

400mm (26in)

B

900mm (36in)

10mm (³/₈in)

10mm (³/₈in)

1000mm (40in)

500mm (20in)

8 or 10mm (⁵/₁₆in or ³/₈in)

200mm (8in)

25mm (1in)

A

450mm (18in)

225mm (10in)

**FRONT ELEVATION**

**SIDE ELEVATION**

15mm (⁵/₈in)

5mm (³/₁₆in)

**SECTION A**

**SECTION B**

### Joining solid timber to make a wide board

It is often necessary to join several strips to make a wide board of solid timber. A suitably wide plank may not be available, or the grain direction in through and through-cut planks may make them unsuitable because of the likely movement of the timber. When joining strips, ensure that they are perfectly square, straight and flat. It is advisable to have some form of jointing method between the faces to be glued, such as tongues in grooves or dowels. To ensure that the board stays flat, it is essential to place sash cramps on both the top and bottom faces.

a tenon saw. Take care not to damage any timber on the other side of the line as this will be difficult to hide and will look unsightly. Remove the waste from the dovetail with a 30mm (1³/₁₆in) chisel. Chisel at an angle in order to make the pitch of the dovetail.

*Make the dovetail for each housing joint.*

### Making the shelf

**10** Next mark out, cut and plane the shelf to size. Cut each corner at a 45-degree angle. The length of the cut is equal to the thickness of the leg – 32mm (1¼in) plus an extra 10mm (³/₈in) each side.

197

**11** Now, cut the dovetail housings in the shelf. Make a router template (jig) from a piece of manufactured board. The slot up the centre will need to match the collar and cutter for your router. Set the cutter to cut 5mm (³/₁₆in) deep into the surface of the shelf. As always when routing, test run a cut in scrap timber to ensure the set-up is correct.

*Make a router template or jig.*

**12** Fix a stop under the jig so that the router will only cut the housing 275mm (11in) long. When the jig is set correctly, lay it on the surface of the shelf and secure it at a 45-degree angle at the corner with a G-cramp. Before cutting, check it again with a mitre square. Rest the router on the template. Start it up and slowly move the cutter into the work. Keep the collar against the left-hand side of the slot, pushing the router forward to the end. Move the router across the end of the slot and pull it back towards you, ensuring the collar stays against the right-hand side of the slot. Repeat this on all four corners of the shelf top.

*Rest the router on the template and cut the slot carefully.*

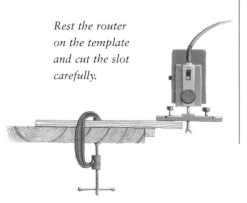

**13** Adjust the stop on the template so that the router will only cut a housing 145mm (5³/₄in) long. Turn the shelf over and cut the bottom housing in the same way.

*Turn the shelf over and make the dovetail housing in the other side.*

**14** Before you assemble the table you will need to fix the internal corners where the two pairs of legs meet. Cut 32mm (1¹/₄in) off one of each pair so that when they are slotted into place, the shorter leg can butt up against the longer leg.

**15** Check the fit of the joints and adjust as required. Sand and apply a first coat of finish to all components, masking the joint areas.

**16** To assemble, slide one long leg into its housing and apply adhesive to the edge that its matching leg will butt up against. Slide in the second leg and press togther firmly. Apply adhesive to the butted edges only, not in the dovetail housing.

*Slide the leg into the housing.*

**17** Remove any excess adhesive with a damp cloth before it is set. When dry, turn the table over and screw-fix each leg in place from underneath the shelf. Drill a 4.5mm (³/₁₆in) hole through the shelf followed by a 3mm (¹/₈in) pilot hole into the leg. Countersink the top of the hole and insert the screw in place.

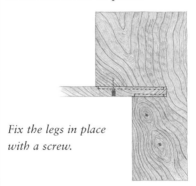

*Fix the legs in place with a screw.*

*Use a power drill to fix the screws in place.*

**18** Sand the table with 150-grit abrasive paper and apply the wood finish of your choice.

**19** Fix two furniture glides to the bottom of each leg. At the top of the legs, position small, clear self-adhesive plastic buffers to prevent the glass top from sliding. The glass top must be manufactured from toughened glass, with all the edges ground and polished by a specialized glazier. Do not use standard glass for this purpose.

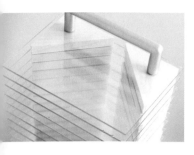

# Free-standing CD rack | *Intermediate*

*As CD collections grow ever larger, safe storage with easy access to CDs becomes an important concern. The design for this CD rack allows for convenient access with CDs stacked alternately to right and left. It is also flexible because you can add extra spacers as necessary by lengthening the rods and make some spacers to a different thickness to accommodate double CDs.*

## Tools

Backsaw

Mitre box (optional)

Mitre square

Block plane

Table saw or radial-arm saw

Screwdriver

Pillar drill and 3mm (¹⁄₈in), 4mm (³⁄₁₆in) and 6mm (¹⁄₄in) bits

6mm (¹⁄₄in) dowelling bit

12mm (¹⁄₂in) Forstner bit and 30mm (1³⁄₁₆in) hole saw

Smoothing plane

Jigsaw

Second-cut file

### Skills required for project

Measuring and marking
*pages 64–7*

Basic sawing *pages 68–71*

Planing *pages 74–81*

Fine sawing *pages 82–5*

Shaping *pages 94–5*

Drilling *pages 96–100*

Using abrasives
*pages 115–17*

Assembling projects
*pages 120–7*

Wood finishing
*pages 130–5*

Using metals and plastics
*pages 146–7*

| MATERIALS | | |
|---|---|---|
| Part | Materials and dimensions | No. |
| | **Solid timber** – hardwood or softwood of your choice to make a rack for 29 CDs | |
| Length for triangles | 2100 x 50 x 12mm (82 x 2 x ¹⁄₂in) | 1 |
| Base | 150 x 165 x 40mm (6 x 6¹⁄₂ x 1⁵⁄₈in) | 1 |
| Handle (optional) | 100 x 50 x 12mm (4 x 2 x ¹⁄₂in) | 1 |

**Other materials:** one 3750 x 140 x 3mm (150 x 5¹⁄₂ x ¹⁄₈in) acrylic sheet; scraps of timber for jigs; two 585 x 6mm (23 x ¹⁄₄in) threaded rods; four with washers (two standard and two dome); six 25mm (1in) 6 gauge countersunk screws; abrasive paper (120-grit, and 400- and 600-grit wet-and-dry); finish.

You will often be faced in woodworking with the need to produce batches of components of the same size and this project demonstrates some simple jigging methods, which will show how you can achieve this.

This free-standing CD rack can be made with hand tools but in order to use the jigs effectively, some machinery would be useful – for example, a table saw for making the timber triangles and cutting the acrylic precisely to size, and a pillar drill for drilling the holes in both the timber and acrylic.

Once you have made the necessary jigs it will be easy to add to existing racks or make matching ones at a later stage. The only dimensional change will be in the length of the threaded steel rods or spacers of different thicknesses.

### Making the timber triangles

First, cut the timber triangles to size. There is a variety of ways to do this.

1 If you are going to use a hand saw (or backsaw) mark the triangles with a cut line. On a scrap piece, make a saw cut, measure the width of the kerf and ensure that the two cuts between each triangle are the same dimension as the kerf, so that you will only need to make one cut between each piece.

*Mark out the triangles and then cut with a hand saw.*

2 Alternatively, if you decide to use either a traditional mitre box (see box top right),

or a mitre frame with your backsaw, make a stop that is fixed to the fence face that will enable each cut to produce a triangle to the required size. After the first cut, turn the timber over so that the new 45-degree corner fits into the stop. Ensure that the edge is hard against the fence face. Continue cutting to make the required number of pieces. Clean up the cut ends with a sharp block plane and/or 120-grit abrasive paper wrapped around a sanding block. If planing, secure the end in a vice and plane with the grain. Check the edge for square with a try square, and the mitre with a mitre square. Be careful to keep the pieces the same size.

3 On the other hand, if you are using a table saw, use the adjustable sliding fence and adjust precisely to 45 degrees. Make a timber fence that fits to it at least 25mm (1in) high and fix with screws. Adjust the height of the saw blade to slightly more than the thickness of the timber and make a cut in the timber fence. Now make an extra piece that will fit to the fence to create a stop. Cut one end of this piece at 45 degrees and align it with the saw cut on the right-hand side.

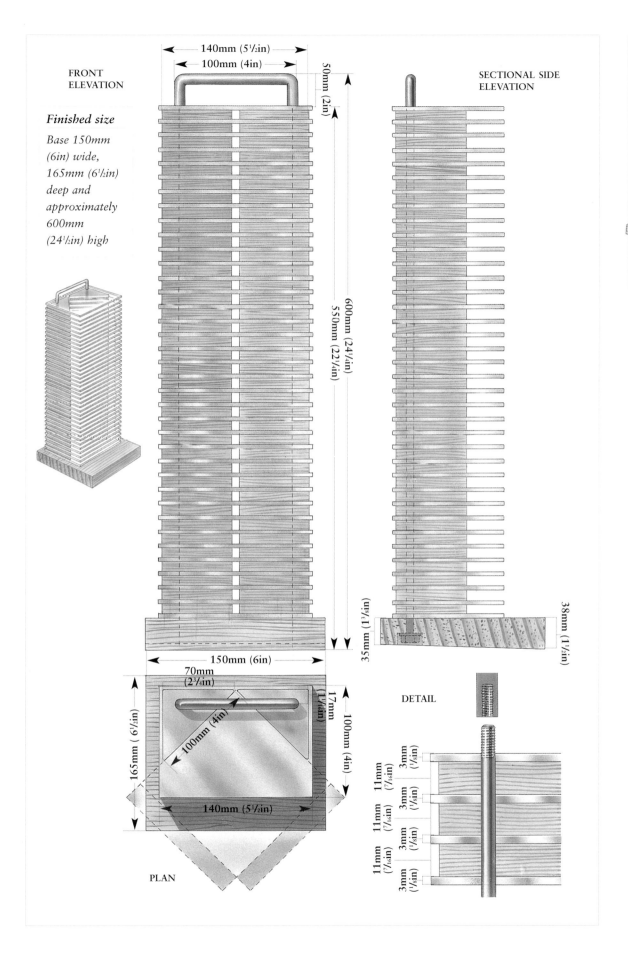

**FRONT
ELEVATION**

*Finished size*

*Base 150mm
(6in) wide,
165mm (6¹⁄₂in)
deep and
approximately
600mm
(24¹⁄₂in) high*

140mm (5¹⁄₂in)
100mm (4in)
50mm (2in)

600mm (24¹⁄₄in)
550mm (22¹⁄₄in)

**SECTIONAL SIDE
ELEVATION**

35mm (1³⁄₈in)

38mm (1¹⁄₂in)

150mm (6in)
70mm (2³⁄₄in)
17mm (¹¹⁄₁₆in)
100mm (4in)
100mm (4in)
165mm (6¹⁄₂in)
140mm (5¹⁄₂in)

**PLAN**

**DETAIL**

3mm (¹⁄₈in)
11mm (⁷⁄₁₆in)
3mm (¹⁄₈in)
11mm (⁷⁄₁₆in)
3mm (¹⁄₈in)
11mm (⁷⁄₁₆in)
3mm (¹⁄₈in)
11mm (⁷⁄₁₆in)
3mm (¹⁄₈in)

### Using a mitre box

A traditional mitre box
is a simple wooden jig,
which is used with a
backsaw to cut square
ends and mitre joints.
It has two raised sides
with slots cut in each
side. The backsaw is
then placed in the slots,
which guide the saw.

201

Fix in place with two 25mm (1in) 6 gauge screws through the back of the fence.

*To make the template, cut a stop with a 45-degree corner and fix it to the fence.*

**4** When cutting the triangles, make a first cut and then turn the timber over and slide it up to the stop. To make the next cut, hold the triangle carefully in place, passing the fence and timber right over the saw before removing the cut piece. Remove the cut piece from the fence. Slide the timber back from the cut line and return the fence back to the starting position. To make the next piece, turn the timber over and cut as before. Continue to cut all the pieces you require for your stand. You will need 58 triangles for 29 CDs.

**Drilling the holes**

Again, the best way to drill the holes in both the triangles and acrylic sheet is to make a jig.

**5** Make a base from scrap manufactured board – about 200 x 300mm (8 x 12in). The base will be fixed to the table of the pillar drill or drill stand.

**6** Ensure that you mark out very precisely the position of the drill centre and the edges where the blocks will be fixed. With a pencil and try square, square a line across the width of the board in the centre. Mark a parallel line on the face 25mm (1in) in from the back

edge of the board. Where these two lines meet, mark two 45-degree lines out to the front edge of the jig. These are the lines indicating the block positions.

**7** Mark two lines parallel to and 20mm (¾in) inside the first pair. The intersection of these two lines is the position for the hole to be drilled.

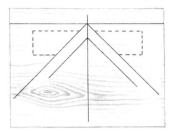

*Mark out the jig for drilling holes in the triangles and acrylic.*

**8** Now make the two blocks from off-cuts that will form the fence. Make sure that the top edge is perfectly flat. Drill two 4mm (³/₁₆in) holes through both blocks. Place one on each side of the first 45-degree lines and drill a 3mm (⅛in) pilot hole into the baseboard through the block. Fix into place with 25mm (1in) 6 gauge screws, ensuring the blocks are fitted precisely on the lines. The jig is made open at the back so that the waste can be removed easily between operations. If this is not done, or if you do not ensure the waste is cleared after each drilling, particles will probably prevent the work sitting precisely against the blocks – causing the hole to be drilled in the wrong place.

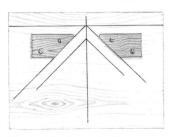

*Fix the blocks to the jig.*

**9** Fix the base in place so that the drill is positioned exactly over its mark and cramp the jig to the drill table.

*Fix the jig to the drill stand.*

**10** Place a 6mm (¼in) dowel bit in the pillar drill. Adjust the depth stop and/or table height to drill a hole just into the baseboard of the jig. Test that the centre of the bit lines up with the centre mark on the base. Adjust as required. Place the cut timber triangle in position. Hold it firmly against the fence of the jig and drill the hole right through. Take it easy so that you produce a clean cut and prevent breaking out the bottom face. Clean away any waste and repeat for each section of the job.

*Drill holes in the timber triangles.*

**Making the acrylic dividers**

**11** Next, prepare the acrylic that will be used for the dividers. This usually comes with a protective paper layer on both faces. Do not remove this until you are ready to assemble the finished project. First, prepare the sheet of acrylic with one straight edge and saw strips 100mm (4in) wide. When cutting acrylic sheets, use a timber push stick on top of the sheet to hold it down firmly, as it tends to jump as it passes the back edge of the saw. The waste particles from the cut tend to be statically charged, so wear a face mask. Hold against the rip fence and cut at a steady speed.

**12** Next, set up the cross-cut fence on the saw to cut each strip into the required number of divisions (30), each 140mm (5½in) long. To ensure the divisions are all the same size, set a stop on the right-hand side of the blade. This stop must not be past the leading edge of the blade; if it is, then the cut piece may twist and jam between the blade and the stop. It may also fly up and cause injury. Hold the strip down firmly and slide it across to the stop. Carefully push the strip forward to the blade to make the cut. Remove the cut division, slide the strip away from the blade and return the cross-cut fence back to the starting position. Repeat the cutting process for all the acrylic divisions.

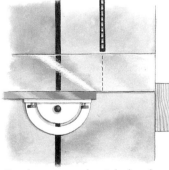

*Set the stop on the right-hand side of the blade.*

**13** Next, drill holes into the acrylic. As the timber sits slightly in from the acrylic,

the drilling position needs to be adjusted (see drawing on page 201). Change the dowelling bit in the pillar drill for a sharp 6mm (¼in) twist bit. The drill speed must be quite fast (1500–2000 rpm). Hold acrylic down firmly while drilling, or damage may result. Both holes are drilled on the long edge. Feed the acrylic sheets into the jig used for the timber. Drill the first hole and then turn through 90 degrees to drill the second hole.

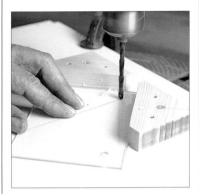

*Drill holes into the acrylic pieces.*

**14** Clean up the edges of the acrylic divisions by placing them in a vice and sanding them with 120-grit abrasive paper. To produce a very fine, clean edge, resand with 400-grit wet-and-dry abrasive paper and then finish with a 600-grit abrasive paper. Remove the sharp edges with the finer paper once you have finished the edge.

### Making the base

**15** Cut and plane the base to the dimensions shown on the drawing on page 201 – 40mm (1⅝in) thick x 165mm (6½in) long x 150mm (6in) wide. Position the two holes by marking a line 12mm (½in) in and parallel to the back edge. Lay a piece of pre-drilled acrylic on top so that the back edge lines up with the line.

Ensure the acrylic is in the centre and mark the hole position through the top onto the base. Drill a 6mm (¼in) hole. Then use a clean-cutting Forstner bit to drill a larger hole, approximately 12mm (½in), underneath, which will accept a washer and nut.

**16** Now plane the taper on the bottom of the base. Pencil gauge a line 8mm (5/16in) up from the bottom. Join this line to the bottom front corner on each end of the base. Lay the face side down on the bench against a bench stop. Hold a smoothing plane at a slight angle to match the taper, and plane the base to shape. Turn the base over when finished and lay it on a true flat surface to check for any twist. Adjust as required by planing.

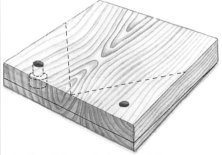

*Drill and shape the base and fit two nuts with washers into the bottom.*

### Making the handle

The handle used here is a proprietary version, the thread of which matches the metal rods into which the timber and acrylic pieces are threaded. Alternatively, you could make a wooden handle, which is fitted to the top of the metal rods.

**17** Cut and plane the handle to size – 140mm (5½in) long x 50mm (2in) high x 25mm (1in) thick. Using the pillar drill, drill a 6mm (¼in) hole at each end through the width to match the holes in the acrylic divisions. These should be 12mm (½in) in from each face.

**18** On the face of the handle, drill a 30mm (1³/₁₆in) hole – 50mm (2in) in from each end and in the centre. The hole should be 25mm (1in) down from the top edge. Again, drill this on the pillar drill with the hole saw. Hole saws can be used in either a power drill or a pillar drill. They are used to drill larger sized holes and are available in sets ranging from 25–90mm (1–3½in). Interchangeable circular cutters fit into a collar, which in turn fits onto the drill bit. Cut between the 30mm (1³/₁₆in) holes with a jigsaw to create a slot in the handle. Hold the handle firmly in a vice while cutting the centre out.

**19** Clean up the inside edges with a second-cut file if required, and finish it with 120-grit abrasive paper. Plane a 5mm (³/₁₆in) taper on the face in the same manner for the rack base.

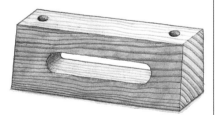

*Make a wooden handle for the rack.*

### Assembly and finish

**20** Cut the threaded rods to the correct length – 585mm (23in) each. Place a nut on the rod before cutting to length. Once cut, remove the nut and this will clean the thread on the end of the cut.

This can also be smoothed off with a second-cut file. Sand the base and the timber triangles with abrasive paper to remove any marks and sharp edges.

**21** All the timber pieces can now have a finish coat of lacquer or other finish of your choice. It is not recommended that you use an oil finish as this may find its way onto the CDs.

**22** Fit the nuts and washers onto the bottom of the threaded rod and insert this into the base.

**23** Now start the assembly of the CD rack by removing the protective cover from the acrylic. Place a piece of acrylic in position on the base and then fit two triangular blocks on the rods, Repeat this process until you have the required number of spaces for the CDs. In order to ensure that everything is straight, it may be necessary to use some small pieces of double-sided tape when initially placing blocks onto the acrylic rectangles.

*Slot the timber triangles and acrylic rectangles onto the threaded rod.*

**24** Now position the handle, fit the domed nuts and washers, and tighten the stack. If using a proprietary

handle, the studding – threaded rod – will screw directly into it. Ensure that you purchase studding that will fit the handle chosen and, if necessary, change the diameter of the drilled holes to suit.

**25** If you use your own wooden handle, fix the nut and washer onto the bottom of the threaded rod and insert this into the base. Then assemble the acrylic sheet and timber triangles, finishing with the wooden handle and top nuts and washers.

**26** If using a shop-bought metal or plastic handle, screw the studding into this first and assemble the acrylic and spacers before applying the base and the nuts and washers.

### Hanging the CD rack on the wall

If you want to hang your CD rack on the wall, the rear projection of the base will ensure that the stack is held away from the vertical surface so that the CDs slope slightly towards the rear. Make a wooden support to fix to the wall with a groove into which the wooden handle can slot. Drill holes through the support to accommodate the screws.

*Make a wall support into which the wooden handle can slot.*

# Oriental influences

The Orient has always fascinated those in the West, presumably because the culture is so very different, and Eastern furniture-making styles and techniques have often exerted an influence.

### TRADE OPENS UP THE WAY
During the 16th century there was much exploration of the East undertaken by Western European countries. They learned about lacquerwork and took East Asian objects of art back home with them. However, it was not until the 17th century that Portugal, Holland and England established regular trading relations with India and China. Lacquered furniture and domestic goods were imported from the East, where Oriental craftsmen also created pseudo-European styles based on designs that were supplied by visiting traders. During this time there were two main styles within Indo-European furniture – Indo-Portuguese, which included furniture decorated with inlaid bone or ivory on ebony and other dark woods, and Indo-Dutch, distinguished by its production of light-coloured wooden furniture with inlaid bone, incised and lacquered, as well as ebony furniture carved with flower shapes.

By the end of the 17th century Oriental decorative tastes were being widely imitated in Europe, and Chinese taste was particularly in vogue. Heavy tropical woods were also imported to Europe, which was used to fashion furniture in Oriental styles. Lacquerwork became so desirable that European craftsmen developed a technique for imitating lacquer known as 'japanning'. During the latter part of the 17th century and the beginning of the 18th century many European countries

experimented with methods of creating lacquer. None came close to the excellence of Oriental resins, but various gums and bitumens were used to create different types of varnishes.

### TWISTS ON ORIENTALISM
The style reached its peak around 1750 in what could be called a craze for all things Oriental, when high gloss lacquer and painted scenes and designs took over from marquetry, gilding and carved work. By this time the Oriental style had evolved and rather than simply trying to imitate everything within Chinese and Indian art, including the figures, shapes and imported lacquers, a more relaxed and playful Anglo-Chinese style emerged. This was the Rococo's twist on Chinese style – pagodas, exotic birds and animals such as monkeys, European figures, icicles and dripping water were all used as decoration within this style. Included in this transformation was a wide range of background colours. Whereas traditional Oriental products usually use black, brown and gold, the European examples included scarlet, yellow, white, blue and green.

### USES OF LACQUER
The different ways that lacquer was used in Europe reflects varying tastes between the 17th and 18th centuries. In the late 17th century it was mainly used to decorate the cases of cabinets that were set upon carved Baroque bases. In the 18th century, however, lacquered bookcase desks, clocks and tea tables were all fashionable in England and Germany, while in Italy and France chests of drawers and corner cabinets were also lacquered. Even whole sets of lacquer-decorated furniture

OPPOSITE LEFT *A beechwood chair shaped and painted to imitate bamboo, from the Royal Pavilion, Brighton.* ◆ OPPOSITE CENTRE *A contemporary bed design by Robin Furlong.* ◆ OPPOSITE RIGHT *An ornate 19th-century Chinese table.* ◆ ABOVE LEFT *A 19th-century Chinese armchair.* ◆ ABOVE CENTRE *A carved iron lock on a Japanese cabinet.* ◆ ABOVE RIGHT *The highly polished finish enhances the smooth lines of this Japanese-style table.*

existed. When there was a resurgence of enthusiasm for Oriental motifs in Britain in the mid-18th century, Thomas Chippendale (see page 173), instigated a Chinese Chippendale style – furniture with pagoda surmounts, fretwork and bamboo interlacing.

In the early 19th century the change of taste towards the plainer, classical style meant that lacquered furniture declined. However, as the Regency style took hold there was a resurgence in interest in the whole area of Chinese taste (see page 187 on the Brighton Pavilion), and it continued to survive in Victorian England with the vogue in painted tin or toleware.

## JAPANESE INFLUENCES
It was in the mid-19th century that trade was opened up with Japan. This country had not developed many specialized types of furniture as its interior architecture, with the garden as the focal point, served the aesthetic and social requirements. However, its lacquering far surpassed even the best Chinese examples. Edward Godwin pioneered the Anglo-Japanese style. He combined his interest in Japanese design with 18th-century ideas, which he found to be

*The simple modern cupboard combines elements of traditional Ming with European style.*

complementary. His favourite materials were ebonized wood, Japanese leather paper and bamboo, and he embraced simplicity and lightness in his work.

In the 1880s the Japanese craze of the 19th century reached its height and there were many oddities such as spindly furniture and lacquer applied to the most inappropriate pieces of furniture. During this decade and the next, Orientalism was particularly dominant in America. Near Eastern objects, as well as those from China and Japan, were chosen for smoking rooms. The 'Turkish corner' became an important part of American households – this was an arrangement of pillows, Oriental rugs and a divan in a corner of a room under a canopy, with plants and exotic accessories completing the scene.

By the start of the 20th century, creating lacquer had become a part of the chemical industry but, nevertheless, an interest in traditional Oriental techniques remained. The Irish born designer Eileen Gray learned the Japanese tradition of lacquer and undertook meticulous experiments, achieving extraordinary tones. Her screens and panels were widely exhibited at the time and influenced later lacquer artists and styles, such as Art Deco.

# Circular plant stand  [ Intermediate ]

*The elegant curves on this plant stand are produced by turning the timber on a lathe. There are two main turning methods – faceplate turning and between-centre turning. This project will give you a chance to practise both because the top and bottom of the plant stand are turned on a faceplate while the connecting spindles are turned between centre.*

## Tools

Bandsaw

Lathe with faceplate and between-centre capacity

Full face shield

Set of turning tools

Smoothing plane or hand saw (optional)

Callipers

Three-jaw chuck

Lathe drill

Cramps

## MATERIALS

| Part | Materials and dimensions | No. |
|------|--------------------------|-----|
| | **Solid timber**, preferably hardwood | |
| Round baulks | 260mm (10½in) diameter x 50mm (2in) thick | 2 |
| Spindles | 300mm (12in) x 140mm (5½in) diameter | 2 |
| Connecting piece | 150mm (6in) x 70mm (2¾in) diameter | 1 |

**Other materials:** adhesive; abrasive paper; finish.

## Skills required for project

Measuring and marking *pages 64–7*

Basic sawing *pages 68–71*

Drilling *pages 96–100*

Making housing joints *pages 110–11*

Using abrasives *pages 115–17*

Assembling projects *pages 120–7*

Using adhesives *pages 128–9*

Wood finishing *pages 130–5*

Turning *pages 142–5*

If you purchased your timber from a turnery supplier, it may be a slice of a log where the grain is travelling from face to face. If you purchased it from a timber yard it is likely to have come from a sawn board and therefore the grain will run lengthways along the board.

*Timber baulks with different grain directions.*

### Making the top and bottom

**1** First, mark out the circumference of the top and bottom of the plant stand on each baulk. Use a bandsaw to shape the timber to approximately 6mm (¼in) bigger than this circumference.

**2** To make the top, select the best face of one of the baulks and screw it onto the faceplate. Remember that you are going to make a rim 15mm (⅝in) deep on the top and so ensure the screws do not project into the timber beyond 12mm (½in).

*Fix the baulk face to the faceplate.*

**3** Mount the faceplate on the machine and adjust the tool rest just under half way from the centre.

**4** Ensure that the plate runs freely and make some marks to give you a guide to the curved base and the centre hole that you will be turning. Making sure that you are wearing a full face shield for protection, start the lathe and begin your cut with the roughing gouge.

**5** First, follow your markings to shape the end of the baulk into what will become the joint with the spindle in step 18 (see drawing opposite). Turn a flat surface in order to produce the shoulder of the joint and then turn the large hole that will accept the spindles in the centre.

**6** Next, turn curve A (see section on drawing opposite), placing the tool rest at an angle across the corner of the piece as you work. Since the top and bottom are the same up to this stage, turn the bottom in the same way.

*Turn the curve on the stand top.*

**7** Next, you will need to turn the outside face of the top and bottom sections of the stand. Begin by fixing the shoulder face of the top to the faceplate. Ensure that it is

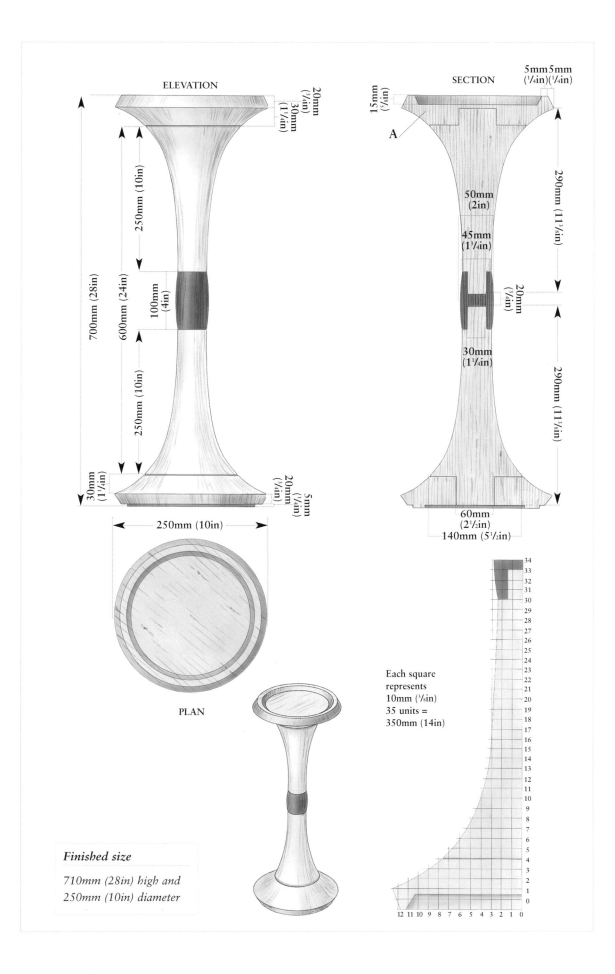

ELEVATION

20mm
(¾in)
30mm
(1¼in)

250mm (10in)

700mm (28in)

600mm (24in)

100mm
(4in)

250mm (10in)

30mm
(1¼in)

20mm
(¾in)

5mm
(¼in)

250mm (10in)

PLAN

SECTION

5mm 5mm
(¼in)(¼in)

15mm
(⅝in)

A

290mm (11³⁄₈in)

50mm
(2in)

45mm
(1¾in)

20mm
(¾in)

30mm
(1¼in)

290mm (11³⁄₈in)

60mm
(2½in)

140mm (5½in)

Each square
represents
10mm (³⁄₈in)
35 units =
350mm (14in)

34
33
32
31
30
29
28
27
26
25
24
23
22
21
20
19
18
17
16
15
14
13
12
11
10
9
8
7
6
5
4
3
2
1
0

12 11 10 9 8 7 6 5 4 3 2 1 0

**Finished size**

710mm (28in) high and
250mm (10in) diameter

*Turning*

Wood turning began
with the invention of
the lathe in Egypt some
time before the 13th
century. It was practised
by the Egyptians,
Assyrians and Romans
and also flourished
in medieval England.
Turned chairs with
triangular seats were
made of indigenous
woods from Norman
times through until the
17th century with little
change and turners
were one of the earliest
types of craftsmen.
Before the end of the
16th century, turners
had produced legs,
posts, balusters and
spindles and they came
into their own in the
17th century when
they began to produce
graceful columns.
Turned decoration on
furniture was widely
used during the
Renaissance period and
has been a feature of
furniture design ever
since. From the 19th
century onwards, more
complex spiral turnings
appeared as a result
of the development in
turning tools. However,
classic, simpler styles,
such as bobbin and
ball turnings have also
retained their popularity.

placed centrally on the faceplate by checking that the overhang on the work is even all the way round. Screw into position and replace on the lathe.

8 Turn a small bevel on the ouside edge of the top. Then carefully turn out the central recess, making sure that it is flat.

9 Take the top off the faceplate and fix the bottom of the plant stand in place. Turn a small bevel on the outside edge, a rim on the bottom surface and a shallow recess, as shown below. It is better not to have a flat base because this may later distort.

**Top**

**Bottom**

*The finished shape of the top and bottom of the stand.*

### Making the spindles

This stand has been designed with two upright pieces with a joint in between, in case the lathe does not have the required length to turn the centre spindle in one. If your lathe has the length capacity, you can turn the centre spindle as one. If your lathe will not accept a 140mm (5½in) diameter, the curve can be adjusted to suit.

10 Mark the centre at each end of one piece. Fix one end to the driving centre in the headstock, with the other end held in the tailstock with a revolving centre.

11 It can be helpful, if you have the equipment, to saw the square or plane into an octagon as this means less material to remove. It is possible, however, to turn from a square shape as long as you are very careful.

*It is easiest to cut the spindle to an octagon shape before turning.*

12 Adjust the tool rest, making sure that the revolving timber will not be in contact with it; very carefully start initial cuts that will remove corners and make the work cylindrical.

*Cut the shape into a cylinder.*

13 Make a template from the grid given with the drawing on page 209 so that you can measure off diameters needed at any stage easily.

14 Set the callipers to the thickest end and turn down to the correct diameter. Do the same at the thinner end. Turn along the full length until you achieve the required shape.

15 Both ends need to be turned down to fit into the holes – the thick end into the top or bottom of the stand and the thin end into the connecting piece. Repeat process on second piece.

*The bottom half of the spindle.*

*Ensure that you are cutting the right shape by using a template.*

16 First, turn the connecting piece to a simple cylinder and then turn the shape of the outside.

*Shape the connecting piece.*

17 Hold it in a three-jaw chuck, and drill or turn the holes that will accept the spindles.

### Assembly

18 The parts can now be assembled. Join the two spindles to the connecting piece, applying adhesive and then cramping. The top and bottom of the stand can now be fixed; glue and cramp these in place.

19 When the adhesive has cured, the whole piece can be sanded down and you can apply required finish.

6 Next, turn your attention to the bottom half of the stool. Mark the holes for the side bars in the lower legs 200mm (8in) up and drill them, ensuring that they are in line with the holes that fix the seat.

7 Cut two metal side bars from the flat bar to 400mm (16in) and round the ends with a file. Mark four holes in each as shown on the drawing on page 213 and drill them. Drill corresponding 6mm (¼in) holes through the legs. Fix the bars in position and secure with nuts and bolts.

8 Cut the footrest to length and plane it to shape, ensuring that the angles are correct so that it fits between the two metal side rails.

*Assemble the side bars and footrest.*

9 Now, make the cross-bar, which goes across the middle between the two metal side bars. Mark and cut the tube to fit; remember that the ends will need to be angled to fit against the side bars. Insert timber dowels in the ends of the tube and screw the cross-bar in place.

10 Next, glue the basic seat frame together ensuring that the components are located correctly. Screw the seat slats in position one by one and then bolt the top ends of the legs to the cross-rails.

*Fix the legs to the seat unit.*

11 With the stool upside down, bolt the side bars to the legs and then screw into the footrest and cross-bar.

12 Next, make the feet. You can finish the metal legs with plastic caps on the tube. Or, you can use left-over timber to make plugs to fit inside the tube.

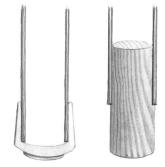

*Use plastic leg caps or timber plugs to finish the feet.*

13 Place the stool upright on a flat surface. Using a pencil on a small block of timber, mark all round the bottom of the legs to show where to angle them at the base so that the stool sits on a flat surface.

*Angle the feet so that the stool will sit on a flat surface.*

14 Cut to these marks and then work a small bevel around the cut edge. Sand so the edges are not damaged.

15 To ensure the structure is rigid, make the V-support between the cross-rails and the bottom cross-bar. The two supports are different, and so measure, mark and label each individually. With the stool assembled, mark the top angle that will connect with the inside face of the cross-rails, and mark the position of the bottom cross-bar.

16 Drill a hole in the V-support to accommodate the cross-bar. Remove the cross-bar from the stool, position both supports and replace it. Check the angled faces against the inside faces of the cross-rails and adapt as necessary.

17 Next, mark the halving joint between the two supports as they fit over the bar. Dismantle, cut the halvings and glue the supports together.

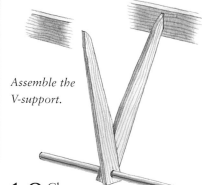

*Assemble the V-support.*

18 Clean-up the supports and replace them and the cross-bar on the stool. Fix the angled faces to the inside faces of the seat cross-rails with adhesive and screws.

19 Disassemble, sand and finish all timber parts; then reassemble to complete.

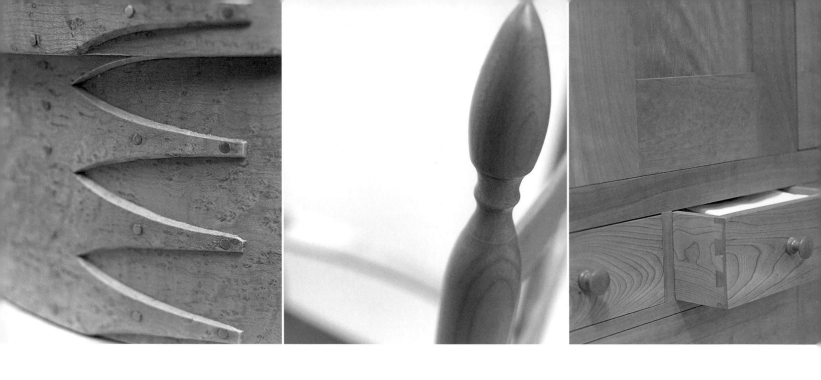

# American traditions

**SHAKER STYLE**

The Shaker religious sect founded its first community in 1787 in New Lebanon. They lived a commune lifestyle and believed that they should be self-supporting in every way. Any unnecessary frill or decoration on an object was sinful. They believed that high craftsmanship contributed to a better life on earth and as such they rejected modern production methods. Their belief that 'beauty rests on utility' found expression in simple, functional furniture and interiors, without the vanities of decoration, but always well made.

The Shakers manufactured and sold objects to obtain what they needed from the outside world and their furniture was most notable in terms of quality and inexpensiveness. Spiritual values pointed the way to a unity of form and construction. Expertly crafted joints and pegs removed any need for screws or adhesives. Function and practicality drove their designs, chairs were light and portable, so they could be easily hung on peg rails when not in use. Finely turned posts and stretchers minimized weight and 'pommel' finials acted as handles rather than simply a

*This maple sewing table would have been shared by two Sisters – the drawers slide out from the front and back allowing access to both users.*

decorative feature, which nevertheless resulted in delicate and pleasingly simple chairs. They also had to be comfortable enough for lengthy meetings and, long before the subject of ergonomics was formally studied, the Shakers designed their furniture to fit the human body. Chair backs tilted backwards slightly to cushion the human back and the back posts of the chairs were fitted with wooden ball and socket feet that could be tilted to prevent floors getting scuffed. Favourite seats were made of woven hand-dyed tape that was easy to attach, sturdy and comfortable. Other furniture was equally practical and suited to communal living. For example, dining tables were often fitted with breadboard ends and double sewing machine tables enabled the Sisters to work companionably together. These simple, elegant pieces, typically made in maple, cherry and pine, became popular in the 1860s and again at the end of the 20th century. Many of the features of Shaker furniture are still copied, but often with little relevance to the ideas that gave birth to their design philosophy. The Shakers did not set out to create a style, but a way of life.

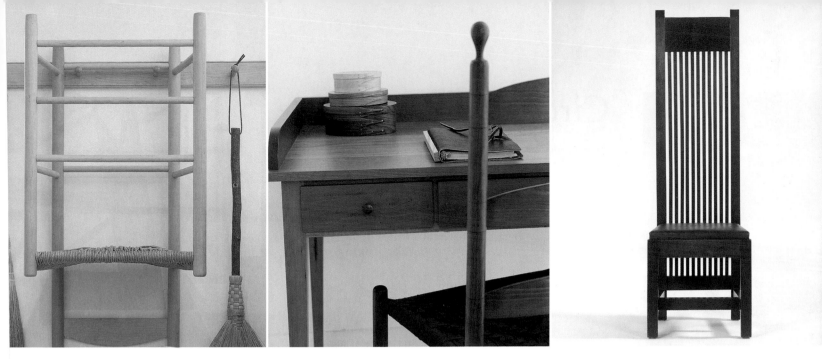

## AMERICAN ARTS AND CRAFTS

The American Arts and Crafts Movement was influenced by the ideas of William Morris (see pages 226–7) but with a slightly different emphasis. It sought to extend the ideas of quality and honesty in design. One of the people responsible for popularizing the movement in the US was Gustav Stickley. He abandoned his eclectic colonial style of furniture and started a new line using plain oak boards. His work was in fact quite heavy. A more elegant line was produced out of the same movement (which was also influenced by Mackintosh) by the architect and draughtsman Harvey Ellis. The American version of the movement managed to marry mass-market furniture with honest craftsmanship. Elbert Hubbard, a rich industrialist, was taken with the whole ethos and he founded a community of craftsmen in New York, called the Roycrofters. Early pieces of furniture produced at their workshop were simple and akin to Morris in style – oak benches, tables and stools that were known as Mission Furniture.

*A cherry rocking chair of the style made in Enfield New Hampshire in 1840.*

This is just one example, but in actual fact, the ideals of the Arts and Crafts movement swept across the whole of America, to an even greater extent than in England, possibly because it appealed to the self-help mentality that prevailed in the country.

The American movement flowered during the 1870s in some of the furniture of the architect and designer, Frank Lloyd Wright. He drew inspiration from the geometric shapes of children's games devised by Froebel, as well as Japanese-style open-plan designs. The open plan and projecting roofs of the Prairie Houses that he designed from 1900–10 encapsulated his idea 'to include furniture as far as possible as organic architecture'. His work still has a profound influence on both architecture and design today.

**6** Now, make the legs round. If turning, you will need a lathe with a long enough bed to accept the length needed; it may make turning easier if the mortises are temporarily filled with softwood plugs inserted dry. If planing, mark the final round on each end and carefully plane the octagon round. The pencil marks on the ends will give you a good guide as to how the rounding is proceeding. Repeat the process to make the other legs round.

**7** Next, prepare the four top rails by marking shoulder lengths and the stopped tenons. Square a line around the rail 30mm (1³⁄₁₆in) in from one end, a further 530mm (21in) along, and then 30mm (1³⁄₁₆in) for the tenon. Cut to length on the radial-arm saw. Square the shoulder lines all around the first rail with a marking knife. Set up the mortise gauge to the width of the mortise – 12mm (½in) – and 10mm (³⁄₈in) in from each face. Scribe the tenon around the rail from shoulder to shoulder line. Hold vertically in a vice and cut down the sides of the tenon on the waste side to the shoulder lines.

**8** Remove and lay flat against a bench hook and cut away the waste at the shoulder set-outs. Replace vertically in the vice. Pencil gauge the width of the tenon 50mm (2in) in, and cut down the tenon to make the haunch. Remove the waste by cutting across the top edge between the shoulders. Remember to cut both haunches on the top edge. Test the fit and adjust as required. Repeat for the other top rails.

**9** Cut a mitre on the ends of the tenons to allow both rails to penetrate the full depth of the mortise. Measure the diagonals to check for square. Cramp the four legs and top rails together with sash cramps.

**10** Prepare the two lower cross-rails. Lay each in turn across the diagonals and mark the shoulder lengths for the mortise and tenon joints with the legs from the dry assembled frame to ensure that the lengths are exact. Square the shoulder lines around each rail and mark the through tenons by scribing along the length with the already-set mortise gauge. Measure the distance between the shoulders and square a line around each rail 15mm (⅝in) either side of the centre for the halving joint. Use the marking gauge to scribe the centre of the face between all these squared lines. Remember to gauge from the face edge on both pieces.

**11** Hold each cross-rail in a vice and cut the tenons. Lay flat and cross-cut the shoulders as for the top rails. Place vertically in the vice and cut the tenon to width to suit the mortise at the bottom of the leg.

**12** Cut the halving joint in the centre of both rails. Secure horizontally in a vice and cut down the shoulder lines to the required depth with a tenon saw. Remove from vice and secure flat on the bench with a G-cramp. Remove the waste with a 25mm (1in) chisel. Take out the bulk of the waste in one or two cuts from one side, and then work back to the gauge lines from both sides. Check the fit and adjust as required. Repeat on the other rail.

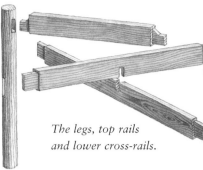

*The legs, top rails and lower cross-rails.*

**13** Assemble the whole underframe dry and check for square.

*The dry assembled underframe.*

**Making the top cross-rails**

**14** Next, make the top cross-rails, which fit across the top of the top rails and form the main support for the table top planks. Prepare the cross-rails by marking them 900mm (36in) long. Set out and cut the cross halving joint in the centre of this pair of rails in the same manner as the lower rails. The only difference is that these are 50mm (2in) in width, and so the halving will be 25mm (1in). Assemble the two halves and check for square.

**15** Next, measure and set out a 30mm (1³⁄₁₆in) wide by 25mm (1in) deep halving in the centre of each top rail. These should still be set up dry in the cramps. Position the two assembled

## Marquetry

*This rich, decorative technique involves layering veneers in order to contrast light- and dark-coloured woods to make up a pictorial design. It was first developed in the 17th century in France, spread to the Low Countries and from there to England by the 18th-century. It was extremely popular until the 19th century and is still used today. Flowers and plants were popular subjects in marquetry in the late 17th century and the technique has often been combined with other forms of decoration, such as gilding (as shown in the image below). In the mid-18th century marquetry fans, shells, swags, pendant husks and floral motifs were used on even the humblest pieces of furniture and panels of marquetry were put on more elaborate pieces. Engraved marquetry was introduced in the second half of the 18th century and consisted of cutting fine lines in the surface of veneers and filling them with a black composition.*

lippings and base to a depth of 6mm (¼in) using a router with a 6mm (¼in) straight bit. Cut the mitres with a tenon saw and test the fit. Adjust as required.

3 Glue the lippings, applying PVA adhesive to both surfaces, and place the tongue in the groove. Position each and hold with sash cramps if required.

4 When the adhesive has cured, use a smoothing plane to plane the excess lipping flush to the surface of both sides of the board, without rounding over. Key both surfaces with a toothing plane.

5 Since veneers can exert a pull on the face of a board, you must put a backing veneer on the underside. Cut one piece for the centre and some strips for a border around the edge. Lay the pieces out, slightly overlapping each other and trim to fit, including the mitred corners where the borders meet.

6 Brush some slightly thinned animal adhesive onto the board's surface to act as a size, and then apply adhesive to the veneer. Lay the veneer in position and, using the veneer hammer, work from the centre and squeeze out the excess adhesive and any air pockets.

*Lay the backing veneer with the veneer hammer.*

7 If it is necessary to relay the veneer because of bubbles, the adhesive can be softened using an iron and damp cloth, and the veneer pushed down again with the veneer hammer. Tap the surface with a fingernail. You will hear if there are any areas that have not adhered.

8 Prepare the face veneers and board. Draw joint lines on the board where the pieces of veneer will meet. Cut the four book-matched leaves the same size to give a total rectangle of 400 x 280mm (16 x 11in). Set this out in its location on the board over the joint lines.

9 Now lay the face veneers. Lay one of the four rectangles as described above. Then lay the second adjoining veneer with the edge to be joined overlapping the first. Using a sharp veneer knife and straightedge, cut through both veneers along the joint line. Soften the adhesive with the iron and remove the waste strips of veneer. Relay both so that the joint is perfect. Lay all four pieces in the same way. Slight movement is possible while the adhesive is wet.

*Lay the first section of veneer with a veneer hammer.*

10 The edge veneer can now be laid around the centre. Trim the border

and prepare the four edge veneers for application. Begin by laying one strip of veneer in position, trimming the corner to the lipping but overlapping at the mitre. Now lay the adjacent strip of veneer, overlap the corner and, using a sharp veneer knife and metal straightedge, cut the mitre at the corner where they meet. Soften the adhesive using the method explained in step 7, remove the waste pieces and press down with the veneer hammer. Repeat on the other three corners and trim the veneers to the edge.

11 Next, mark the position of the grooves on the tray – these are the two long thin grooves for the side strips and the two angled grooves for the two handles. Cut these with a router. To run the angle grooves, use a G-cramp to cramp a 20mm (¾in) thick block 40mm (1⅜in) in from the end, parallel to the end. Use this fence to plunge cut the groove, and set the bit to protrude 22mm (⅞in) from the baseplate. Steady the router and cut the groove 250mm (10in) long and 50mm (2in) in from each edge.

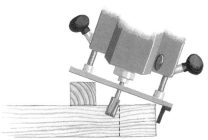

*Use a router to cut the grooves.*

12 Change the router bit and, with the aid of a fence, run the other two grooves 12mm (½in) from the edge and 6mm (¼in) wide to suit the side strips. These should be 380mm (11in) long in the centre and 6mm (¼in) deep.

**13** Plane the thin side strips to size, cut to length and adjust them to fit the grooves.

*Fit strips in the grooves.*

**14** Plane the material for the two handles, initially keeping the pieces square. Mark the handle hole positions, drill a 25mm (1in) hole in each end and remove the waste from between the two holes with a coping saw. Carefully pare the edges with a chisel to true up.

**15** Mark and cut the tongues that will join the handles to the tray. Run an 8mm ($^5/_{16}$in) groove in the centre bottom edge of each handle 15mm ($^5/_8$in) deep.

**16** To work the tapers, mark and plane the two angles on the faces, and then mark the ends; cut and plane. Plane the angle on the bottom 8mm ($^5/_{16}$in) on one side. Check the fit and adjust as required.

*Mark out and cut tongues and tapers on the handles.*

**17** Set up the router to run a small rebate on the bottom edge of the tray 2 x 2mm ($^1/_{16}$ x $^1/_{16}$in). There is also a bevel on the top of the tray. Mark this on all four sides and plane.

**18** Sand all components, glue the thin side strips in place and then the handles. Apply the required finish.

# Arts and Crafts heritage

The rapid technological progress and industrialization that occurred in the second half of the 19th century meant that mass furniture production appeared for the first time. Some theorists reacted against this and advocated a return to handwork.

## ARTS AND CRAFTS MOVEMENT

The Arts and Crafts movement in Britain was led by the artist and social reformer, William Morris. This movement blamed the Industrial Revolution for the disintegration in society and looked back to the art and society of the Middle Ages for a more harmonious approach. Morris suggested that products would be better if they were simple and made by hand by craftsmen. He fought against machine production and sought to replace huge industrial cities with smaller communities in which craftsmanship could flourish once again. In 1861 he started the firm of Morris, Marshall and Faulkner to promote his beliefs. He discovered, however, that the sole use of handwork made most products too expensive for the mass market.

However, his ideas influenced architects, designers and makers into and throughout the 20th century. His ideal of a community of artists and craftsmen later became a reality with groups like the Werkstätten, which was founded at the beginning of the 20th century in Vienna. His social and ethical concerns reappeared later in the Bauhaus school (see pages 274–5).

*A Voysey chair designed in 1906.*

Sidney and Ernest Barnsley and Gimson continued the movement into the 20th century in Britain. Their approach to design was based on clean lines and unadorned surfaces. They showed a fresh appreciation for the materials that they used and a respect for quality and understanding of construction.

Not all observers were anti-machine however. In the wake of Morris's movement, the Art Furniture movement arose in the 1870s and 1880s. Charles Eastlake was its most important advocate. He warned against formal exaggeration and demanded simple lines and straightforward construction.

## ART NOUVEAU

At the end of the 19th century Art Nouveau made its appearance, born out of the wish to create an entirely new style independent of traditional styles. Initially inspired by English ideas, it soon found its own language on the Continent where it had a greater influence.

The first success of the movement was in Belgium with Victor Horta who employed mahogany, maple and pale fruitwoods along with sumptuous upholstery. Henri van de Velde was more rigorous than Horta, finding a style based on the contrast between curving lines and smooth, filled planes.

In France, Emile Gallé wished to create an alliance of industrial arts and in 1901 the School of Nancy was founded. The furniture exponents

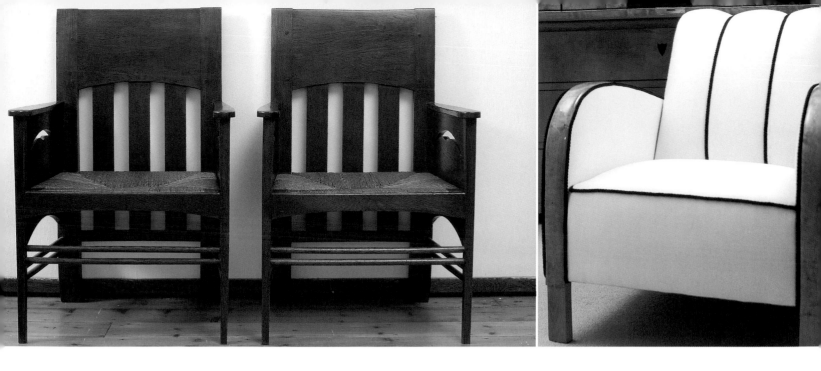

OPPOSITE LEFT *Produced and sold by Morris, Marshall and Faulkner in 1875, this Sussex armchair has became a classic.* ◆ OPPOSITE CENTRE *The beaten iron strap handles on this c1900 cabinet are a common Arts and Crafts feature.* ◆ OPPOSITE RIGHT *This oak table with two flaps is a typical Arts and Crafts style.* ◆ ABOVE LEFT *Oak armchairs with pierced side panels designed by Charles Rennie Mackintosh for the Argyle Street Tea Rooms, Glasgow in 1897.* ◆ ABOVE RIGHT *A Swedish Art Deco chair made out of birchwood c1920–30.*

of the group included Majorelle, Gallé, Gruber and Vallin. The furniture produced there used nature, especially the flower, as its central theme.

Germany found this ornate, floral style did not sit well with new machinery. Instead, they laid the emphasis on function, not superficial decoration. One important designer, Richard Riemerschmid, made furniture in mahogany, ash and poplar, using only the occasional scroll as decoration.

## MACKINTOSH

In Scotland in about 1890, the architect Charles Rennie Mackintosh and his group began to create their own aesthetic. His furniture was slender and geometric in form, which contrasted with the rustic simplicity of the contemporary English style. His pieces were based around straight lines and rectangles combined with a gently curving, linear ornament – a style connected to the Art Nouveau movement but much simplified. His work had a great influence on European design and the angular construction of his furniture pointed a way for the future.

## BEYOND MACKINTOSH

Although many designers were seduced by Art Nouveau, some eventually called for change. Otto Wagner and Adolf Loos founded the

*An elegant Arts and Crafts hatstand made of oak.*

Vienna School, calling for a style that gained its expression purely from the materials used to make a piece and the construction methods employed on it. Their furniture was always simple, well proportioned and in harmony with its surroundings.

The Arts and Crafts movement had an impact all over Europe, and artists began to form communities. In 1903 Josef Hoffman founded Wiener Werkstätten with Koloman Moser. He expounded Morris's theories but the movement also had upper-class clients for whom they made costly furniture with veneers of fine woods. They did, however, make simple oak furniture of pure quality. Loos and Wagner joined this group and by 1908 exotic woods and rich veneers combined with sharper angularity to anticipate Art Deco furniture.

## LATER DEVELOPMENTS

The European Arts and Crafts and Art Nouveau movements developed during World War I into Art Deco. There was a need for rebirth after the exuberant Art Nouveau and the movement drew its inspiration from the late 18th century. Its main criteria was for form to follow function. Decoration was only to be contained within the shape itself, which meant, for example that marquetry and carving were allowed. The premier wood was ebony, which was rare and costly. Exotic veneers were employed, and there was a revival of Oriental lacquerware (see pages 206–7).

# Modular storage cubes  *Advanced*

*This storage system is flexible and expandable. Two alternative methods are outlined below: firstly, using pre-veneered MDF and secondly, using particle board with lippings. Be sure to check the sizes before you begin because you may need to alter them to suit your own storage needs.*

### Tools for method one

Table saw

Router with 6mm (¼in) straight cutter

G-cramps

Sash cramps

Electric iron

Second-cut file

Drill and 3mm (⅛in) and 4.5mm (³⁄₁₆in) bits

Screwdriver

Sanding block

Hacksaw

### Skills required for project

Measuring and marking *pages 64–7*

Basic sawing *pages 68–71*

Grooving *pages 90–3*

Drilling *pages 96–100*

Making housing joints *pages 110–11*

Using abrasives *pages 115–17*

Assembling projects *pages 120–7*

Using adhesives *pages 128–9*

Wood finishing *pages 130–5*

Veneering *pages 136–9*

Using metals and plastic *pages 146–7*

### MATERIALS

| Part | Materials and dimensions | No. |
|---|---|---|
| | Manufactured board – particle board, plywood or MDF | |
| Cube sides | 2400 x 1200 x 16mm (8 x 4ft x ⅝in) | 1 |
| | **Solid timber** | |
| Lippings if required | 1800 x 25 x 16mm (71 x 1 x ⅝in) | 1 |
| | **Ply sheet** | |
| Tongues for lippings | 450 x 450 x 6mm (18 x 18 x ¼in) | 1 |

**Other materials:** two 30mm (1³⁄₁₆in) 8 gauge countersunk screws per door; pegs; adhesive (PVA); masking tape; abrasive paper (120-grit); 4.5mm (³⁄₁₆in) diameter steel rod; finish (veneer, plastic, laminate or paint).

The desired visual finish will affect the construction sequence. If you are using the first method, with pre-veneered board, then you do not need to use lippings. If using the second method, with manufactured particle board, you may need to fix lippings to all four edges (unless you intend to use a painted finish).

The materials listed will make three basic cubes. The most common size for manufactured board is 2400 x 1220mm (8 x 4ft), giving 18 squares, plus some extra for doors and internal fittings, though more may be needed depending on your requirements.

If you use pre-veneered board, medium-density fibreboard (MDF) would be suitable. This can be bought cut-to-size. If all the edges are to be lipped, then you can use particle board (chipboard) or plywood.

If cutting the board yourself, use a power saw and straightedge, or a table saw. Cut the whole sheet to make three 400mm (16in) wide strips. Cross-cut these to produce the squares.

### Method one: construction using pre-veneered MDF

This method uses a system of routed edges. Wear a face mask when working with MDF as the dust can be hazardous.

1 Cut the sheets precisely to size on a table saw. Ensure that all the parts for the four sides and the back are identical.

2 The edges of the panels are joined together with routed edges. There are two types of groove (shapes A and B), which fit together. All the edges of the back panel will be shape A. Each side panel will have two B edges and one A edge – remember to leave the front edges square.

3 To make shape A, remove the shaded area shown below, either with a table saw or router. Then make the 6mm (¼in) groove with a router – set this up so the base sits on the panel face and the fence runs along the edge. To make shape B, set the fence so that the groove is in the position shown – this time the router base needs to sit on the panel edge and the fence will run along the face.

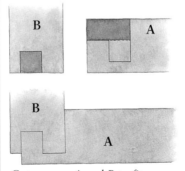

*Cut grooves A and B to fit the edges together.*

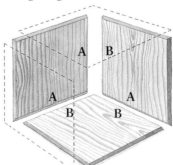

*Cut the panels so that an A edge is always adjacent to a B edge.*

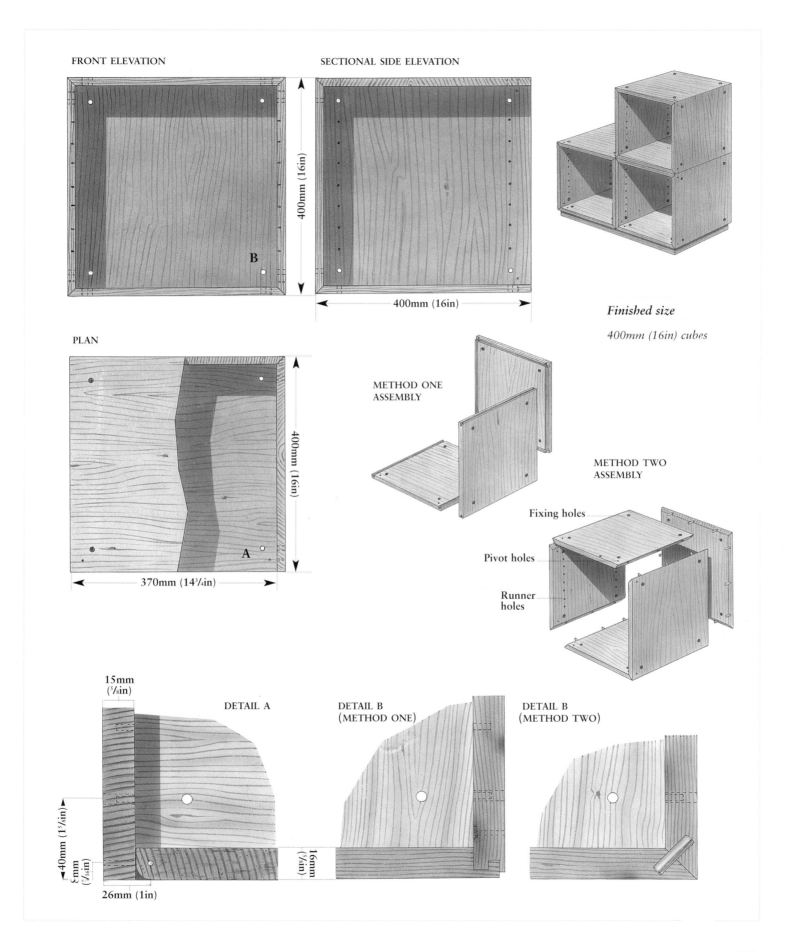

FRONT ELEVATION

SECTIONAL SIDE ELEVATION

400mm (16in)

400mm (16in)

B

PLAN

400mm (16in)

370mm (14³/₄in)

A

Finished size

400mm (16in) cubes

METHOD ONE
ASSEMBLY

METHOD TWO
ASSEMBLY

Fixing holes

Pivot holes

Runner
holes

15mm
(⁵/₈in)

DETAIL A

DETAIL B
(METHOD ONE)

DETAIL B
(METHOD TWO)

40mm (1⁵/₈in)

16mm
(⁵/₈in)

26mm (1in)

**4** Before assembly, sand and finish all the internal faces. Glue the four side joints and place sash cramps along each side to pull the top and bottom up.

*Glue the side joints together, before fitting the back panel.*

**5** Apply adhesive to the back panel and push lightly down to close the joint. Additional cramps may be required if the joint does not close. Remove excess adhesive and check for square. Adjust as required.

*Apply adhesive to the back panel and push lightly into place.*

**6** Since you are using pre-veneered board you will need to apply a matching veneer to the front surfaces. This is best done when the cube itself has been assembled. In this case, the veneers can be mitred at the corners. Use a pre-glued veneer and simply iron it on. This type of veneer has a thermo-setting heat-melting adhesive, which is

similar to that used in hot-melt glue guns. The pre-glued veneer has the adhesive on the back. When melted with the iron, apply an even pressure to the surface with a sanding block, rubbing over the veneer for a few seconds until the adhesive cools enough for it to fuse.

**7** Clean off any overhang with a second-cut file, and sand smooth with 120-grit abrasive paper.

**8** Using this method, there will be a small rebate on the four edges and around the back where a thin edge of veneer and MDF will show. You can apply a finish or, if you want, a small strip of timber can be glued into the rebate. Alternatively, paint it black or another contrasting colour. The first option is the method that has been used to make the prototype as shown. The rebate has been finished but left unfilled since it creates a visual line between each cube when they are joined together.

**Method two: construction using particle board with lippings**

**1** If using this method, attach lippings to each of the edges that will make up the front face of the cube. Plane the solid timber lippings perfectly square to a size just over the thickness of the board. It will be easier to leave these full length – 1800mm (71in) – or at least cut into two lengths of 900mm (35½in) for planing.

**2** When the lippings are finished, cut the squares so that their dimension plus the width of the lipping (where relevant) is slightly over the final measurement of 400mm (16in) to allow for planing.

**3** Hold each panel vertically in a vice and set up a router with a 6mm (¼in) cutter to a depth of 10mm (³⁄₈in). Use the fence as a guide and run the groove in the centre of the front edge on four of the five pieces. Secure the edge lipping onto the bench with a G-cramp and run a matching groove along its length. Make a series of tongues by cutting ply strips 16mm (⅝in) wide and the same thickness as the groove – 6mm (¼in).

*Make tongues to fit in the grooves in the lippings and sides.*

**4** The lippings will need to be mitred at the corners before they are glued to the sides. Cut these on a radial-arm saw for accuracy.

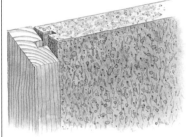

*Mitre the lippings at the corners before fixing the joint.*

**5** Apply a little PVA to the face edge of the panel and edge lipping, and a little into the groove. Insert the tongue into the groove and then position the lipping. Align the long point of the mitre with the end of the panel. Hold in position with masking tape.

**6** When completely dry, use a smoothing plane to plane the lipping so that it is perfectly flat with the surface of the board. Take care not to roll the surface.

7 If you want a natural wood finish, a veneer can now be applied to both top and bottom surfaces. Use a veneer with a thermo-setting adhesive. Simply iron it down to the surface and immediately follow the iron with a sanding block or roller to push the veneer down. Trim the edges with a second-cut file and sand the surface with 120-grit abrasive paper.

*Plane the lippings flat and then apply veneer if required.*

8 Five panels are needed for each cube. The front or open face edge of each cube will be the panels that have been lipped and left square. The other edges of each panel will need to be mitred to 45 degrees. The back will need to be mitred to 45 degrees on all four edges.

9 Hold each panel upright in a vice and gauge a line parallel to the short point of the already mitred lipping (see step 4). Using a smoothing plane at a 45-degree angle, plane the edge down to the gauge line to produce the mitre. Repeat on the opposite and back edges, leaving the lipped edge square. Plane the mitre on all four edges of the back panel.

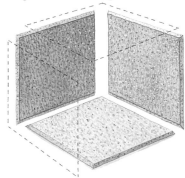

*All the edges except the front four will be mitred to 45 degrees.*

10 To aid in the assembly of the cubes, three locating dowels can be drilled into each mitre. The dowels on the side mitres need to be drilled at 90 degrees to the joint, while the dowels for the back are at 45 degrees to the joint. Position one dowel in the centre and then two more dowels 50mm (2in) in from each edge. Use a try square to mark these points along the edges. Mark the centre of the dowel hole 6mm ($\frac{1}{4}$in) up from the inside face (the short side of the mitre). Mark the holes on each mitre face before you start to drill.

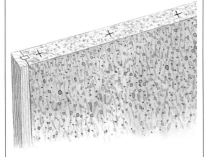

*Mark the positions of the dowels.*

11 Use a 6mm ($\frac{1}{4}$in) dowelling bit to drill each hole 12mm ($\frac{1}{2}$in) deep. Use a depth stop or masking tape to prevent drilling through the side. When drilled, place dowel centres in the holes. Position the corresponding panel in its correct alignment and push together. The dowel centres will mark the position of the holes on the other side of the joint.

12 Repeat this for all the joints around the side panels. The dowels in the back are set out the same. The only difference is the direction in which the holes are drilled; they must fit when the mitred edges are assembled.

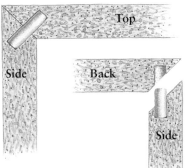

*The corner joints.*

13 Before assembly, sand all the surfaces and apply the finish to the internal faces. Cut the dowels to 20mm ($\frac{3}{4}$in) lengths. Dry test your work and adjust as required. Apply PVA to the mitre joint and in the dowel holes, and insert the dowels in the side joints. Stand vertically on a flat surface and bring all four side panels together (see drawing on page 229). Position two web cramps around the work and apply a little pressure – just enough to close the joints. Apply adhesive to the dowel holes and mitres of the back panel. Lay the back panel in position on top of the cube and tap down lightly to close the joints. Roll the cube over to one side and close the back joint up with the aid of sash cramps.

14 Remove excess adhesive and check the cube is square. Loosen or apply pressure to the cramps to bring the work up true. If the back and sides were cut square and the job has no twist, it must be true.

Whichever method you have followed, you should now have one completed cube. Make additional cubes as desired. The instructions for connecting the cubes together and fitting them out with doors, shelves and drawers are the same.

**Expert tip**

Use blocks between the work and cramps to prevent any marking of the surface occurring.

## Making pivots with screws

The pivots are made from modified 30mm (1³/₁₆in) 8 gauge screws. Mark a 45-degree line back from each corner where the pivots are required. Drill the 3mm (⅛in) pilot holes and insert the two screws in the door or flap. Remove the screws, cut off the heads and cut another slot in the end in which a small screwdriver will fit. Place the door or flap in position with a washer in between. Use a screwdriver to insert the screws just below the surface of the cabinet.

## Drilling the holes

Holes are needed to connect the cubes together, run drawers or hold shelves. While you could just drill the holes needed for a particular application, here all the holes have been drilled so that the cubes are flexible and you can rearrange them at a later date.

**1** Construct two jigs so that all the holes can be drilled in exactly the right position. On the first jig, there are four holes, one on each corner, which will be used for fixing the cubes together, and two small holes on each of the front edges, which can be used for door or flap pivots. Make the first jig out of a sheet of thin plywood exactly the size of the outer face of the cubes, marking up from the holes shown on the drawing on page 229.

**2** The second jig is also made from a sheet of thin plywood, which will fit the inside face of the cube and has a line of smaller holes that will hold the shelves and drawer runners. These holes will be 40mm (1⅝in) in and spaced to suit your requirements – for example, approximately 30mm (1³/₁₆in) apart with a diameter of 4.5mm (³/₁₆in).

**3** Construct each jig and then position and drill the holes required.

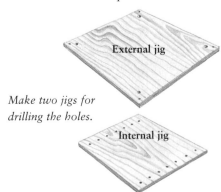

*Make two jigs for drilling the holes.*

## Making the doors/flaps, shelves and drawers

**4** Make the doors out of manufactured board, ensuring that they are lipped and finished to complement the cubes (see steps 1–7 on pages 230–1). Finish with a 2mm (¹/₁₆in) clearance all round. The doors will fit the opening and be hinged on pivots (see box left), which are inserted through two of the eight small holes near the front edge, thus enabling the doors to be left- or right-handed, and flaps to hinge down from the bottom or up from the top. Plane a small round on the pivot side to enable each door to swing past the inside face.

**5** The shelves are held in position with mini-wires – pieces of steel rod 4.5mm (³/₁₆in) in diameter. The legs are inserted into a pair of interior holes, while the projecting piece runs in a groove along the side edges of the shelf. Cut the steel rod to length with a hacksaw and bend each length in a vice to suit the hole spacing. Cut the number of shelves required with a table saw and edge the front. Hold with the side up in a vice. Set the router to run a groove in the centre of the shelf – the required depth for the rod. Stop the groove short of the front so that it cannot be seen. Insert the rods in the holes and check the shelves for fit.

*Fit pieces of steel wire to the inside of the cube to support the shelf.*

*Shelf components.*

**6** The drawer runners follow the same principle as those used for the shelf, but are made of timber and not metal. The runners fit into grooves on the drawer sides and are held in place by the width of the drawer. The drawers are made with simple housing joints in the front and back, with the bottom grooved in. They are made from the same manufactured board with a barefaced tongue and groove joint on the sides. See pages 272–3 for more on making drawers.

*The drawers are fixed with runners.*

*Two finished drawers.*

# Folding chair  Advanced

*It is often useful to have extra chairs available for unexpected visitors.*

*This attractive chair takes up very little room when folded away and a set*

*of them could even be mounted on a wall if you are short on space.*

## Tools

Mitre square

Radial-arm saw

Drill and 3mm (⅛in),
4.5mm (³⁄₁₆in), 6mm (¼in),
10mm (⅜in) and
countersink bits

Mortise gauge

G-cramp

12mm (½in) and 30mm
(1³⁄₁₆in) chisel

Marking knife

Marking gauge

Tenon saw

Sash cramp

Spanner

Jigsaw

Smoothing plane

Second-cut file

Sanding block

Screwdriver

### Skills required for project

Measuring and marking
*pages 64–7*

Basic sawing *pages 68–71*

Planing *pages 74–81*

Fine sawing *pages 82–5*

Chiselling *pages 86–9*

Making mortise and tenon
joints *pags 104–9*

Using abrasives
*pages 115–17*

Assembling projects
*pages 120–7*

Using adhesives
*pages 128–9*

Wood finishing
*pages 130–5*

Using metals and plastics
*pages 146–7*

## MATERIALS

| Part | Materials and dimensions | No. |
|---|---|---|
| | **Hardwood** | |
| Legs | 650 x 50 x 22mm (26 x 2 x ⅞in) | 4 |
| Cross-rail | 375 x 60 x 22mm (15 x 2⅜ x ⅞in) | 1 |
| Hinge block | 375 x 40 x 40mm (15 x 1½ x 1½in) | 1 |
| Seat front rail | 410 x 50 x 22mm (16 ½ x 2 x ⅞in) | 1 |
| Grip rail | 150 x 20 x 22mm (6 x ⅞ x ⅞in) | 2 |
| | **Plywood** – 10mm (⅜ in) thick | |
| Seat | 400mm (16in) square | 1 |
| Back | 316 x 370mm (12½ x 14½in) | 1 |

**Other materials:** two 6 x 50mm (¼ x 2in) domed nuts with bolts and washers; eight 12mm (½in) 6 gauge nuts with countersunk bolts and washers; fourteen 32mm (1¼in) 8 gauge countersunk screws; four 25mm (1in) 6 gauge countersunk screws; two 50mm (2in) 8 gauge round-head screws; one 50mm (2in) barrel bolt; two pairs of narrow butt hinges; adhesive (PVA); abrasive paper (120-grit); finish.

### Making the legs and cross-rail

**1** Prepare the material for the four legs, face side, face edge, width and thickness. There are two pairs of legs – the outside pair (A), and the inside pair (B). They need to be marked left- and right-handed (see drawing opposite).

**2** First, make the angles on the top and bottom of each leg. The first pair (A) are marked 600mm (24in) long. Square a line around the leg at this length. Mark the centre point across the squared line at each end. From this point, use a mitre square and pencil to mark a 45-degree line back to the edge. Turn the mitre square over and mark a second 45-degree line towards the opposite edge to create the

point. Square this line around the edges. Repeat to complete the marking out on both ends of the (A) legs. Cut these ends on the set-out lines (45 degrees) with a tenon saw. Set out the other pair of legs (B) 575mm (20½in) long. Mark out the 45-degree points and cut as before.

**3** Next, mark the positions towards the middle of the legs where the pair will cross and be joined. Measure up 300mm (12in) from the bottom on all four legs. Square a line across the face and mark the centre 25mm (1in) in from the edge. Drill a 6mm (¼in) hole through each leg at this location.

**4** Next, mark the positions where the cross-rail will be joined to the two (B) legs – this is held in place with through

mortise and tenon joints. Lay the 575mm (20½in) pair of legs side by side on a flat surface. Measure up 25mm (1in) past the drilled hole, and then a further 60mm (2⅜in). Square a mortise line back in 3mm (⅛in). Return this line around to the opposite side. Use a mortise gauge to scribe the width of the mortise 12mm (½in) in the centre face of each leg. Remember to gauge from the face side.

**5** Secure the work on a firm, flat surface with a G-cramp. Take care to keep the sides of the mortise straight and square. Drill out the bulk of the waste in the mortise. Finish by working from both sides and paring back to the set-out lines at the ends with a 12mm (½in) chisel, and a wider 30mm (1³⁄₁₆in) chisel on the sides. Repeat on the other leg.

**6** Next, cut the cross-rail to length – 360mm (14¼in). Measure in 20mm (¾in) from each end. Square this around the timber with a marking knife. This is the shoulder line for the tenon. Set a marking gauge to 3mm (⅛in) and scribe a line from the shoulder line on the face side back to the end, and then across the end and back down the other side to the opposite shoulder line. Repeat from face edge to face edge and then mark out the tenon on the other end of the rail in the same way.

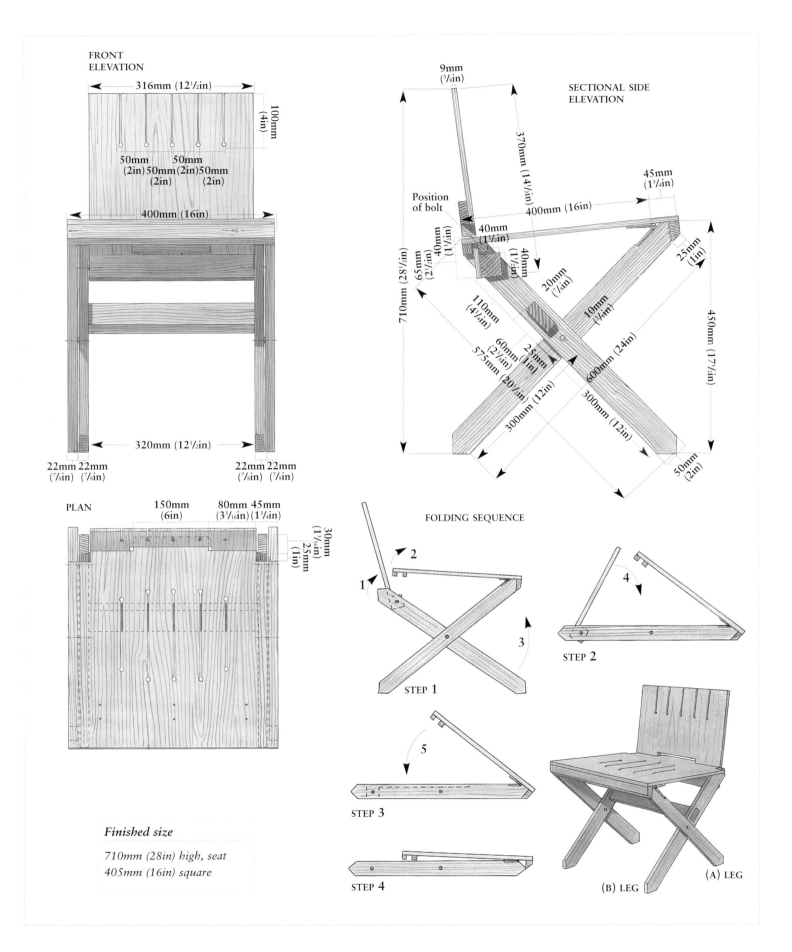

FRONT
ELEVATION

316mm (12½in)

100mm
(4in)

50mm
(2in) 50mm (2in) 50mm
(2in)

400mm (16in)

320mm (12½in)

22mm 22mm
(⅞in) (⅞in)

22mm 22mm
(⅞in) (⅞in)

PLAN

150mm
(6in)

80mm 45mm
(3³⁄₁₆in) (1¾in)

30mm
(1³⁄₁₆in)
25mm
(1in)

*Finished size*

*710mm (28in) high, seat*
*405mm (16in) square*

9mm
(³⁄₈in)

SECTIONAL SIDE
ELEVATION

370mm (14½in)

45mm
(1¾in)

Position
of bolt

40mm
(1½in)

400mm (16in)

25mm
(1in)

40mm
(1½in)

40mm
(1½in)

20mm
(⅞in)

10mm
(³⁄₈in)

450mm
(17½in)

710mm (28½in)

65mm
(2½in)

110mm
(4¼in)

600mm (24in)

60mm
(2⅜in)

25mm
(1in)

575mm (20½in)

300mm (12in)

300mm (12in)

50mm
(2in)

FOLDING SEQUENCE

1

2

3

STEP 1

4

STEP 2

5

STEP 3

STEP 4

(B) LEG

(A) LEG

235

**7** Stand the rail vertically in a vice and saw down on the waste side of the gauge lines to the shoulder line. Lay flat against a bench hook and cut the shoulders with a tenon saw. Clean the faces of the tenon with a sharp chisel. Test the fit and adjust as required.

**8** Next, set out the pivot position where the (B) legs will be joined to the chair back. Set out a point in the centre of each leg – a further 110mm (4¼in) up from the cross-rail. Drill a 4.5mm (³⁄₁₆in) hole through each leg.

*The two sets of legs and the cross-rail.*

**9** Apply adhesive to the tenons on the cross-rail and glue to the (B) legs. Place in a sash cramp and ensure that the frame is square. Wipe off the excess adhesive and allow to dry.

**10** Join the legs together with the domed nuts and bolts. Tighten with a spanner, placing a washer each side and between the legs.

*The completed underframe.*

## Making the seat

Make the seat initially as a separate component.

**11** Cut the seat to the outside shape 400 x 400mm (16 x 16in). Mark the clearance cut-outs in the two back corners 45mm (1¾in) square across from the edges and 55mm (2³⁄₁₆in) in from the back. Cut away the waste with a tenon saw or jigsaw. Mark a second cut-out for the grip rail a further 80mm (3³⁄₁₆in) across and 30mm (1³⁄₁₆in) wide. This will leave a 150 x 30mm (6 x 1³⁄₁₆in) tongue on the underside of the seat. Mark the position of the front rail across the full width and the rear gripping rails 150mm (6in) in the centre of the back edge. Do not put the seat slits in yet.

**12** Cut the front rail to match the width of the seat. Drill four holes of 4.5mm (³⁄₁₆in) diameter across the front of the seat, making sure that they are evenly spaced and 10mm (³⁄₈in) in from the edge. Countersink the top. Hold the rail in position and drill a 3mm (⅛in) pilot hole through each clearance hole into the top edge of the rail. Apply the adhesive to the edge and fix in place with 32mm (1¼in) 8 gauge countersunk screws. Turn the seat over and plane a 45-degree angle on the bottom edge of the front section to match the angle on the leg.

**13** Cut two 22 x 22mm (⅞ x ⅞in) grip rails 150mm (6in) long. The first rail should be fixed 32mm (1¼in) in, and the second rail should be flush with the back. Fix these in the same manner as for the front rail with three screws in each.

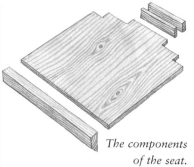

*The components of the seat.*

## Making the back

Make the back initially as a separate component.

**14** Cut the backboard 370mm (14½in) high x 316mm (12½in) wide. Use a try square and marking gauge to mark out the cut-out for the tongue slot in the centre 65mm (2½in) up from the bottom edge, 35mm (1⁵⁄₁₆in) high and 150mm (6in) long. Hold firm on a flat surface with the set-out overhanging the surface. Drill a 10mm (³⁄₈in) hole through the back within the set-out. Place a jigsaw through the hole and cut around the set-out to remove the slot. Clean all the edges up with a second-cut file and 120-grit abrasive paper.

**15** The back is fixed to the legs with a hinge block, measuring 65 x 40mm (2½ x 1½in). Fit it so that it finishes flush with the outside edges and the bottom of the chair back. Glue and screw in place as you did with the front rail in step 12.

*Fit the hinge block to the back.*

**16** Mark the diagonals on the ends of the hinge block and drill a 3mm (⅛in) pilot hole in the middle where the lines meet. Hold the back in position between the back legs with a washer separating them. Insert a 50mm (2in) 8 gauge round-head screw with washer at each end of the assembly. Tighten with a screwdriver just enough to allow the hinging action to operate smoothly.

*Fit the back to the legs.*

### Fitting the front hinges

**17** The front hinges will be set in position as shown in the drawing on page 235: one half of the hinge will be screwed to the top of the (A) legs and the other leaf fitted to the bottom of the ply seat. As there is not enough thickness for screws to be used through the seat, you will either need to rivet or bolt this section into place.

**18** Chisel out the top of one leg to suit half the thickness of the hinge – approximately 3mm (⅛in). Square a line across the edge of the leg 55mm (2³⁄₁₆in) down from the end. Gauge back to the end 3mm (⅛in) deep on both sides. Place several saw cuts with a tenon saw to the gauge line and remove the waste with a chisel. Hold the leg in its upright position.

Place the hinge in the recess and against the underneath of the seat. Mark all the holes in the hinge leaf with a pencil. Fix one leaf to the leg with two 25mm (1in) countersunk screws. Drill the 4.5mm (³⁄₁₆in) holes through the seat and fix the hinge with two 12mm (½in) 6 gauge nuts and countersunk bolts with washers. Repeat on the other leg.

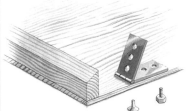

*Drill the hinge to the underside of the seat.*

### Assembly

**19** Check that the whole chair system opens and closes as necessary.

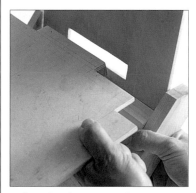

*When the chair is up, the seat latches into the slit in the back.*

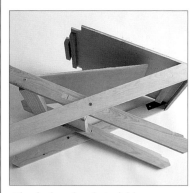

*Check that the chair folds away and opens correctly.*

**20** Set up the chair in the open position. At this point, there will be movement in the chair and so fix a barrel bolt to the underside of the seat in the centre, which can then be bolted in securely to the back when the chair is up. With the seat in the upright position, drill a hole through the inside grip rail, the ply back and into the outside grip rail. Extend the bolt and hold it in place; drill holes through the seat. Secure with nuts and bolt as for the hinges.

*Fit a bolt to secure the seat to the back when the chair is up.*

### Finishing

**21** Disassemble the chair. Sand the various components to remove any marks and sharp edges.

**22** Cut the vertical slits in the back and the seat, if required. Drill a 10mm (⅜in) hole, 100mm (4in) down from the top, in the centre of the back. Two more holes are required 50mm (2in) apart towards each side. Cut a slit square down from the top to the centre of each hole with a jigsaw. Clean up the edges with abrasive paper. The slit in the seat can be cut in a similar manner. This will require a hole at each end of the slit, and a saw cut in between.

**23** Apply a finish of your choice.

# Single bed  Advanced

*This bed design offers an interesting use of wood in woven strips for the headboards and footboards. The dimensions given on the drawing on page 240 are to fit a standard, single-bed mattress but, as mattresses tend to vary slightly in size, you should double check both the width and the length before you begin work to ensure that it will fit the bed properly.*

### MATERIALS

| Part | Materials and dimensions | No. |
|---|---|---|
| | **Solid timber:** a light wood is preferable | |
| Headboard and footboard | | |
| Legs | 1050 x 60mm (42 x 2⅜in) diameter | 2 |
| | 850 x 60mm (34 x 2⅜in) diameter | 2 |
| Cross-rails | 900 x 40mm (36 x 1½in) diameter | 4 |
| Dowels | 800 x 12mm (32 x ½in) | 14 |
| | 50 x 8 mm (2 x ⁵⁄₁₆in) | 8 |
| Woven strips | 850 x 50 x 3mm (34 x 2 x ⅛in) | 24 |
| Head-to-foot components | | |
| Bed rails | 2000 x 150 x 30mm (78¾ x 6 x 1³⁄₁₆in) or length to suit mattress | 2 |
| Cleats | 2000 x 40mm (78¾ x 1½in) square or length to suit mattress | 2 |
| Mattress support slats | 900 x 75 x 20mm (35½ x 3 x ¾in) | 14 |

**Other materials:** four 100 x 8 mm (4 x ⁵⁄₁₆in) bolts with barrel nuts; twenty-eight 50mm (2in) 8 gauge countersunk screws; twenty-eight 25mm (1in) 8 gauge countersunk screws; adhesive (PVA); abrasive paper (120-grit); finish.

## Making the headboard and footboard frames

**1** Prepare the cylindrical components (see box on page 241) for the head and footboard and then cut to length on a radial-arm saw. One pair of legs is 800mm (32in) long and the second pair is 1000mm (40in) long. The cross-rails joining the legs on the headboard and footboard are 840mm (33in) long.

**2** Next, mark out the positions of the holes in the legs, which will accommodate the cross-rails. The centres for the bottom rails are 200mm (8in) up from the bottom, and the centres for the top rail are 20mm (¹³⁄₁₆in) down from the top of each leg. Mark a line in the centre of the legs to ensure that the holes will be in line. Hold each leg in a vice with the centre line on top. Place a 25mm (1in) auger drill bit in a hand brace. Position the drill bit on the set-out and drill the hole to a depth of 30mm (1³⁄₁₆in). Care must be taken to drill the holes square. Check both ways as you drill. A depth

stop or a piece of tape around the bit will help you to drill to the correct depth.

**3** Next, turn the pegs at each end of the cross-rails. If you have a lathe, place each rail in the lathe and turn the ends down to 25mm (1in) diameter and 30mm (1³⁄₁₆in) long. Shape the next 12mm (½in) of the rail down to a 30mm (1³⁄₁₆in) diameter and create a 6mm (¼in) chamfer back to the overall size (see detail on drawing on page 240). Follow all the safety procedures when operating a lathe. If you do not have a lathe, shape the ends by sawing around each shoulder line, then make the rounds with a chisel and smooth off with a file.

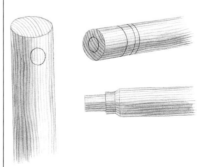

*Mark out and cut the joints in each leg and cross-rail.*

**4** Check each joint for fit and then dry assemble both end frames. Adjust as required.

### Tools

| |
|---|
| Radial-arm saw |
| Brace and 25mm (1in) auger drill bit |
| Lathe, if available |
| 25mm (1in) chisel |
| Router with 3mm (⅛in) straight cutter |
| G-cramp |
| Pillar drill and 12mm (½in) bit |
| Drill and 3mm (⅛in), 4.5mm (³⁄₁₆in) and 12mm (½in) bits, countersink bit and 8mm (⁵⁄₁₆in) doweling bit |
| Sash cramps |
| Box square |
| Tenon saw |
| Dowel centres |
| Screwdriver |
| Smoothing plane |

### Skills required for project

Measuring and marking *pages 64–7*

Basic sawing *pages 68–71*

Planing *pages 74–81*

Fine sawing *pages 82–5*

Chiselling *pages 86–9*

Grooving *pages 90–3*

Drilling *pages 96–100*

Using abrasives *pages 115–17*

Assembling projects *pages 120–7*

Using adhesives *pages 128–9*

Wood finishing *pages 130–5*

Turning *pages 142–5*

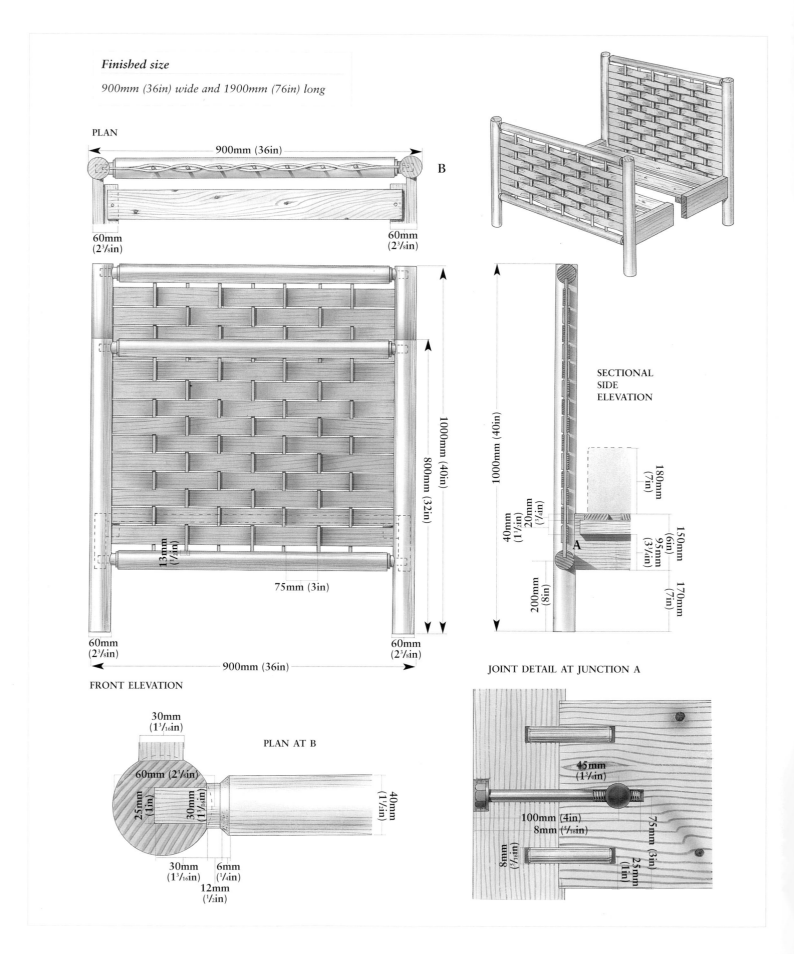

*Finished size*

*900mm (36in) wide and 1900mm (76in) long*

PLAN

B

900mm (36in)

60mm
(2³⁄₈in)

60mm
(2³⁄₈in)

1000mm (40in)

800mm (32in)

13mm
(½in)

75mm (3in)

60mm
(2³⁄₈in)

60mm
(2³⁄₈in)

900mm (36in)

FRONT ELEVATION

SECTIONAL
SIDE
ELEVATION

1000mm (40in)

40mm
(1½in)

20mm
(¾in)

180mm
(7in)

150mm
(6in)
95mm
(3¾in)

170mm
(7in)

A

200mm
(8in)

JOINT DETAIL AT JUNCTION A

30mm
(1³⁄₁₆in)

PLAN AT B

60mm (2³⁄₈in)

25mm
(1in)

30mm
(1³⁄₁₆in)

40mm
(1½in)

30mm
(1³⁄₁₆in)

6mm
(¼in)

12mm
(½in)

45mm
(1³⁄₄in)

100mm (4in)
8mm (⁵⁄₁₆in)

8mm
(⁵⁄₁₆in)

75mm
(3in)

25mm
(1in)

**5** Next, work the grooves on the inside faces of the legs, which will accept the woven timber strips. The groove is best cut with a plunge router. Make a jig from some spare manufactured board for attaching to the router baseplate. Cut two guides for the jig – the same width as the diameter of the round leg. Fix the two guides to the baseboard so that the round section will fit neatly in between. Drill a hole through the top of the baseboard in the centre, long enough for the cutter to penetrate. Fix the router baseplate to the jig so that it lines up with the hole. Set a 3mm (⅛in) straight cutter to cut a groove 16mm (⅝in) deep.

**6** Hold one leg down on a flat surface with a G-cramp. Ensure the previously drilled holes are directly on the top. The groove must run between these two holes. Position the router and jig over the leg so that the jig rests on the top edge. Following all the safety procedures for operation, start the router and plunge the cut to the correct depth. Move the router along the leg the required length between the holes. Continue routing until you achieve the required depth. Turn the router off and wait for the cutter to stop before removing it. Repeat on the other three legs.

*Make a jig to attach to the end of your router and then run a groove in each leg.*

**7** Next, mark the positions of the dowels in the cross-rails. Mark a straight line along their length with a pencil. Start with the centre and measure out towards each end at 75mm (3in) spacings along this line. There should be seven holes in total. Place a 12mm (½in) bit in a pillar drill and bore the holes at these set-outs to a depth of 12mm (½in).

*Rout grooves in the legs and holes in the cross-rails.*

### Weaving the timber strips

If you have your own machinery, you could saw the woven strips from larger pieces of timber and plane them on a thicknesser. If you do not have the correct equipment, approach your timber yard to see if they can do this for you. An alternative is to use 3mm (⅛in) plywood as illustrated.

**8** The vertical lines of the cross-weave are formed by dowels. Cut these to length to fit from the top to bottom cross-rail on each end frame, including the depth of the locating holes – 25mm (1in) each.

**9** Insert the dowels into one of the cross-rails. Cut two strips of plywood to length approximately 850mm (34in) long and have a trial weaving of the strips. Remember to allow for the amount that will sit in the side grooves. Check the length and trim as required. Once the correct length is obtained, cut the remaining strips.

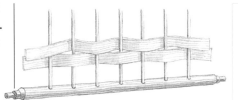

*Try weaving the strips.*

**10** Glue the seven dowels in place between the two cross-rails and then place the rails into the legs, dry. When that adhesive has cured, glue and cramp one leg to the cross-rails with sash cramps. Put some adhesive in the groove and reweave the strips. Ensure they fit all the way into the groove.

*Part assembly of the headboard.*

**11** Fit the second leg by placing the rails into the holes and the strips into the groove. Spread adhesive in the holes and groove in the second leg. Locate the pegs in the holes and the strips in the groove before final cramping. Repeat on the other end frame.

*Fully assembled headboard.*

### Making circular timber

The head and footboard both use circular timber. You may be able to purchase this, but if it is not available you will need to make it. One option is to turn the timber on a lathe, but the components are quite long. Another way of producing cylindrical material is to plane from square.

To use the latter method, set out an octagon on the ends (see page 246) and mark a parallel line down each edge for the corners of the octagon. Plane the bevel edges, then shape to a round by removing the remaining corners. Finish with abrasive paper to produce a smooth round.

## Making the bed rails and cleats

The main structural supports for the bed are the two large bed rails that connect the head and footboards. The bed rails are attached to the legs with two dowels and a bolt (see detail on drawing on page 240). On the inside of these are square cleats that support the mattress slats.

**12** Prepare the two rails and mark out the length. To ensure the holes connecting the bed rails and legs are the correct size, you will need to have the bolt and barrel nut to hand. On the inside face of each leg, cut a small flat to allow the end of the bed rail to sit flat. Measure up 170mm (6¾in) and 320mm (12⅝in) from the bottom. Square these lines across the leg with a box square and pencil. Mark two lines along the leg 30mm (1³⁄₁₆in) apart, ensuring they are in the centre of the leg. Cut across the top and bottom lines with a tenon saw to a depth of 4mm (³⁄₁₆in), and pare away the surface with a 25mm (1in) chisel to produce a flat surface.

**13** In the end of the bed rails, set out the dowel location 25mm (1in) from each edge on the centre line. Drill the holes 25mm (1in) deep with an 8mm (⁵⁄₁₆in) doweling bit. Insert a pair of dowels and bring the joint together. The centres will mark the correct location for the matching holes in the leg. Drill these 25mm (1in) deep.

**14** On the outside of the leg 225mm (9in) up, drill an 8mm (⁵⁄₁₆in) diameter hole through the leg for the bolt. Hold the bed rail in position and place the drill

back in the bolthole to mark the position on the end of the rail. Remove the leg and drill the hole in the rail to a depth of 60mm (2³⁄₈in). Mark out the barrel nut hole on the inside face 75mm (3in) up from the bottom edge and 45mm (1¾in) in from the end. Drill a 12mm (½in) hole 20mm (¾in) deep to accept the nut. On the outside of the leg, you can counterbore the bolt head, if required.

*Drill holes in the bed rails for the bolt and nut.*

**15** Next, mark the location of the cleats on the inside face of the bed rails. Scribe a line parallel to the top edge, 20mm (¾in) down. Cut two 40 x 40mm (1½ x 1½in) cleats 20mm (¾in) shorter than the length of the bed rails. Fix in place – 10mm (³⁄₈in) in from each end with 50mm (2in) 8 gauge countersunk screws at approximately 150mm (6in) spacings. Drill a 4.5mm (³⁄₁₆in) countersunk hole in the centre of the cleat. Apply adhesive, hold in position and drill the 3mm (⅛in) pilot holes. Insert the screws and tighten.

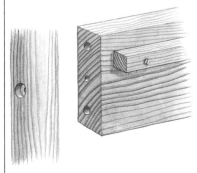

*Fix the cleat in place on the inside face of the bed rail.*

## Assembly

**16** Assemble the two bed rails on the head and footboards with locating dowels. Put the 8mm (⁵⁄₁₆in) bolt in its hole. Secure the barrel nut in its hole, and the screw, so that the joint is brought up tight. Repeat on the other three corners.

*Secure the barrel nut and screw.*

**17** Cut 14 slats to length to fit between the bed rails on the cleats. Drill a 4.5mm (³⁄₁₆in) hole, countersunk at each end of the slats. Remove any sharp edges with a smoothing plane and abrasive paper.

**18** Place each slat in position – evenly spaced along the bed. Drill the 3mm (⅛in) pilot holes through the slats into the cleats and fix with 25mm (1in) 8 gauge screws.

*Screw the slats to the bed.*

**19** Disassemble the bed and apply your chosen finish before final assembly.

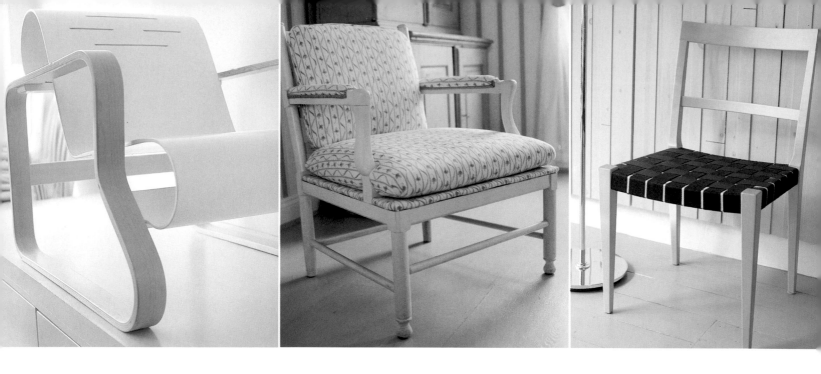

# Scandinavian design

Scandinavian design conjures up ideas of simplicity and the use of natural materials, based on the culture and weather of the various countries. Scandinavia enjoyed long periods of peace during the 19th and early 20th centuries. The style of living there was based on a peasant tradition. The comparatively late industrialization and low population density gave the countries a feeling of stability so they didn't feel the need for new forms of housing or furnishing and kept to their traditional values. After World War II, however, liberal socialism combined with rapid industrialization swept across Scandinavia and changed the social structure. This, inevitably, had an impact on furnishings.

Scandinavian designers held the Vienna School as their ideal (see page 227) and, while the Bauhaus movement was taking Europe by storm in the 1920s and 1930s, they remained true to it. They finished industrial products by hand, giving the furniture a personal quality, which was one of the reasons it became so famous after World War II. Scandinavia was relatively unscathed during the war, while other European countries had witnessed the terrible things that technology could do. As such, the traditional craftsmanship and warm, natural materials used in Scandinavian design became popular throughout Europe after the war. The simple but classic designs that emerged at this time show how designers in Scandinavia have maintained an interesting but functional look to pieces made out of natural solid timber, laminates or preforms and later metals and plastics. The desire for well-designed and beautiful homes has led to a clean and honest approach that is applied to both structure and fittings.

## SWEDEN

One of the fathers of modern Swedish furniture was Carl Malmsten. He was influenced by the Arts and Crafts movement, nature and traditional Swedish design. He believed it was his duty to furnish people's homes in a way that combined utility with beauty. He mapped out the path that most Scandinavian furniture design has followed since – cultivated craftsmanship in conjunction with functional correctness. This traditional approach nevertheless made use of modern manufacturing processes. At the same time, one young designer, Bruno Mathsson was building chairs made of wooden frames that rested on flexible plywood legs. Josef Frank moved to Stockholm from Vienna in 1934 and took the playful lightness of his design with him.

## FINLAND

At the beginning of the 20th century Finland was battling for political independence. The peasant culture began to fascinate young craftsmen and a new Finnish style was born – National Romanticism. Alvar Aalto was one such craftsman and his work is dealt with in depth on page 267.

## DENMARK

Architect Kaare Klint was one of the founders of modern Danish furniture design. Rather than turning away from the influences of earlier centuries he drew upon other periods and 'renewed' them in his own unique way. He took elements from late 18th-century English furniture, Chinese and Egyptian designs and eliminated the stylistic characteristics in order to create timeless forms. His designs do not show a craving for

◆ OPPOSITE LEFT *Alvar Aalto's 'Paimio' armchair (designed in 1924) was made out of birch ply.* ◆ OPPOSITE CENTRE *A Swedish Gripsholm Gustavian armchair made in c1930 after a 1780s style.* ◆ OPPOSITE RIGHT *A 1932 'Monat' chair, designed by Bruno Mathsson, who had been inspired by Aalto's designs.* ◆ ABOVE LEFT *Alvar Aalto's 'Chair 43' (designed in 1936–7) made from steamed birch bentwood.* ◆ ABOVE CENTRE *Solid oak book shelf, designed by Lloyd Schwan.* ◆ ABOVE RIGHT *The 'Ant' stacking chairs, designed by Arne Jacobsen in 1955.*

newness but are a restatement of classic solutions that combine comfort and dignified simplicity.

The country was particularly interested in the Thonet process of manufacturing bentwood parts (see page 266). A company founded by Fritz Hansen was one of the major organizations that worked on its development. His son Soren Hansen brought out a new chair made of laminated wood in 1950. In 1952 Arne Jacobsen produced the famous 'Ant' chair – the seat and back were made of one piece of plywood and it had steel legs. This was probably one of the first Danish chairs to be designed expressly with mass production in mind.

The architect Borge Mogensen developed inexpensive, practical furniture based on a system of dimensions that he devised himself. His mastery of materials was very like Klint's. Finn Juhl's style was accepted abroad as well as being popular at home. His 1945–55 style dissolved the traditional chair into two separate, defined components – the frame and the seat.

*The 'Wishbone' chair, made from beech, was designed by Hans J Wegner in 1950.*

Hans Wegner's style falls somewhere between Klint's discipline of form and Johl's temperament. His designs were amenable to mass production – so much so that five factories merged under the name of Salesco to devote themselves to manufacturing his furniture. The standard of design in Denmark was high, as illustrated by the work of Hans Wegner, along with his master cabinetmaker Johannes Hansen. Much of Wegner's furniture from the 1940s and 50s shows how machinery and handwork could be combined to give the most elegant designs. The components are shaped or bent to exquisite forms and joined in such a way as to enable the form of the piece to flow without undue interruption. Machinery was used initially to ensure the most precise joints, and handwork was used for the final shaping and finishing.

The export of Danish furniture began in the early 1950s – many talented designers including Borge Mogensen, Ole Wanscher, Hans Wegner, Grete Jalk, Poul Kjarholm and Arne Jacobsen took up the challenge of form and material to create rare syntheses of precision construction, imagination and truth to materials that has earned Danish furniture its international reputation.

# Octagonal birdhouse  | *Advanced* |

*This design has been sized for small garden birds. It has individual*

*compartments and stands on its own central support. The base is*

*attached with dowels that can be removed for cleaning purposes.*

## Tools

Try plane

Pair of compasses

Marking gauge

25mm (1in) chisel

Hand saw or power saw

Smoothing plane

Hammer

Nail punch

Pillar drill with 6mm (¼in) and 30mm (1³⁄₁₆in) drill bits

Hole saw

Jigsaw or coping saw

Sliding bevel

### Skills required for project

Measuring and marking
*pages 64–7*

Basic sawing *pages 68–71*

Planing *pages 74–81*

Fine sawing *pages 82–5*

Drilling *pages 96–100*

Using abrasives
*pages 115–17*

Assembling projects
*pages 120–7*

Using adhesives
*pages 128–9*

Wood finishing
*pages 130–5*

### MATERIALS

| Part | Materials and dimensions | No. |
|---|---|---|
| | **Softwood** or **hardwood** (exterior grade) | |
| Support pole | 1800 x 40mm (6ft x 1⅝in) or adjust to suit requirements | 1 |
| | **Plywood** (exterior grade) | |
| Roof | 250 x 100 x 6mm (10 x 4 x ¼in) | 8 |
| Walls | 105 x 100 x 6mm (4³⁄₁₆ x 4 x ¼in) | 8 |
| Internal partitions | 250 x 100 x 10mm (10 x 4 x ⅜in) | 8 |
| Base | 200 x 200 x 12mm (8 x 8 x ½in) | 1 |

**Other materials:** eight 75 x 6mm (3 x ¼in) diameter dowels; 20mm (¾in) panel pins (exterior grade); adhesive (exterior grade); masking tape; abrasive paper (120-grit), finish (exterior grade).

**1** With the try plane, plane the upright support pole to 40mm (1⅝in) square. Then, mark out an octagon on one end of the pole. Draw diagonals from corner to corner. To find the equal 45-degree lines across the corners, place the point of a pair of compasses on one of the corners, and rotate from the centre point to the outside edge. Mark a line across the corner to the opposite edge. Repeat the measuring process to mark the 45-degree lines across the

other corners. Next, set a marking gauge and scribe the points along the length of the pole.

**2** Secure the timber on a flat surface or in a vice and plane the octagon to shape using the try plane. At each point of the octagon, plane a 10mm (⅜in) flat edge, along 300mm (12in) from the top. The bottom of this flat-edged length of pole can be finished with a chisel to give a square-stopped end.

**3** Cut the internal partitions to a shape of 245mm (9⅝in) long by 80mm (3⅛in) wide. Taper the top by measuring up 85mm (3⅜in) along the outside edge and drawing a line up to the top of the opposite edge. Use a hand saw or power saw and true the edges with a smoothing plane.

**4** Plane a bevel along the side and top edges and taper to 22.5 degrees off each face. This is best set out with a sliding bevel. Mark the bevel on the top edge and pencil gauge a line along the inside face to represent the amount to be removed. Hold on edge in a vice and plane to the line. Check with the bevel as you go.

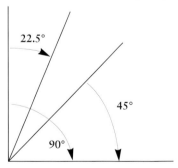

*Bisect a 45-degree angle to produce a 22.5-degree angle.*

**5** Use adhesive to position the partitions on the small flat edges of the support pole with the bottom of each resting on the 300mm (12in) stopped end. Secure them in place with 20mm (¾in) panel pins. To prevent movement while the

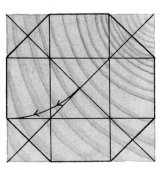

*Setting out an octagon.*

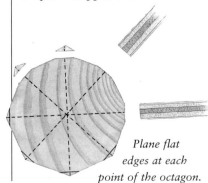

*Plane flat edges at each point of the octagon.*

adhesive dries, wrap masking tape around the outside, ensuring the partitions are still evenly spaced.

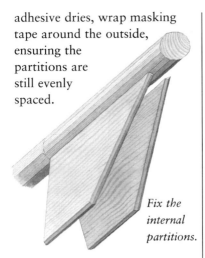

*Fix the internal partitions.*

**6** Cut the eight walls to 85mm (3⅜in) wide and to 105mm (4⅛in) long. Measure the positions of the two holes in each wall at 15mm (⁹/₁₆in) and 48mm (2in) up from the middle of the bottom. Mark these and use a pillar drill to drill the 6mm (¼in) bottom hole. Use a 30mm (1³/₁₆in) hole saw to make the top hole.

**7** Next, bevel the side edges of each wall to 22.5 degrees (see step 4). Plane one wall and then fit the rest individually by measuring them against the finished edge of the first.

**8** In contrast, the bottom edge of each wall is slightly curved. Mark a pencil line along the length in the centre of each wall. Measure up 54.5mm (2³/₁₆in) from the bottom. Place the point of a pair of compasses on this spot and scribe the curve along the bottom edge. Cut this curve with a jigsaw or coping saw, and smooth with 120-grit abrasive paper.

*Make the eight walls.*

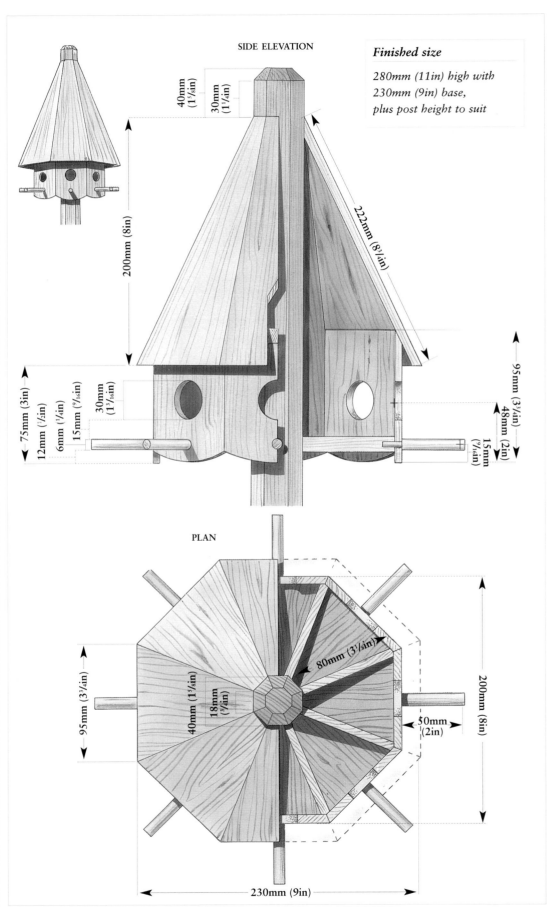

SIDE ELEVATION

*Finished size*

*280mm (11in) high with 230mm (9in) base, plus post height to suit*

40mm (1⅝in)
30mm (1¼in)
200mm (8in)
222mm (8¾in)
95mm (3¾in)
48mm (2in)
15mm (⁹/₁₆in)
75mm (3in)
12mm (½in)
6mm (¼in)
15mm (⁹/₁₆in)
30mm (1³/₁₆in)

PLAN

80mm (3⅛in)
95mm (3¾in)
40mm (1⅝in)
18mm (¾in)
200mm (8in)
50mm (2in)
230mm (9in)

**9** Next, mark and cut the base. Set out the octagon in the centre of a 200mm (8in) square board. Drill and chisel the octagonal hole for the upright from both sides. Slide this up the pole from the bottom and mark the point at which it meets the outside edge of the partitions. Remove from the upright. Adjust the shape with a hand or power saw. Test fit and adjust as required.

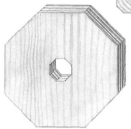

*Make the base and check it for size.*

**10** Next, fit the walls to the partitions. Lay one wall piece on top of its two partitions so that the bevelled edges of each match up. Plane to fit if necessary and fix in place with adhesive and pins.

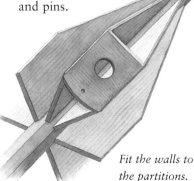

*Fit the walls to the partitions.*

**11** With the structure lying flat, plane the bevel at the top of each wall to match the bevel on top of the partition. Make the eight roof sections in the same way that you made the walls in step 6. Cut the basic pieces to 225 x 95mm (8⅞ x 3¾in) and plane an angled bevel on the top of each section so that it will sit against the upright pole.

**12** Position one of the roof sections on top of its wall and two partitions. Check the fit at the top and adjust the bevel as required. Mark the tapering sides on the underneath by tracing along the right-hand partition with a pencil. Cut and plane the bevel on this right-hand edge only. Repeat this on a second roof section but bevel the left-hand edge. Lay the two sections together in their adjacent locations and test their fit against one another. Plane and adjust as required.

**13** Once a neat fit has been obtained, set the sliding bevel to the edge. Mark the width at the top and bottom of the first section. Hold the timber in the vice and plane it to match the sliding bevel. Fix that completed roof section in place with adhesive and pins.

**14** Place the second section in position and mark it out. Plane to shape, but do not fix this yet as it will be used for a template for the remaining pieces.

**15** Trace the shape of the second roof section onto the remaining pieces of timber. Cut these to shape, making sure that they are slightly oversized.

*Make and fit the roof sections.*

Plane the bevel on all the right-hand edges. Working anti-clockwise, position each in turn, and check and mark the width, top and bottom. Plane the bevel along this edge to suit the sliding bevel and then fix as before. The last section may need a little extra fitting before you fix it in place.

**16** The base of the birdhouse is held in position by dowels. Cut the dowels to 75 x 6mm (3 x ¼in). Put the base in position and drill through the 6mm (¼in) hole in each wall. Drill 25mm (1in) into the edge of each face of the base. Fix the base in place with the dowels. The dowels can be removed and the base taken away for cleaning.

*Side view of the dowels.*

*Insert the dowels to hold the base in position.*

**17** Plane a 10mm (⅜in) chamfer around the top of the upright support pole. Sand all the surfaces in order to remove any set-out lines and marks that may be left, and apply an exterior finish to all the outside faces. Leave the inside of the birdhouse in natural timber.

bradawl. Start from the centre two and work outwards, adjusting the end of each slat to allow the back slats to fit between them when they are inserted – a 40mm (1⅝in) space is needed for the back slats. Remember that as these are being fitted you will need to dry cramp the main frame joints.

**26** Drill 3mm (⅛in) pilot holes in the back rails and screw the slats in place one by one, using steel 30mm (1³⁄₁₆in) 8 gauge screws. When all the slats are in position, mark the front curve as shown on the drawing on page 251.

*Fix the seat slats into place.*

**27** Remove the screws and cut and shape the front ends of each slat. Sand the slats and apply the first coat of finish.

**Making the back slats**

The back slats are laminated in a jig to achieve more of a curve.

**28** On one face of a piece of softwood, scale up the grid on the drawing on page 251 of the shape of the back slats and plot the two curved lines of a slat.

**29** Using a bandsaw, very carefully saw down on the waste or slat area sides of both lines.

**Alternative for making seat slats**

If you are unable to find a piece of timber in the same species as the rest of the chair at this size, it is possible to use six lengths of timber 25mm (1in) thick. First, cut the upper surface to shape and then glue the resulting piece of waste to the underside of the slats. Finish the shaping as before.

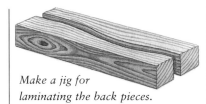

*Make a jig for laminating the back pieces.*

**30** Prepare the thin strips of constructional veneer ready for laminating. Cut them about 10mm (⅜in) wider than the final slat, since you will need to plane the edges after laminating. There will be four strips per slat. Make sure that you have some thick sheets of paper or polythene to line the faces of the jig and set up some sash cramps to apply pressure while the adhesive cures.

**31** Make a package of four strips for one slat – sandwiched between the two pieces of sheet polythene. Put it into the jig dry. Tighten up the cramps to check that the strips are fully under pressure and then remove from the jig.

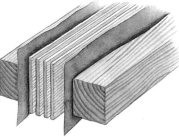

*Dry assemble the package.*

**32** Apply adhesive to the inside faces of the strips. Replace the glued bundle between the polythene, return to the jig and cramp tightly. Leave the jig in the cramps overnight so that the glue cures. Make four more slats.

**33** Plane one edge of a slat straight and mark its width with a marking gauge set at 60mm (2⅜in). Plane the edge to the correct width. Hold in

the jig, with the marked edge above the surface of the jig. Place in a vice and plane length.

*Place the jig in a vice and plane.*

**34** Mark the length and the narrowing shape at the bottom of the back slats (40mm/1⅝in wide and 100mm/4in long with round corners). Cut the shaping, plane and sand the edges. Shape the other slats in the same way.

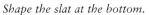

*Shape the slat at the bottom.*

**35** Mark screw positions on the centre line at the bottom of each slat and 25mm (1in) from the end. Place the first slat between the two seat rails, and adjust length of the shaping at the bottom to fit flush on the bottom of the back rail. Mark hole centres with a bradawl, drill pilot holes and screw in place. Repeat with each slat.

*Screw the back slats into place.*

36 Mark out the curve across the top of slats. Disassemble and cut on bandsaw. Sand and apply first finish coat.

### Final assembly

Assemble the chair before adding the buttons and the leather arms.

37 Sand all components to remove any marks. Glue up the two side frames first by applying the adhesive to the tenons on each end of the side rails and in the holes for the 20mm (³/₄in) dowels. Place each side frame in sash cramps and tighten. Check for square and ensure that it is free of wind. Remove excess adhesive, and leave to dry.

38 Remove from the cramps and complete the assembly by applying the adhesive to the tenons on the other rails. Position each rail and cramp up the whole frame. Check for square and wind. Remove excess adhesive and leave to dry.

39 Remove from the cramps and sand off any marks. Apply the final finish to the frame, seat and back slats.

40 Refit the seat and back slats with the brass screws on the lower back rail. The other ends will be 'floating' over the front and top back rails. It would be possible to screw through the outside face into these rails – however this would show. Therefore make 'buttons' to hold the slats in place. The buttons are made with a flat face so that they can be screwed under or behind the slats and will locate in holes drilled into the rail (see main photograph, page 255).

41 Take the 25 x 20mm (1 x ³/₄in) strip and mark the 11 buttons, each 30mm (1³/₁₆in) long. Mark the position of the screw holes in the centre and then drill and countersink using a 4.5mm (³/₁₆in) bit and a countersink bit. Cut the buttons to length and drill the holes to accept 6mm (¹/₄in) dowels in the end, 10mm (³/₈in) down.

42 Cut the dowels to length and glue into the holes. Shape the top either round, or chamfer the edge and end on the face.

*Make the buttons and cut the dowels to length.*

43 Using one button as a pattern, mark where the dowel will enter the rails on the bottom edge of the top rail for the back and behind the front rail for the seat. Fix the slats with the buttons by inserting the dowel into the hole. Mark with a bradawl where the screw will be positioned. Drill a pilot hole and fix into place with 30mm (1³/₁₆in) 8 gauge steel screws.

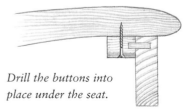

*Drill the buttons into place under the seat.*

### Making the leather strap arms

The chair is very comfortable without any upholstery but, rather than using solid arms, use leather straps as a contrast to what is otherwise an all-wooden piece.

44 Make the strap supports/ tensioners by cutting four pieces of 20mm (³/₄in) dowel to the same length as the width of the straps, and mark and drill an 8mm (⁵/₁₆in) clearance hole at right angles in the centre of each rod to accept the threaded studding. Drill the same size holes in the four legs at heights to suit. T-nuts are used to hold the threaded studding to the dowel, and a hexagonal (Allen key) nut that shows on the outside of the legs is used to tighten and stretch the straps. For the screw or bolt, use four short lengths of 6mm (¹/₄in) threaded studding.

45 Mark the leather straps to length and ensure they are long enough to fold over to make the 'eye' for the dowel and be secured beneath.

46 Determine the length between the eyes and fold the strap over, marking the end of the overlaps. Take the straps to your local boot maker or upholsterer to have the overlaps sewn. Cut a slot in the end of the eye so that the bolt can be screwed through the dowel and T-nut. Fit the straps and tension as required.

*Fit the leather straps in place.*

# Garden bench   Advanced

*The design for this garden bench provides a strong basic frame with a comfortably shaped seat. There are three different options given for the back of the seat: a back with curved top rails, three cross-rail panels and a cross-weave effect. This bench is a two-seater, but it is possible to modify the dimensions and extend the length slightly if you wish.*

## MATERIALS

| Part | Materials and dimensions | No. |
|---|---|---|
| | **Any hardwood with resistance to weathering,** such as oak, elm or teak; if you use a softwood, make sure that it is treated | |
| Legs | 620 x 60 x 60mm (25 x 2½ x 2½in) | 4 |
| Side rails | 700 x 100 x 25mm (28 x 4 x 1in) | 2 |
| Longitudinal rails | 1425 x 100 x 25mm (56 x 4 x 1in) | 2 |
| Arms | 770 x 100 x 25mm (31 x 4 x 1in) | 2 |
| Back rail | 1450 x 100 x 25mm (57 x 4 x 1in) | 1 |
| Seat bearers | 500 x 100 x 32mm (19⅝ x 4 x 1¼in) | 2 |
| Seat slats | 1250 x 100 x 25mm (49 x 4 x 1in) | |
| **Option 1:** back with curved top rails | | |
| Curved back rails | 450 x 150 x 25mm (17¾ x 6 x 1in) | 2 |
| | 750 x 150 x 25mm (29½ x 6 x 1in) | 1 |
| Vertical uprights | 450 x 45 x 25mm (17¾ x 1¾ x 1in) | 2 |
| Angled uprights | 400 x 45 x 25mm (15¾ x 1¾ x 1in) | 2 |
| Back rail | 1200 x 70 x 30mm (47 x 2¾ x 1⅛in) | 1 |
| Dowels | 450 x 15mm (17¾ x ⅝in) | 5 |
| | 300 x 15mm (12 x ⅝in) | 6 |
| Sheet of plywood or particle board for set-out | | |
| **Option 2:** back with three cross-rail panels | | |
| Horizontal rails | 1200 x 70 x 70mm (47 x 2¾ x 2¾in) | 2 |
| External vertical stiles | 600 x 50 x 50mm (23½ x 2 x 2in) | 2 |
| Internal vertical stiles | 380 x 47 x 47mm (15 x 1⅞ x 1⅞in) | 2 |
| Cross-rails | 460 x 60 x 60mm (18 x 2½ x 2½in) | 6 |
| **Option 3:** back with cross-weave effect | | |
| Horizontal rails | 1200 x 50 x 50mm (47 x 2 x 2in) | 2 |
| External vertical stiles | 600 x 45 x 45mm (23½ x 1¾ x 1¾in) | 2 |
| Internal vertical stile | 400 x 30 x 30mm (16 x 1³⁄₁₆ x 1³⁄₁₆in) | 1 |
| Vertical strips | 400 x 15 x 15mm (16 x ⅝ x ⅝in) | 14 |
| Horizontal strips | 1145 x 15 x 15mm (45 x ⅝ x ⅝in) | 5 |

**Other materials:** 50 x 3mm (2 x ⅛in) 500 gauge galvanized jolt head nails; adhesive (exterior grade); abrasive paper (120-grit); finish (exterior grade).

## Making the main frame

**1** Plane all the components with a jack plane to the finished size. Your timber merchant may do this for you, which will save time and effort.

**2** First, make the legs. Mark the height of the legs 595mm (23½in) for the front and 615mm (24¼in) for the back. Square a line around and cut to length with a tenon saw. Mark out an octagon on one end of one leg (see page 246) and then set a pencil gauge to scribe the points along the leg length. Secure the timber and plane the octagon to shape with the try plane. Repeat to make the other legs.

**3** Next, make the two end frames – the two side rails are fixed to the legs with stopped mortise and tenon joints. Begin by making the mortises in the legs – square two lines across the face edge 205mm (8½in) and 285mm (12½in) up from the bottom. Use a mortise gauge to scribe the width of the mortise 12mm (½in) in the centre of the leg between the squared lines.

**4** Lay flat and secure with a G-cramp on a firm surface. Use a drill with a 10mm (⅜in)

*Finished size*

Approximately 600mm (24in)
high, 1400mm (55in) long and
760mm (30in) deep

FRONT ELEVATION

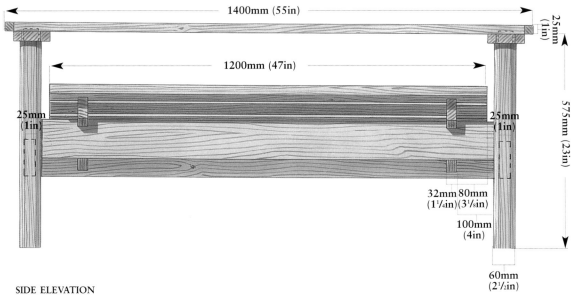

1400mm (55in)

1200mm (47in)

25mm
(1in)

25mm
(1in)

25mm
(1in)

575mm (23in)

32mm 80mm
(1¼in)(3⅛in)

100mm
(4in)

60mm
(2½in)

SIDE ELEVATION

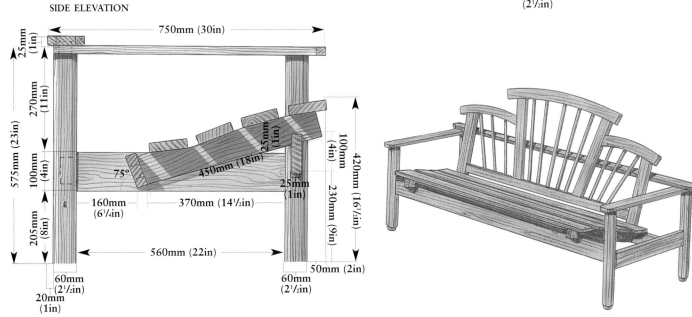

25mm
(1in)

750mm (30in)

270mm
(11in)

25mm
(1in)

575mm (23in)

100mm
(4in)

75°

25mm
(1in)

450mm (18in)

100mm
(4in)

420mm (16½in)

160mm
(6¼in)

370mm (14½in)

25mm
(1in)

230mm (9in)

205mm
(8in)

560mm (22in)

50mm (2in)

60mm
(2½in)

60mm
(2½in)

20mm
(1in)

258

OPTION 1: BACK WITH CURVED TOP RAILS

OPTION 2: BACK WITH THREE CROSS-RAIL PANELS

OPTION 3: BACK WITH CROSS-WEAVE EFFECT

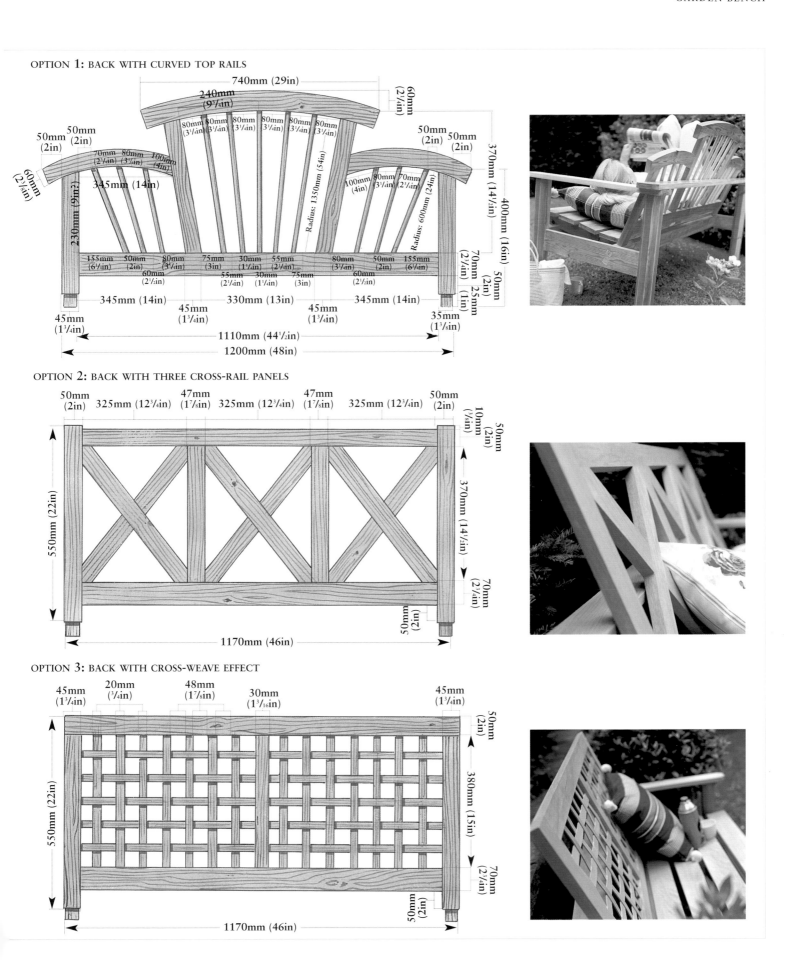

259

bit to drill the bulk of the waste out of the set-out mortise to a depth of 40mm (1⅝in). Use a depth stop or place masking tape around the bit to maintain the correct depth. Remove the waste from the mortise with a 12mm (½in) mortise chisel to the squared lines.

**5** Finish the width with a 25mm (1in) bevel-edge firmer chisel, paring back to the gauged lines. Ensure you chisel straight to keep the mortise true.

**6** Next, cut the side rails 640mm (25¼in) long. Set out the shoulder lines 40mm (1⅝in) in from each end. Square these around the rails with a marking knife. Scribe the tenons 12mm (½in) thick. Place vertically in a vice and cut down to the shoulder lines with a tenon saw. Remove and lay flat against a bench hook. Cut on the waste side of the shoulder line to remove the waste on both sides. Stand upright again and cut 6mm (¼in) off the width on each edge. Cut across the shoulder lines to reveal the tenon. Test for fit and adjust as required.

*Mark and cut the joints between the legs and side rails to make two end frames.*

**7** Now, mark the mortise and tenon joints for the front longitudinal rail. The rail is 230mm (9in) up and 100mm (4in) high. Set out and cut the mortises in the front legs, 40mm (1⅝in) deep. Cut the rail 1356mm (53½in) long and set out and cut the tenons.

**8** Now, cut the bottom longitudinal rail 1330mm (52⅜in) long. Square a shoulder line 28mm (1⅛in) in from each end. Set the marking gauge to 25mm (1in) and mark the double tenon on each end. Scribe a line off each edge from the shoulder line to the end, across the end and back down to the shoulder line. Hold flat on a saw stool and cut down the waste side to the shoulders with a ripsaw. Remove the centre with a 25mm (1in) chisel from both sides. Maintain a square cut to ensure the rail fits against the side rail.

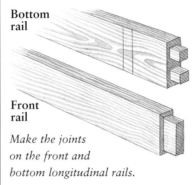

**Bottom rail**

**Front rail**

*Make the joints on the front and bottom longitudinal rails.*

**9** Next, mark and cut the through mortises on the side rails, which will accommodate the bottom longitudinal rail. These will need to be cut at an angle so that the rail sits in the correct position. Measure 160mm (6⅜in) across from the back leg on the bottom edge. Square this across the bottom edge, sloping up to the back. Mark a 75-degree bevel up each face with a sliding bevel and pencil. Mark a second line 25mm (1in) parallel. Lay the side rail on a flat surface and stand the back rail on end between these bevelled lines. Keep the bottom corner flush with the bottom of the side rail. Trace the tenon width onto the rail to mark the mortise sizes. Mark the mortises on both sides of the side rails. Bore a hole in the centre of each

mortise with a 20mm (¾in) auger bit in a brace. Chisel the mortises square from both sides with a 25mm (1in) chisel. Test the fit and adjust as required.

**10** Next, set out a square stub tenon at the top of both the front and back legs. The measurement from the bottom of each leg is 575mm (22½in), giving a larger tenon on the two longer back legs. Set a marking gauge to 12mm (½in) and scribe the width of the tenon. Lay flat and cut on the waste side of the shoulder line down to the gauge line on all four sides. Hold the leg vertically in a vice and cut the sides with the tenon saw.

**11** Now, make the arms of the bench. Cut them to a length of 730mm (28¾in). Set out the stopped mortises that match the stub tenons on the top of the front legs – 36mm (1⁷⁄₁₆in) square x 20mm (¾in) deep. Square the first line across at 62mm (2½in) along from one end. Square the second line a further 36mm (1⁷⁄₁₆in) along. Gauge the width with a marking gauge set at 32mm (1¼in) from both edges.

**12** The front stopped mortise is cut with a 25mm (1in) chisel. First cut a small mortise the size of the chisel down to the required depth of 20mm (¾in), and then work back to the set-out lines.

**13** Set out the through mortises of the same size for the back legs in the underside of the arms – 12mm (½in) in from the end. Transfer the mortise set-out on the bottom to the top. Drill this mortise right through the arm and chisel square to the set-out.

**14** The front end of the bench arm can be shaped: in this case, a bevelled 45-degree corner has been cut, which echoes the angles in the octagonal legs.

*Cut a mortise in the shaped arm and fit it to the tenon on the leg.*

**15** Assemble the end frames dry. If all is well, sand all marks off with 120-grit abrasive paper and glue up with exterior grade adhesive. Check the frame for square and twist. Apply pressure with sash cramps until the adhesive has set. Remember to remove any excess with a damp cloth before it dries.

*The completed end frame.*

**16** Next, cut the upper back rail square and to a length of 1400mm (55in). Set out a stopped mortise on each end to fit over the tenon that protrudes through the arm. The mortise is 32mm (1¼in) in from each end and only 8mm (⁵/₁₆in) deep. Cut this in the same way as you did before. The ends of the back rail can also be shaped with a 45-degree corner.

**17** Cut the mortises in the bottom longitudinal rail. First, set out a mortise 12mm (½in) wide and 123mm (4⅞in) on the face side along from the shoulder line at each end. Scribe a line 10mm (³/₈in) down and 80mm (3³/₁₆in) down from the top edge to give a 70mm (2¾in) long mortise. Cut these mortises 20mm (¾in) deep in the same manner as before. On the top of this rail, set out a mortise 37mm (1½in) in from each shoulder line, 35mm (1⁵/₁₆in) long and 12mm (½in) wide. Hold the rail securely in a vice, and drill and chisel the mortise out in a similar manner to the other mortises.

*Cut two mortises in either end of the back rail to fit onto each arm.*

**18** Assemble the glued end frames, two longitudinal rails and back rail dry. Keep them cramped and check for fit and square. Adjust as required.

*The components of the main frame.*

**19** Disassemble and glue the main frame together. Place in cramps again and ensure the frame is square and true. When dry, remove from cramps and clean all surfaces with abrasive paper. You now have a strong frame to which you will add the seat and back.

### Making the seat

**20** Mark out the two seat bearers 475mm (18½in) long. Set out and cut the 70mm (2¾in) wide x 12mm (½in) thick tenons at one end to fit the 20mm (¾in) deep mortises in the face of the back rail.

*Fit each seat bearer into the back longitudinal rail.*

**21** Mark the position of the bearer on the front rail. Square these marks down the inside face of the front rail. Scribe a line across this squared line 25mm (1in) down. Measure the distance between this scribed line and the inside of the bottom edge of the back rail. Square a line across the bottom of the bearer this distance from the shoulder. Mark the bevelled line on the face side at a 75° angle. Mark a second parallel line 25mm (1in) further forward. Measure up 25mm (1in) on the inside bevel. Square a line off the bevel between the two. Remove the centre by cutting down to the line and chiselling away the waste to create the housing.

## Using a trammel

A trammel is used to draw large circles. It works like a protractor, enabling you to mark out accurate curves. A trammel has a pair of points that are attached to a timber arm. Each point is adjustable along the arm to provide varying centres. One point can usually be replaced with a pencil.

### Additional tools for back option 1

Trammel

Jigsaw

**22** The top edge of the bearer has a shape cut for the seat slats to sit on, which makes it more comfortable. Square lines across the top edge from the front at 80mm (3³⁄₁₆in), 180mm (7in), 290mm (11½in) and 400mm (15¾in). At the front end, measure down 12mm (½in) from the 290mm (11½in) mark to create the shape. Cut to shape with a hand saw and clean up with abrasive paper. Position the bearers in the mortises and over the front rail.

**23** Check the fit and adjust as required. Apply adhesive and fix in place with a 50mm (2in) galvanized nail through the back of the front rail to hold the bearer in place.

*The shaped bearers in position on the end frame.*

**24** Mark and cut the four seat slats 1200mm (47in) long. After giving the slats a light sand, apply a little adhesive to the back of each slat and hold in place ensuring the overhang at each end is equal. Fix through the top of the slats with two 50 x 3mm (2 x ⅛in) jolt-head galvanized nails into each bearer. Remember to angle each nail to increase the holding power. Punch the nails below the surface.

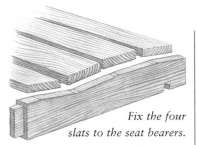

*Fix the four slats to the seat bearers.*

The drawing on page 259 shows the three alternative bench backs.

### Option 1: back with curved top rails

The curved effect of the top rails is marked out with a tool called a trammel (see box, left).

**1** First, mark and cut the tenons on the lower end of the vertical uprights 25mm (1in) long, 35mm (1³⁄₈in) wide and 12mm (½in) thick. Test the fit in the top of the back longitudinal rail.

**2** Next, cut the back rail 1170mm (46in) long. Set out a 25mm (1in) tenon at each end – 12mm (½in) thick and 50mm (2in) wide. Cut these in the usual manner.

**3** Mark out and cut a matching mortise in each upright 60mm (2½in) up from the shoulder line of the tenon, for the bottom rail. Cut these in the usual manner.

*Cut the joints between the back and the bottom rail.*

**4** Next, set out and draw a full scale drawing (set-out) of the back on a sheet of plywood or particle board (see drawings on pages 258–9 for measurements). This will help you to set out the curved rails and angled uprights.

**5** Lay the bottom rail over the set-out and mark the position of the two angled uprights on the top edge. Be careful to keep the shoulder lines at each end in the correct location and set out the mortises on the top of the rail. Chisel the two mortises 25mm (1in) deep, 12mm (½in) wide and 35mm (1³⁄₈in) long. Chisel out and check for fit.

**6** Next, prepare the timber pieces from which you are going to cut the curved rails. Position one of the lower curved rail pieces over the top of the set-out. Set a trammel to a 600mm (24in) radius. Place the base of the trammel arm on the top edge of the bottom rail position on the set-out and use the trammel to trace the curve of the lower edge of the rail on the timber piece.

*Mark the curve on the timber with a trammel.*

**7** Fix the rail over the saw stool and hold firm with a G-cramp. Cut the curve with a jigsaw. True the cut edge with abrasive paper. Lay over the set-out and check the shape. If all is right, change the radius on the trammel to 660mm (26in) and scribe the top curve. Cut as before. Repeat this for all three curved back rails, using the measurements given on the drawings on pages 258–9. Clean up the curves with abrasive paper.

**8** Next, mark and cut the mortises and tenons on the curved rails. Position each of the three curved rails in its correct location over the set-out and transfer the shoulder lines from all the upright pieces onto the edge of the rails. The two lower curved rails have a tenon on the inside end while the other end is cut at an angle. A mortise is also cut in from the outside end to match the tenon on the vertical upright. The top curved rail has a mortise cut in at each end and the ends cut at a bevel.

**9** Set a sliding bevel to the angles the mortises are to be cut and mark the bevels down the face. Gauge the width of the mortises on the edges and at the ends for the tenons. Hold each in a vice and drill out and cut the mortises as before. Note all these mortises are at an angle.

**10** Stand each lower rail in the vice and cut the tenons in the ends. Cramp horizontally to a flat surface and cut the shoulder lines. Cut the tenon 25mm (1in) long and parallel to the shoulder. Cut it 50mm (2in) wide and trim the waste.

**11** Next, mark the shoulders for the tenons on the uprights from the set-out – there should be one at the top of each vertical upright and one at the top of each angled upright. Note the shoulders are at an angle. Cut these tenons as before. Test each for accuracy.

**12** Fit the angled uprights to the back rail and to the top curved back. Check for an accurate fit over the set-out and mark the mortises in the outside edges. Cut as before.

**13** Dry assemble the whole frame in cramps and check for fit. Adjust as required. Mark the position of the centres of the splayed dowels on the inside edges of the back rail, top curved rail and lower curved rails. Lay the dowel across from top to bottom to find the splay. Mark each angle on the face. Mark the length of each dowel to fit 15mm (⅝in) into each rail (see the drawing on pages 258–9). Number each dowel as the lengths vary, and cut to length with a tenon saw.

**14** You can now disassemble the frame. Drill each dowel hole 20mm (¾in) deep in the centre of each edge. Hold the drill with the lead screw of the auger on the centre line. Tilt the drill and bore the hole at the angle marked on the face. Test that each of the dowels fits and is leaning at the angle required.

*Splay out the dowels and fix to the curved rails.*

**15** At this stage carry out a dry assembly of the complete back frame and, if all is well, disassemble, apply adhesive and cramp. Ensure the frame is square and free of wind. Remove all excess adhesive and leave to dry.

**16** After a final sand, the back frame can now be fitted to the main frame. Apply the adhesive to the tenons at the bottom of the uprights. Insert the frame and push it onto the back rail. Fix each upright to the rail with two nails.

*Finished bench with back in place.*

**Option 2: back with three cross-rail panels**

**1** Start by making a back frame consisting of two horizontal rails, two external vertical stiles and two internal vertical rails. First, make the two external vertical stiles: cut them to 550mm (22in) in length and set out the tenons at one end of each, which will fit into the back longitudinal rail (see step 1, option 1). Set out two mortises on each stile 50mm (2in) up from the

shoulder line and 20mm (¾in) down from the top – to accommodate each horizontal rail. The mortises are 25mm (1in) deep, 50mm (2in) long and 12mm (½in) wide in the centre of the edge.

2 Make the two horizontal rails by cutting to 1170mm (46in) in length and set out the tenons at each end. These are 25mm (1in) long, 50mm (2in) wide and 12mm (½in) thick. Cut the tenons. Test the fit and adjust as required.

3 Set out the mortises, which will accommodate the internal vertical stiles. Square a line across the edge of each rail 340mm (13⅜in) along from each shoulder. Square a second line the width of the internal stiles – 45mm (1¾in). As with the other mortises, gauge a line 12mm (½in) wide in the centre. Cut each mortise in the usual manner, 25mm (1in) deep.

4 Cut the two internal vertical stiles 420mm (16½in) long, and set out 25mm (1in) tenons at each end to suit the mortises.

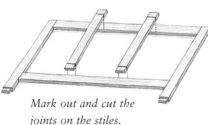

*Mark out and cut the joints on the stiles.*

5 Test the frame dry. Adjust as required and glue up. Ensure the frame is square and free of wind.

6 Now, make the cross-rails, which will fit into the back frame. Set out a halving joint on each pair of cross-rails 450mm (17¾in) long. The halvings are in the centre of each rail. Mark the width of

the timber and square it around the rail. Set a marking gauge to half the thickness and then scribe a line in between the set-out lines.

7 Lay flat against a bench hook and hold with a G-cramp. Cut with a tenon saw to the line. Place several other cuts across the timber between the set-out lines. Remove the waste with a chisel. Check the bottom for flatness. Repeat on the other rails. Test the fit of the three pairs and adjust the components as required.

8 Mark a centre line down the length on the face of each end with a pencil. Hold the assembled cross-rail under the back frame so that the pencil lines align with the intersections of the vertical and horizontal rails. Trace the shapes onto the face of the cross-rail.

9 Cut the cross-rails to length. Square the corner marks down each edge of the rails. Hold flat and cut the ends of the rails to produce pointed tips. Cut, test the fit and adjust as required. Repeat for all three crosses.

*Cut and fix the halving joints where the two cross-rails meet.*

10 Apply a little adhesive to the halving and the pointed ends. Insert the crosses into the back frame so that the faces are flush. Tap a 50mm (2in) nail at each end of the

cross-rails into the back frame. Leave to dry. Sand all surfaces flat. Remove any sharp edges and fit the back to the seat and main frame.

**Option 3: Back with cross-weave effect**

This third option is made up of three vertical stiles and two horizontal rails. Plywood strips are interwoven within this frame to create the cross-weave effect.

1 Follow the step instructions given for option 2 to cut three vertical stiles and the horizontal rails to length. Fix stiles and rails together to make the basic frame as before with mortise and tenon joints.

2 Next, rout a 3mm (⅛in) groove along the inside edge of each of the frame members to accommodate the cross-weave strips.

3 Now, cut two vertical and two horizontal beech strips to length about 385mm (15¼in) long and 1150mm (45¼in) long respectively and have a trial weaving of the strips. Remember to allow for the amount that will sit in the grooves. Check the length and trim as required. Once the correct length is obtained, cut the remaining strips.

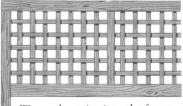

*Weave the strips into the frame.*

4 Put some adhesive in the grooves and reweave the strips. Ensure they fit all the way into the grooves.

## Fitting doors

There are two alternative ways of fitting doors to the linen cupboard. Here, the top doors are held in place with two hinges in each side. The bottom door is a fall, which is held secure with a pivot hinge in the bottom.

*Door on side hinges.*

*Door as a fall.*

**19** The top can be removed and 3mm (⅛in) pilot holes drilled, and then secured temporarily with 30mm (1¼in) 8 gauge screws.

*Screw the top in place.*

### Fitting out the cabinet

**20** Take the two ply shelves and cut to fit neatly in place between the rebates on the internal rails. Cut slightly over size with a hand saw and trim to fit with a smoothing plane. Secure in place with a little adhesive in each rebate.

*Fit the ply shelves.*

**21** Now gather the pieces that will make the two top doors, the fall and the two bottom drawer fronts. The grain should run horizontally through all of these. Each piece can be cut approximately to its vertical size and planed to fit between the front legs with a 3mm (⅛in) clearance. Now mark the positions of the centres of the handle cut-outs and drill with a Forstner bit or a hole saw using a pillar drill.

**22** The top two doors are cut from the one piece already fitted. Crosscut this through the centre vertically and plane precisely to fit. Fit the top doors to the cabinet with hinges on the sides and the bottom one as a fall (see box left and pages 120–7).

**23** Because the legs form a recess within the cabinet sides, normal drawer-running methods cannot be used. Here the drawer runners are fixed to the inside of the cabinet, projecting from the line of the legs as shown in the drawing on page 269. Prepare, mark and cut the runners. Fit each with two 30mm (1³⁄₁₆in) 8 gauge countersunk screws through the side panel. Ensure that the screw heads are well below the surface.

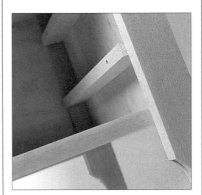

*Fit the drawer runners.*

### Making the drawers

**24** The two drawers are joined at the corners with dovetail joints. Cut the timber to length. The sides are 300mm (12in) long, and the back and front are cut to the distance between the runners, plus 12mm (½in) for the side grooves. Note the width of the material for the back is smaller than that of the sides and front to fit the plywood bottom.

**25** Mark the thickness of the material on the ends of all the pieces. Square this around each. Determine the number of dovetails required. The side pieces will have the tails cut on each end. Measure 12mm (½in) across from the left-hand edge on the squared line. Divide the remaining width up into even parts equal to the number of tails required.

**26** Mark the width of each tail – 12mm (½in) – to the left of each division. Set a sliding bevel to a pitch of 1:6 as before. Mark the sides of each dovetail using the sliding bevel. Square the tails across the end and bevel down the other side to match. Clearly mark the waste in the pin sockets.

**27** Cut the sides of the dovetails with a dovetail saw and remove the waste using a coping saw. Then pare back to the shoulder lines with a chisel. Cut the pins as shown on pages 182–3.

**28** With the router, run a 6mm (¼in) wide groove 6mm (¼in) deep. Run the top edge of the groove to line up with the bottom edge of the back, but set inside the bottom edge on the side pieces and front. Apply adhesive to the contact surfaces and assemble the drawer. Cramp if required and allow to dry, ensuring the drawer is square and free of wind.

**29** Remove from cramps and clean up the joints. Cut the drawer bottom and slide into the groove. Check for square and fix in place through the bottom of the drawer into the edge of the back with three 12mm (½in) 5 gauge countersunk screws. Make the other drawer.

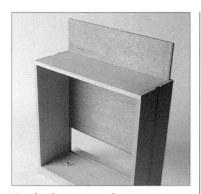

*Fit the drawer together.*

**30** Running the drawers requires a groove along each side of the drawer. Adjust the router to cut a groove wide enough for the runner in the centre of the side. The depth is already set to 6mm (¼in). Adjust the fence to run the groove. This will need to have several passes along the drawer, adjusting each time until a width of 20mm (¾in) is obtained. Clean groove with a chisel and abrasive paper.

**31** False decorative fronts are attached to the drawers. Place each drawer in the cabinet and apply two small pieces of thin double-sided tape on the front. Push all the way in. Hold the false front in position and bring the drawer forward to meet the back of the false front. The tape will hold the two together. Remove and place face down on a flat, smooth surface. Drill four 12mm (½in) screws through the inside of the drawer into the decorative front. Replace drawer to check alignment and adjust as required. Repeat for the other drawer leaving enough room for the fall above to operate.

### Finishing

**32** Sand and apply required finish. A strap or flap stay can be added to the fall to prevent straining the hinges.

# Modernism and beyond

The transition from the 19th to 20th century was marked by many social, political and technological changes. In the arts the old ways were questioned and new ideas brought different approaches to all manner of problems. New technologies were established that, by the end of the 20th century, caused very great changes. This evolution was both interrupted and quickened by the conflict in Europe between 1914 and 1918. Mobilization and the resulting carnage meant the loss to some countries of a whole generation, but it also forced progress in technology, changed social attitudes and gave art and design new practical, visual and aesthetic aims. The 1920s and 1930s were times of very varied experiences, none more so than in art and design. The cataclysm of World War I marked the turning point because what came out of it was disillusionment, poverty but also a desire to experiment.

## DE STIJL AND BAUHAUS

Although occupied by German forces, Holland had avoided much of the fighting and been largely spared by the war, so it was in a better position to lead the way. Gerrit Reitveld had worked during the war years on radical designs that discarded any reference to the past, drawing exclusively upon rectangular and cubic forms. He was a constructionist and a member of a group that explained its theories in a magazine called de Stijl, and the name has since been used to refer to the group itself. Their ideals valued abstract, rectangular forms that only used the primary colours of red, blue and yellow.

*The design of this chair, by Le Corbusier has the ergonomics of the human form in mind.*

OPPOSITE LEFT *A child's chair, designed in 1928 by Erick Dieckmann, a member of the Bauhaus school.* ◆ OPPOSITE CENTRE *Designed by Charlotte Perriand, working with Le Corbusier, Le Petit Confort chair is made out of chromed bent tubular steel with dark leather upholstery.* ◆ OPPOSITE RIGHT *Designers used minimal materials for maximum style as shown in this table, made in 1929–33.* ◆ ABOVE LEFT *Classic tubular steel chairs with red leather seats and backs, called 'Basculant' and designed by Le Corbusier.* ◆ ABOVE CENTRE *Mies van der Rohe's 'Daybed', designed in 1929.* ◆ ABOVE RIGHT *A glass and steel table designed by Eileen Gray in 1927.*

They felt their choice of geometric forms had a higher spiritual level and believed that, through total simplification and abstraction, the art and design world could transform individual, selfish civilization into a spiritual, idealistic one.

The basic ideas of the de Stijl group were developed by the Bauhaus in the 1920s. This was the focal point for a new movement after the war in Germany. Started in Weimar in 1919 by the architect Walter Gropius, it approached the education of architects, artists, designers and makers in a new way. The most progressive practitioners were invited to become lecturers, the studio and workshops were linked and the subjects ranged through architecture, design, graphics and the performing arts. Newness and invention was paramount to this movement – students were taught to probe and seek out a solution that was both a rational result of the tools and materials that they were using as well as an exact fulfilment of its function. This approach was so 'right' for the time that its influence was felt across the world.

## INTRODUCTION OF METAL

Bauhaus designers often used furniture materials other than timber, and it was at this time that Marcel Breuer first experimented with metal furniture. In 1924–5 he used non-resilient chrome tubing to construct a number of totally new designs, notably an armchair that was related in formal structure to Rietveld's work. It emphasized the angular form but instead of upholstery Breuer used canvas, and the frame was made of metal. Architect Mies van de Rohe also began working in metal, creating work in steel strip. In 1928

Breuer designed a tubular steel chair, which was later manufactured by Thonet. This became the accepted prototype for many such chairs afterwards. It combined maximum comfort with minimum materials – one piece of continuously curved metal tubing – eliminating the need for costly joints. It fuelled the urge to reduce form to its minimum, then referred to as 'functional' design. Some resulting furniture was crude, but, done well, this approach led to extreme elegance in design. Breuer designed chairs, tables, cabinets and beds using this method.

In 1929 Mies designed the celebrated Barcelona chair, which was named after the international exhibition for which he designed the German Pavilion, where his chair was an integral element. The chair's frame consisted of two crossing curves of steel bars. This has become a classic piece of 20th century furniture design.

Many other architects and designers also used metal in their designs including the famous French architect, Le Corbusier. Initially he used simple Thonet bentwood chairs in his interiors. Then, along with his associate associate Charlotte Perriand, he designed metal furniture that was closely related to Bauhaus work. However, while the German interest lay in the individual design of pieces, Le Corbusier saw design as a technical, social and economic problem for which a general solution could be found. He reduced all furniture to three categories – tables, chairs and open or enclosed shelves, and then set about designing standard forms for each. Another designer who experimented with new materials and processes was Eileen Gray (see also page 207).

# Dining chair  Advanced

*This chair has simple classic but modern lines. Dining chairs are normally made without arms, but there are often two chairs in a set called carvers, which are versions with arms. Instructions and measurements are given for both.*

### MATERIALS

| Part | Materials and dimensions | No. |
|---|---|---|
| | **Hardwood** | |
| Front legs | 450 x 35mm (18 x 1³⁄₈in) diameter | 2 |
| Back legs | 850 x 35mm (33½ x 1³⁄₈in) diameter | 2 |
| Front rail | 400 x 65 x 20mm (16 x 2½ x ¾in) | 1 |
| Back rail | 400 x 65 x 20mm (16 x 2½ x ¾in) | 1 |
| Top rail | 320 x 35 x 20mm (13 x 1½ x ¾in) | 1 |
| Cross-rails | 420 x 95 x 20mm (16½ x 3¾ x ¾in) | 2 |
| Arms for carver | 400 x 90 x 22mm (16 x 3½ x ⅞in) | 4 |
| | **Bending plywood** | |
| Chair seat | 450 x 400 x 1.5mm (18 x 16 x ¹⁄₁₆in) | 5 |
| Chair back | 560 x 450 x 1.5mm (22 x 18 x ¹⁄₁₆in) | 5 |
| | **Off-cuts of manufactured board** | |
| Two preform moulds | 450 x 50 x 20mm (17¾ x 2 x ¾in) | 28 |
| | 600 x 100 x 20mm (23⅝ x 4 x ¾in) | 16 |

**Other materials:** six 25mm (1in) 8 gauge brass countersunk screws; adhesive (PVA); abrasive paper (120-grit); finish.

### Making the underframe

The underframe is made up of four legs, a front rail, a back rail, two cross-rails and a back rest top rail.

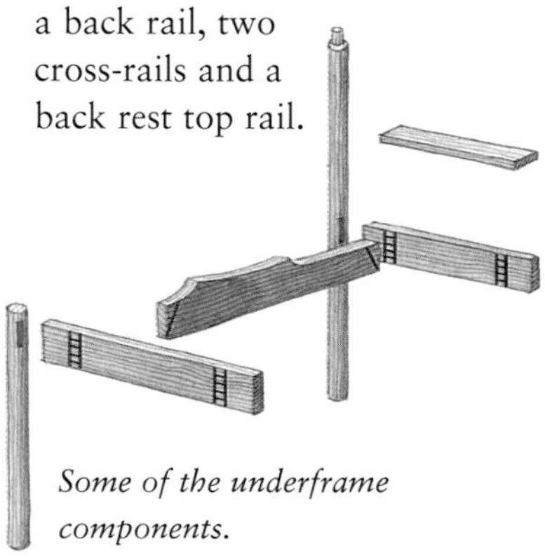

*Some of the underframe components.*

**1** Prepare the two back and two front legs. Saw these square with a radial-arm saw, leaving a little extra on the length. You will make these round later either by turning or planing. Plane each to an octagonal shape in order to make marking out and cutting the joints easier (see page 246). Mark the length and the position of the rail joints using a box square. Measure up 310mm (12¼in) on the back legs and 345mm (13⅝in) on the front legs.

**2** Then mark out a mortise on each leg 55mm (2³⁄₁₆in) further up. Set a marking gauge and mark the mortise between the lines. Hold the leg on a solid surface with a G-cramp and drill out the bulk of the waste from the mortise to a depth of 25mm (1in). Use a depth stop or masking tape to prevent drilling all the way

through. Chisel the mortise to the set-out lines with a 10mm (³⁄₈in) mortise chisel. Clean up the sides of the mortise with a 25mm (1in) paring chisel. Take care to chisel true to the set-out.

**3** Next, prepare the front rail. Cut to 370mm (14⅝in) long on a radial-arm saw. Square a line across the bottom edge at both ends – 25mm (1in) in from each end, leaving 320mm (12⅝in) in between. Set a sliding bevel to a pitch of 1:6 and mark the shoulder across both faces. Return the squared line across the top edge.

**4** Cut the tenons on the ends of the rail to match the mortises in the front legs. Hold vertically in a vice and cut down to the shoulder line on the waste side of the line with a tenon saw.

**5** Remove from the vice and lay flat on the bench. Hold in place with a G-cramp and cut the shoulder line to remove the waste. With the marking gauge already set, scribe a line down each side of the tenon and then saw away the sides so that the tenon is 55mm (2³⁄₁₆in) wide. The end of the tenon will also be bevelled parallel to the shoulders. Cut this with the tenon saw and check the fit. Adjust the components as required.

FRONT ELEVATION

SIDE ELEVATION

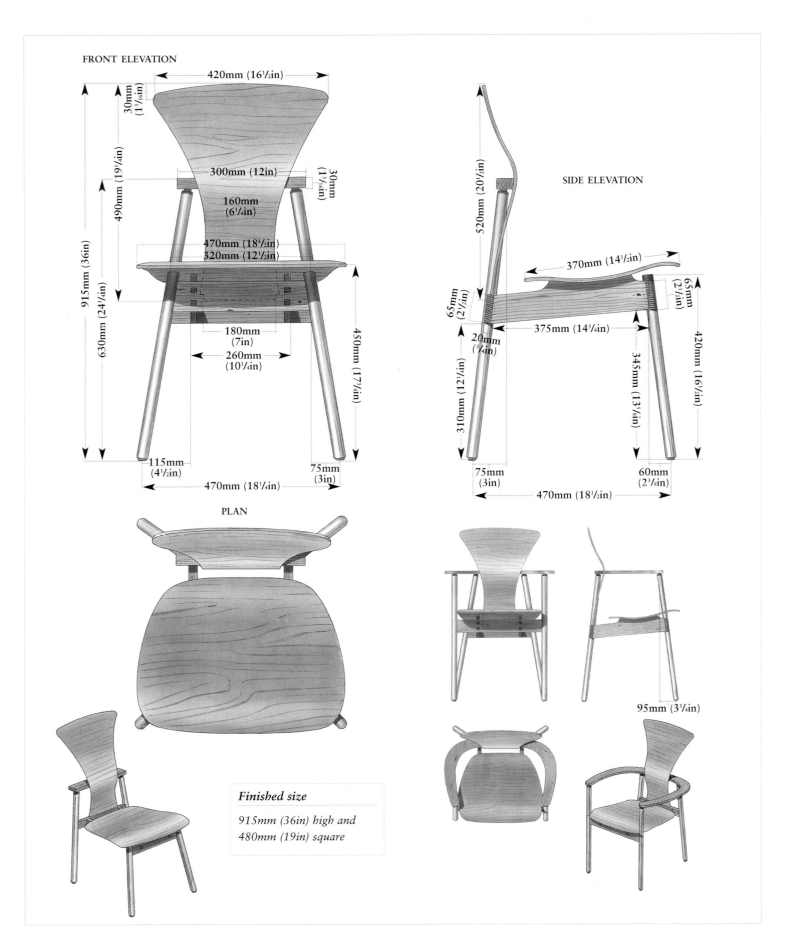

420mm (16½in)

30mm (1³⁄₁₆in)

300mm (12in)

30mm (1³⁄₁₆in)

160mm (6¼in)

490mm (19¼in)

470mm (18½in)

320mm (12½in)

915mm (36in)

630mm (24¾in)

180mm (7in)

260mm (10¼in)

450mm (17¾in)

115mm (4½in)

75mm (3in)

470mm (18¼in)

520mm (20½in)

370mm (14½in)

65mm (2½in)

65mm (2½in)

375mm (14¾in)

20mm (¾in)

310mm (12¼in)

345mm (13⅝in)

420mm (16½in)

75mm (3in)

60mm (2³⁄₈in)

470mm (18½in)

PLAN

95mm (3¾in)

### Finished size

*915mm (36in) high and
480mm (19in) square*

6 The back rail is set out the same as the front with one exception – it needs to be slightly longer as it is lower down the legs. To find the length, assemble the front rail and legs. Lay the back legs on top of the front ones with the bottoms flush. Mark the back legs at the top and bottom edge of the rail 5mm (³/₁₆in) below these points, giving the shoulder lines. Set this out on the bottom edge of the back rail. Mark the bevels on the face and complete the set-out. Cut the tenon in the same manner as for the front rail.

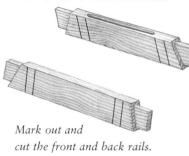

*Mark out and cut the front and back rails.*

7 Set out the two cross-rails of the seat frame by marking the bevel across the face at one end at a pitch of 1:85. Mark the shoulder line – parallel to the bevel 30mm (1³/₁₆in) along. Measure up this line 35mm (1³/₈in) from the bottom edge. This represents the distance that the back rail is lower than the front rail. Measure a 375mm (14³/₄in) line perpendicular to the bevel from this point to the bottom edge – this indicates the length between the shoulders on the bottom edge. Mark the other shoulder line at a pitch of 1:7, and then the tenon length of 20mm (³/₄in).

*Carefully mark out all the cut lines on the cross-rails.*

8 Set out the cut-outs for the cross-rails. Measure up the front of each shoulder line 65mm (2⁵/₈in), and mark a line along the length from shoulder to shoulder. From the front shoulder, measure back 50mm (2in), and then a further 200mm (8in) on the top edge. Make a curve from this point back towards each end down to the previous line along the length. Cut these with a jigsaw, and clean up with a plane or chisel.

9 Cut the cross-rails slightly over length. They will be cleaned up when assembled.

10 The width of the double tenons on the cross-rails is 12mm (¹/₂in). Divide the 65mm (2⁵/₈in) shoulder line into five equal spaces. Cut down these on the waste side to the shoulder lines and crosscut away the waste on the outside. Remove the waste between the tenons with a coping saw, and then pare back to the shoulder line with a chisel.

*Cut the tenons on the cross-rail.*

11 To set out the double mortises in the front and back rails, find the centre of the bottom edge of both rails and measure out 110mm (4³/₈in) each side, plus the thickness of the timber. Square a line across the faces of both rails. Measure up five spaces of 12mm (¹/₂in) from the bottom edge. The second and fourth are the through mortises. Set these out on all four faces. Cut the mortises with a 10mm (³/₈in) drill bit and then a chisel. Check the fit and adjust as necessary.

*Mark and cut the double mortises for the front and back rails.*

12 Dry assemble the chair frame and check the shoulders of the rails. It will be necessary to adjust the shoulders with a chisel in order to achieve neat fitting joints.

*The main seat frame assembled dry.*

13 It is at this stage that the octagonal legs should be planed or turned to a round shape. At the top of the back legs, turn a 25mm (1in) diameter dowel 35mm (1⁵/₁₆in) long.

14 Mark out the top rail. Here the tops of the back legs are rounded to fit the holes in the rail. Mark out the rail and these angled holes by holding the rail behind the legs and marking the positions of the dowel tops. Square the lines across the face and mark the centres for the holes. Drill the holes in the centre on this set-out. These holes will also be at an angle in order to match the marks on the edge. This is best achieved on a pillar drill with a Forstner bit. Cut the rail to an approximate length of 300mm (12in) on a radial-arm saw.

*Fit the legs to the
top rail.*

**15** Set up a router with an 8mm (⁵/₁₆in) straight bit and cut a groove 160mm (6³/₈in) long and 8mm (⁵/₁₆in) deep in the centre of the top edge of the lower back rail.

### Assembling the underframe

You should now be able to assemble the whole underframe dry, before securing the components with adhesive.

**16** The cross-rail joints are wedged through mortise and tenons, so disassemble and cut the slots for the wedges. Cut the wedges from any piece of waste. Sand off any set-out marks.

**17** Assemble the seat frame, cross, front and back rails by gluing and cramping the joints. Insert the wedges. Ensure the frame is completely square and free of wind.

**18** When the adhesive has cured, plane off the excess tenons and wedges on the outside face.

**19** Fix the four legs to this frame by gluing the tenons and cramping. Pull the joints up tight with the cramps. Check that each pair of legs is in line with the other and that there is no twist in the frame.

**20** Finally, fit the top rail over the dowels and wedge these joints into

place. Skim any projection with a smoothing plane and sand as necessary.

*Fit the legs and cross-rails together.*

### Using preforms to mould the seat and back to shape

The interesting feature of this chair is the preformed seat and back. If produced in a factory these would be made from sheets of constructional veneer, but for our purposes it is better to make them from thin plywood. First it is necessary to make the moulds that will form these individual sheets of plywood into the required shape. The seat is a single curvature, while the back has a single curve but also wings that are slightly curved at the top of the central shape. Very precise work is necessary to make these moulds.

**21** First, determine the availability of suitable plywood, particularly as regards to the thicknesses that are available. The final form does not need to be any thicker than 10mm (³/₈in), and so if you use 3mm (¹/₈in) ply you will need three layers. If you use 1.5mm (¹/₁₆in) plywood, you would achieve a thinner form using five layers, resulting in a thickness of 7.5mm (⁵/₁₆in). Since it is desirable for the grain direction on both outside faces to run the same way,

particularly on the back preform, you will need an uneven number of layers.

**22** Now, make the seat mould. First, make the sides of the mould by setting out a curve on the off-cut of manufactured board to suit grid shape on the right. Set out another line parallel, equal to the thickness of the form. Cut both lines with a jigsaw. This will give two matching sides (top and bottom) with a space for the form to go between.

**23** Next, cut the lateral strips to length and fix them into the sides as shown below. Make sure that the top edges are flush. Check fit and finish by shaping or sanding to the correct curvature.

**24** Cut and fix the two end pieces, which stabilize the mould when pressure is applied. Finally, cut the ply top of the mould and glue in place.

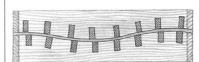

*Make the seat mould.*

*Fix the top of the seat mould.*

**25** Try the mould dry with the pieces of ply you have cut for one seat form. Cramp the jig together to press the sheets to the shape.

Grid for
seat mould

Each square =
20mm high x
10mm wide

Grid for
back mould

**26** If all is well, apply adhesive to the faces to be glued and cramp the mould, leaving it cramped long enough for the adhesive to cure. Remove from the mould, mark out the shape from the grid on page 279, trim with a jigsaw and sand the edges.

*Cramp the ply in the mould.*

**27** The back mould is made in a similar way to the seat, except that at the top there is a slight curve on each side (see drawing on page 277). Make the centre of the mould in the same way as you made the seat mould (see page 279 for grid). In addition, make a second mould for the wings of the back – this takes in the curve of the first mould along its side edges. Cut and fit into the first mould as shown below.

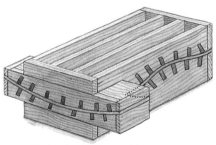

*Make the back mould.*

**28** When this mould is finished, follow the above procedure to produce the preform and, when it is complete, cut the correct shape and finish the edges.

## Final assembly

**29** Sand and apply the required finish to all components and then set the preforms in position. The bottom of the back will need to be trimmed to fit into the groove on the top edge of the back rail. A 10mm ($^3/_8$in) wide x 8mm ($^5/_{16}$in) high cut-out in each corner is required.

**30** The back will be glued at the bottom into the groove and held in position with two 25mm (1in) 8 gauge brass countersunk screws into the top rail. Drill the two 4.5mm ($^3/_{16}$in) holes through the back, followed by 3mm ($^1/_8$in) pilot holes. Countersink the top of the holes to let the heads of the screws sit just below the surface.

*Screw the back in position.*

**31** The seat will be held on the cross-rails with four screws. Check the fit of the seat on the cross-rails. Plane the top edge of these for a neat fit. Drill holes through the seat, as for the back. Apply adhesive to the cross-rails and screw in place. Sand and apply required finish.

## Making the carver chair

The carver chair is based on the standard chair described above, with just a few changes.

**1** The seat frame is the same except that the front legs are straight and extend up past the seat to support the arms. The front rail is longer and the tenons are square.

*The front rail is longer on the carver.*

**2** The front legs are also longer – mark and cut to length. Cut a dowel top in the front legs as you did for the back legs in step 14. Fit the back legs and top rail as before, and then fit the longer front legs in position. The ply back will be the same, as will the seat, except for slight shaping around the legs.

**3** Make and fit the arms. They are made in pairs with 22mm ($^7/_8$in) timber. The arms are made from two pieces that are joined together with halving joints on the sharp back curve. Join the two pieces together before marking and cutting the shape.

*Make the curved arm.*

**4** When the arms are ready, drill the hole that will accept the top of the leg. Place in position and check that each fits on the top of the top rail. Mark and cut so that they join in the centre of the back. Glue in place. The top of the leg can be wedged, while the back parts can be glued to the top of the top rail. Sand and finish.

# The swinging avant-garde

In the second half of the 20th century, technological advances dramatically changed many aspects of everyday life and furniture design also began to develop in previously unknown directions. Advances made due to the exigencies of World War II led to the development of more modern manufacturing processes and materials, which were enthusiastically embraced by designers. For example, Du Pont created nylon in 1939 and a new lightweight plastic – polyethylene – was first used commercially by the Tupper Corporation. The new materials gave designers more scope and had a dramatic effect on the forms of furniture.

### THE UNITED STATES
In the United States, Charles and Ray Eames completely rejected right angles and entered a new sphere of 'sculpted' furniture based on the latest technology. They designed the first mass-produced moulded fibreglass shell chair, the 'DAR' chair, in 1950. They also combined steel and aluminium, in conjunction with leather or fabric, for the 'Aluminium group' chair of 1958 and the 'GRP la Chaise'. David Rowland's 'GF 40/4' stacking chairs made use of steel rods with laminated ply. A rounded 'womb-like' shape was one of the most distinctive to emerge for chairs. Eero Saarinen's 'Womb' chair was constructed of latex foam on a moulded plastic shell, reinforced with fibreglass on chromium-plated steel supports. He had envisioned an enveloping chair when he designed it – one where the sitter could draw their legs up but still be supported elsewhere. It employed very generous, wide proportions and was covered in foam rubber padding and fabric. The aim of his design was to reduce the number of parts and minimize the manufacturing process. George Nelson's 'Coconut' chair of 1956 was manufactured by Herman Miller, of which he was the design director from 1946. This company devoted much of its time to studying the process for moulding plywood, as well as solving the problems of attaching metal legs to plywood seats and moulded plywood parts to one another. They also paid particular attention to the new plastics that were used in the aircraft-manufacturing field.

### GREAT BRITAIN
Britain's industrial capacity suffered greatly in World War II and rationing of timber and tubular steel was in place as early as 1940. The 1950s heralded a new era in design in England, with inspiration from Italy, Scandinavia and America. Light, spacious interiors and vivid colours were favoured in this period, and motifs such as molecular patterns and space-age imagery were popular. Ernest Race won justifiable acclaim with the medal-winning 'BA aluminium chair'. This was the result of real ingenuity – he used aluminium taken from scrapped war planes. This innovative technical spirit was carried forward by Robin Day, who created the 'Polyprop' chair in 1963, a stackable chair which had a strong polypropylene one-piece shell and was the first that could be injection moulded. This is a truly modern classic and can still be seen everywhere – in offices, schools etc. It perfectly suited the furniture production of the time, as it was light and cheap to produce. Another influential designer of the decade, Vernon Panton created the first single moulded fibreglass form with his 'Stacking' chairs of the 1960s, which had no need for any embellishment.

OPPOSITE LEFT *Eames's model 'LCM', designed in 1945.* ◆ OPPOSITE CENTRE *A chair from Eames' 'Aluminium Group', designed in 1958.* ◆ OPPOSITE RIGHT *Race's 'Rocking chair', designed in 1948.* ◆ ABOVE LEFT *Panton's plastic cantilever chair, designed in 1960.* ◆ ABOVE CENTRE *Albini's 'Luisa' chair, designed in 1955.* ◆ ABOVE RIGHT *The 'Karuselli' chair, designed by Y. Kukkapuro in 1964.*

In the 1960s Britain was swinging with new ideas, attitudes and trends. This change of attitude was apparent in many aspects of popular design. And furniture was no exception, reflecting the upbeat mood of the age with the introduction of fun pieces – the 'Series Up' polyurethane foam chairs popped out of the packing containers that compressed them and Peter Murdock's 'Polka Dot' children's chair was made of bright laminated paperboard that could be packed flat. These were some of the first examples of successful mass-produced furniture.

## SCANDINAVIAN DESIGN

Scandinavian design of the 20th century was characterized by classic lines that resulted in high-quality furniture. Designers were sympathetic to natural materials but not afraid to take advantage of machine production, which they employed to create bold shapes and curves. When one thinks of Scandinavian design, beautiful wooden pieces spring to mind, but in the second half of the century many designers turned to new materials and proved that a similar feeling could be evoked without timber. Chairs with moulded fibreglass forms and metal frames and bases were characteristic of this period. Arne Jaacobsen's

*Pesce's Donna chair, designed in 1969.*

innovative 'Swan' and 'Egg' chairs show how latex foam padding can be applied over the top of a fibreglass shell to create simple, inviting curved shapes that swivel on cast aluminium star-shaped bases. The 'Egg' chair, which has been in production since 1957, has a sense of comfort and stability and is also strongly sculptural.

## ITALIAN DESIGN

In Italy designers produced some classic modern pieces. Earlier pieces were based on more traditional shapes but Italian design quickly took a lead in innovation with Magistretti's 1961 stackable chair 'Selene' and Joe Colombo's 1967 'Colombo' chair, which was the first all-plastic chair to be made by injection moulding.

There was an explosion of ideas around the world during the 1970s and 80s. Two major groups were Studio Alchmia under Alessandro Mendini and the Memphis group, led by Ettore Sottsass. Kukkapuro, who designed the 'Karuselli' chair in 1964 became associated with the Memphis group during the 1980s. They rejected ascetic modernism and were radical, inventive and over the top. Anything went, as long as it was modern, progressive and decorative.

# Feature shelving  Advanced

*The design of this feature shelving unit looks both modern and attractive. It provides plenty of shelf space and includes a small drawer within one of the shelves. The back piece (inserted as six separate panels of plywood) is optional – if you do want to add it, then follow the instructions on page 288. If not, then follow the drawing opposite.*

## Tools

Smoothing plane

Sliding bevel

Marking knife

Tenon saw

Panel saw

G-cramps

Router with 6mm (¼in) and 12mm (½in) straight cutter and 12mm (½in) rebate cutter with a ball race

Marking gauge

25mm (1in) paring chisel

Drill and 3mm (⅛in), 4.5mm (³⁄₁₆in), countersink and 10mm (³⁄₈in) dowelling bits

Screwdriver

Sash cramps

Dovetail saw

### Skills required for project

Measuring and marking *pages 64–7*

Basic sawing *pages 68–71*

Planing *pages 74–81*

Fine sawing *pages 82–5*

Grooving *pages 90–3*

Drilling *pages 96–100*

Making housing joints *pages 110–11*

Making dovetail joints *pages 112–14*

Using abrasives *pages 115–17*

Assembling projects *pages 120–7*

Using adhesives *pages 128–9*

Wood finishing *pages 130–5*

### MATERIALS

| Part | Materials and dimensions | No. |
|---|---|---|
| **Solid timber – hardwood** | | |
| Triangle | | |
| Long sides | 2100 x 310 x 25mm (82 x 12½ x 1in) | 2 |
| Bottom short side | 1520 x 310 x 25mm (60 x 12½ x 1in) | 1 |
| Plinth | 1500 x 50 x 25mm (59 x 2 x 1in) | 2 |
| | 300 x 50 x 25mm (12 x 2 x 1in) | 2 |
| Shelves | | |
| Top | 2200 x 200 x 25mm (86 x 8 x 1in) | 1 |
| Second | 2050 x 220 x 25mm (81 x 8¾ x 1in) | 1 |
| Third | 1900 x 240 x 25mm (75 x 9½ x 1in) | 1 |
| Fifth | 1600 x 260 x 25mm (63 x 10¼ x 1in) | 1 |
| Shelf/drawer | 1800 x 270 x 25mm (71 x 10½ x 1in) | 1 |
| Build-up | 1800 x 150 x 25mm (71 x 6 x 1in) | 1 |
| Thickness battens | 1800 x 75 x 25mm (71 x 3 x 1in) | 1 |
| | 420 x 50 x 25mm (16¾ x 2 x 1in) | 4 |
| Dowels | 50 x 10mm (2in x ⅜in) diameter | 30 |
| Support battens | 1800 x 75 x 20mm (71 x 3 x ¾in) | 2 |
| | 2100 x 75 x 20mm (82 x 3 x ¾in) | 2 |
| | 2400 x 75 x 20mm (94½ x 3 x ¾in) | 1 |
| Drawer | | |
| Sides | 400 x 50 x 15mm (16 x 2 x ⅝in) | 2 |
| Back | 800 x 50 x 15mm (32 x 2 x ⅝in) | 1 |
| Drawer runner | 400 x 8 x 8mm (16 x ⁵⁄₁₆ x ⁵⁄₁₆in) | 2 |
| **Plywood** – the approximate sized triangles will be base x height x 6mm (¼in) thick; do not cut these until the carcase is assembled | | |
| Top back | 370 x 300mm (14½ x 12in) | 1 |
| Second back | 530 x 230mm (21 x 9in) | 1 |
| Third back | 740 x 210mm (29 x 8¼in) | 1 |
| Fourth back | 950 x 210mm (37½ x 8¼in) | 1 |
| Fifth back | 1200 x 260mm (47 x 10¼in) | 1 |
| Sixth back | 1440 x 320mm (56 x 12½in) | 1 |
| Drawer bottom | 800 x 400 x 6mm (32 x 16 x ¼in) | 1 |

**Other materials:** forty 30mm (1³⁄₁₆in) 8 gauge countersunk screws; fifty 12mm (½ in) 6 gauge countersunk screws; six 50mm (2in) 8 gauge countersunk screws; adhesive (PVA); abrasive paper; finish.

## Making the triangular carcase

**1** First, make the slanting front face of the two long sides of the triangle (see drawing opposite, side elevation) – the sides measure 300mm (12in) at the base tapering to 200mm (8in) at the top. Cut and plane both sides to shape. Apply a face-edge and face-side mark to the opposite side. Do all the setting out from this back edge.

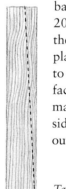

*Taper the front edge of the sides.*

**2** On a piece of manufactured board, make a set-out, either full-sized or scaled, for the mitres on each corner. Remember that the top one is a more acute angle than the two at the bottom. Set up a sliding bevel to the mitre joint.

**3** The overall measurements of the two sides are 2043mm (80½in) long and the bottom is 1500mm (59in) long. Mark these lengths with the mitre joints on the side faces. Mark the joints across each face.

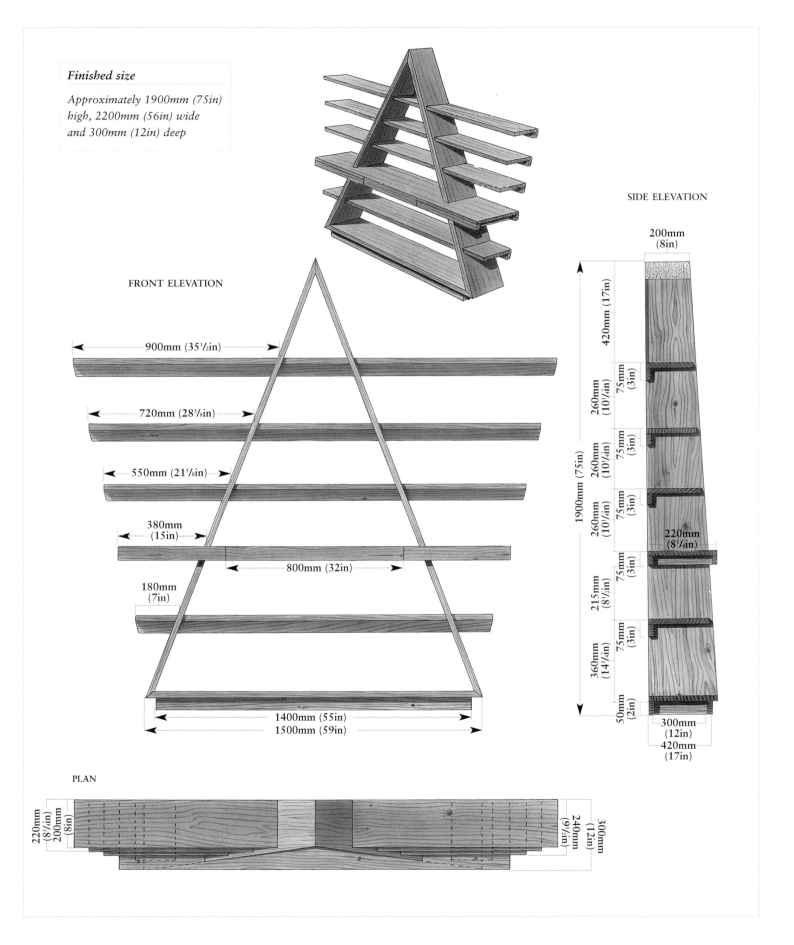

**Finished size**

*Approximately 1900mm (75in)
high, 2200mm (56in) wide
and 300mm (12in) deep*

SIDE ELEVATION

200mm
(8in)

420mm (17in)

260mm
(10¼in)

75mm
(3in)

260mm
(10¼in)

75mm
(3in)

1900mm (75in)

260mm
(10¼in)

75mm
(3in)

220mm
(8¼in)

215mm
(8½in)

75mm
(3in)

360mm
(14¼in)

75mm
(3in)

50mm
(2in)

300mm
(12in)

420mm
(17in)

FRONT ELEVATION

900mm (35½in)

720mm (28⅜in)

550mm (21⅝in)

380mm
(15in)

800mm (32in)

180mm
(7in)

1400mm (55in)

1500mm (59in)

PLAN

220mm
(8¾in)
200mm
(8in)

240mm
(9½in)

300mm
(12in)

*Cramp the top mitres together.*

### Fixing the rear battens

**20** Next, prepare the five rear battens that support the shelves. Check that they all fit into the slots already cut in step 17, that they are the correct length and that when positioned they are all parallel with each other and the base.

*Ensure the rear battens are parallel.*

**21** Glue and screw them into place through the back using 30mm (1³⁄₁₆in) 8 gauge countersunk screws. You will now have a triangular cabinet with four internal shelves in place and with five extending battens to support the outside shelves.

### Making the back and plinth

**22** Prepare the plywood backs for fitting. Since the back will not be one whole piece, rebates need to be made around each opening in the

sides and in the rear battens into which the ply backs will fit. Use a 12mm (½in) rebate cutter with a ball race, and cut the rebates 6mm (¼in) deep and 12mm (½in) wide.

*Cut rebates for the back panels.*

**23** Now mark each of the six back pieces of timber – because of the angled ends you will be able to cut economically from a single sheet of plywood. Cut and fit each back into the rebates and fix with 12mm (½in) 6 gauge countersunk screws.

*Screw the back panels in position.*

**24** Now fit the bottom plinth. Prepare the timber and mark out and cut the dovetails in the corners. Glue the four sections of the plinth together. When dry, sand the surface.

**25** Fix the plinth in place by pocket screwing through the bottom edge, using

three 50mm (2in) 8 gauge countersunk screws along each long edge.

*Screw the plinth into place on the bottom of the unit.*

**26** Now, prepare the external shelf extensions. You will already have these pieces from when you measured them before step 15. Using the jig as shown in step 16, drill the holes for the dowels and offer up to the unit so that you can ensure that the shelf ends fit into the housings.

**27** When the outside ends are finished, the shelves can be placed into position. The rear battens and the shelves can be pocket screwed together. Drill pocket holes 8mm (⁵⁄₁₆in) in diameter and a clearance hole of 4.5mm (³⁄₁₆in). Check that all fits well, apply the adhesive, and cramp and screw the shelves into place.

*Check the fit and then fix the outer shelves into position.*

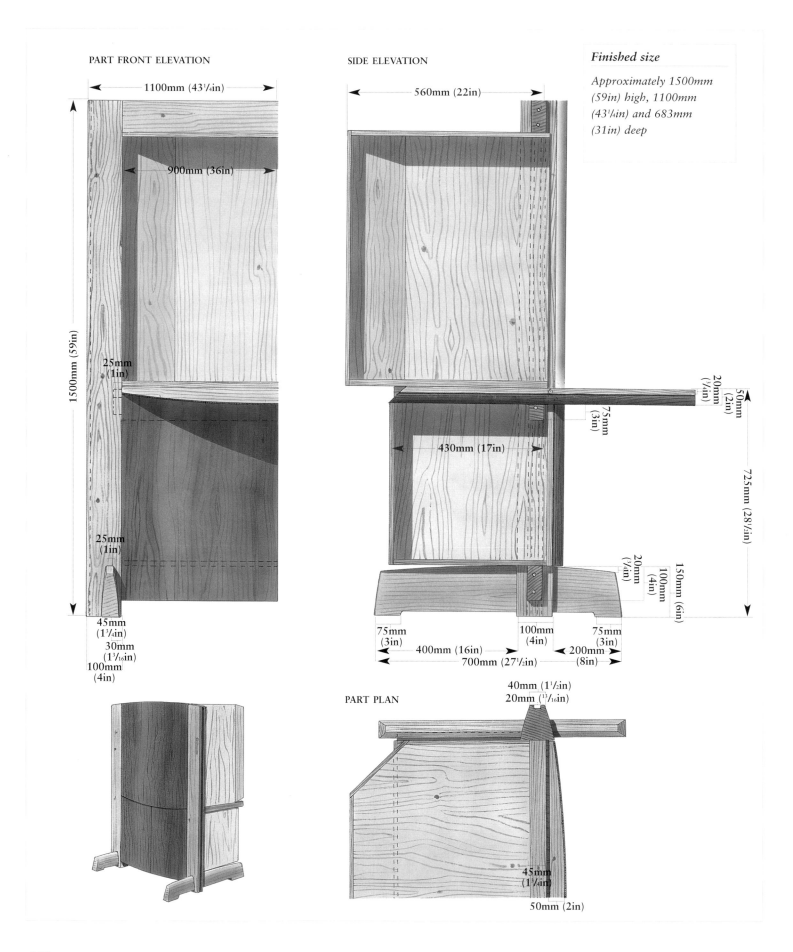

PART FRONT ELEVATION

1100mm (43¼in)

900mm (36in)

1500mm (59in)

25mm
(1in)

25mm
(1in)

45mm
(1¾in)
30mm
(1³⁄₁₆in)
100mm
(4in)

SIDE ELEVATION

560mm (22in)

20mm
(¾in)

50mm
(2in)

75mm
(3in)

430mm (17in)

725mm (28¹⁄₂in)

20mm
(¾in)

100mm
(4in)

150mm (6in)

75mm
(3in)

100mm
(4in)

75mm
(3in)

400mm (16in)

200mm
(8in)

700mm (27¹⁄₂in)

*Finished size*

*Approximately 1500mm
(59in) high, 1100mm
(43¼in) and 683mm
(31in) deep*

PART PLAN

40mm (1¹⁄₂in)
20mm (1³⁄₁₆in)

45mm
(1¾in)

50mm (2in)

292

edge from both sides. Use the power plane and try plane to shape these. Make a taper along the top edge, starting 20mm (³⁄₄in) along from each end of the housing that will be cut in step 7. Shape with a smoothing plane. Recut each end on the radial-arm saw at a slight bevel.

5 The feet are also shaped at the bottom to prevent them from rocking on the floor: remove 10mm (³⁄₈in) from the centre with a jigsaw or bandsaw. Mark a line parallel to the bottom edge 10mm (³⁄₈in) up. Square the ends 75mm (3in) in from each end. Cut this out, rounding the corners as you go.

6 Now, mark out the halving joints between the bottom of the upright posts and feet – note that these are made with housings where the shaped sections meet.

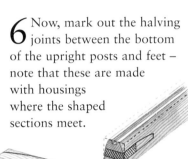

*Mark out the positions of the halving joints.*

7 Cut the joint in one of the upright posts using a tenon saw and then trace the shape of the post onto the top of one foot to mark the position of the joint. Cut to shape. Use a tenon saw and chisel to cut the housings. Repeat to cut the joints in the other post and foot.

8 Fit each foot onto its post to check the fit and square of the joint. Apply adhesive to the joint once the fitting is complete and leave to dry.

*Test the fit of the halving joint.*

## Making the horizontal fall/support rails

These front-to-back rails have grooves in them, along which the pins on the bottom of the fall/work surface run. In order to reduce wear, let in some metal channel sections and give the pins bearings. These rails are halved, glued and screwed to finish flush with the inside of the main column. They are further reinforced by the inclusion of the top and bottom storage section sides.

9 Mark out and cut the two horizontal support rails to a length of 430mm (17in). Work two grooves, one for the fall pins (preferably inserting a metal channel) and another for the fixed work surface, inside the cabinet. The pin groove is 6 x 6mm (¼ x ¼in), and matches the width of the pin and bearing (if used). Set up the router as before and run this groove 45mm (1³⁄₄in) down from the top edge. The groove for the work surface is 20mm (³⁄₄in) wide x 10mm (³⁄₈in) deep. Set up and run this groove from the same edge, 12mm (½in) down.

10 Set out the halving joint at one end, which will be fixed to the upright posts. Set these out as a pair 70mm (2³⁄₄in) long, and square around

the outside face and both edges. Scribe the depth with a marking gauge, 20mm (³⁄₄in) from the outside face. Hold vertically in a vice and cut down to the squared lines on the waste side. Lay flat against a bench hook and cut the shoulders.

11 Set out the stopped housing on the inside of each post to match, positioning the top of the rail 737mm (29in) from the bottom of the post. Lay each post flat and hold firm. Cut the shoulders with a tenon saw and remove the waste with a chisel, ensuring that the stopped housing is square. Test the fit to check that the face of the rail finishes flush with the post and is square.

12 Screw and glue the rails in place. Use three 40mm (1³⁄₈in) 8 gauge countersunk screws on each end. Drill the holes for the screws, taking care that the holes do not interfere with the grooves.

*Fit the support rails into place.*

## Making the three cross-rails

The top and bottom are simple straight rails, but the centre rail is shaped so that it supports the work surface when it is open and in use.

13 Set out the mortises in the posts to locate the cross-rails. The bottom mortise

is 60mm (2³⁄₈in) up from the bottom of the post and 90mm (3½in) long. Mark the centre mortise 605mm (23⁷⁄₈in) up and 55mm (3⅛in) long, and the top mortise 10mm (⅜in) down and 80mm (3³⁄₁₆in) long. Square all the mortises across the inside face of both posts.

**14** Set the mortise gauge to scribe the mortises 25mm (1in) wide between the squared lines. Lay posts on a firm surface and secure with a G-cramp. Remove the bulk of the waste by drilling several holes 20mm (¾in) in diameter to a depth of 25mm (1in) in the centre of the set-out. Use a mortise chisel to cut the mortise to length, and straighten the sides with a 25mm (1in) firmer chisel.

**15** Cut the three cross-rails to 950mm (37½in) long and cut a 25mm (1in) long tenon on each end. Square a shoulder line around each end, set a marking gauge to 10mm (⅜in) and scribe the tenon from the shoulder line out across the end and back to the opposite shoulder from both faces. Hold each rail vertical in a vice and cut down each side of the tenon on the waste side to the shoulder line. Secure each rail on a flat, firm surface, and cut along the squared shoulder lines on the waste side with a tenon saw. Cut the tenon to width by removing 10mm (⅜in) from each side in the same manner. Test the fit of each joint and adjust as required until you achieve a neat fit.

**16** Shape the top edge of the middle cross-rail to accommodate the slide in the fall or work surface. Square a line across the centre on the face side. Mark a curve on

this face 30mm (1³⁄₁₆in) down at the centre, to finish the full width at each end. To do this, bend a thin piece of timber to shape, and mark with a pencil. Cut this shape on the bandsaw or jigsaw on the waste side, and smooth out with 100-grit abrasive paper.

**17** To enable the whole unit to be assembled and disassembled, it is best to use barrel nuts and bolts instead of adhesives to hold the mortise and tenons tight.

**18** From the outside, drill the holes central to the post and into the mortise to accommodate the 8mm (⁵⁄₁₆in) bolts. Drill two in the bottom and top rails 25mm (1in) in from each edge, and one in the middle of the centre rail. Remember that the middle rail will be fitted over the end of the horizontal support rail. Hold the middle rail in the mortise and drill through the hole again into the end of the tenon. Remove the rail and drill the hole in the end to a depth of 85mm (3³⁄₈in).

**19** Square a line 45mm (1¾in) along from each shoulder. Measure 25mm (1in) in from each edge for the top and bottom and the centre of the middle rail. Drill holes into each face at this set-out to match the barrel nuts.

*Use barrel nuts and bolts to secure the mortise and tenon joints.*

*Fit the bottom rail in place.*

*Fit the middle rail into place after the support rail has been fitted.*

**20** Fit this whole frame together. Insert the bolts and nuts, and tighten. Check the frame for size, twist and square. Adjust as required.

*Assemble the whole frame.*

### Making the fall/work surface

The work surface is made from flat board while the shaped front is constructed by using curved fillets. These support a thin sheet of veneer plywood that is glued to them to give the curved surface.

**21** Cut the ply board to 895 x 675mm (35¼ x 26⅝in). Cut two frame uprights 675mm (26⅝in) and fix along the two side edges of the ply on the back with PVA.

**22** Next, cut the curved fillets. You will need to construct each rib so that its centrepoint is 30mm (1¼in) higher than the ends. Cut and set out one rib 795mm (31¼in) long. Mark 20mm (¾in) on each end and 50mm (2in) in the centre. Bend a thin piece of timber between these points and trace the curve. Cut to shape on a bandsaw or jigsaw. True the curve with abrasive paper. Use this as the template for all the other ribs, including those for the lower doors. There are 12 in all.

**23** Now, fit the curved fillets to the back of the work surface. Start by fixing the top and bottom ribs between the two uprights. Cut and fit a centre upright in between. Fix with adhesive so that the top edges are flush. Cut and fix five more ribs with PVA between the uprights, dividing them to accommodate the centre upright. Test the fit in the opening of the main frame. Plane until you obtain a 3mm (⅛in) clearance on each side.

**24** Drill a 3mm (⅛in) hole 10mm (⅜in) up from the bottom and 10mm (⅜in) from the back edge of the frame uprights for the pins. Insert the pins into these holes. If required, the pins can be made by cutting the heads off some screws and placing a slit in the end for a screwdriver. The pins should not protrude more than 6mm (¼in) from the edge of the fall.

*Make the fall/work surface.*

**25** Remove one side of the frame and place a washer on the pin before placing it into the frame. Check the fall fits the grooves in the horizontal support rails and make any necessary adjustments. Once satisfied, remove the fall from the frame so that you can fit the ply top.

*Check the fit and adjust if necessary.*

*Check the hinging system of the fall.*

**26** Cramp the thin veneered plywood sheet to the curve and fix with adhesive onto all the curved ribs and uprights. Use a G-cramp to secure a scrap block over the full length of each upright until dry.

**27** Trim the face ply to finish flush on the edges.

### Making the top storage area

**28** Next, make the fixed work surface by cutting to the shape on the drawing on page 292 – 548mm wide (21½in) and 920mm (36¼in) long. Fit into the top grooves in the horizontal support rails. The back corners are cut off at 45 degrees from the ends of the support rails.

**29** Cut the side panels to fit from the fixed work surface up to the bottom edge of the top cross-rail, plus 20mm (¾in) for the corner battens. The back edge will need to be bevelled at an angle to match the work surface. The front top corner will need a section cut around the cross-rail. Fix the side upright panels in position, screwing to the main uprights and the work surface.

**30** Cut and fit the top. This will also need the back corners cut off at an angle to match the work surface. Screw this to the underside of the top frame rail. Cut and fit the corner battens to go around the side and back edges of the top. Then screw the side panels to the corner battens.

*Complete the back of the top storage section.*

**31** Fit the two angled panels to the back of the work surface, the top and side panels. Finally, fit the back panel in place and screw to the work surface and the angled panels. Cut each in turn to fit, with angled edges. Fit out with shelves to suit your needs.

### Making the bottom storage area

**32** Fit the sides to the main frame and the horizontal support rails, fixing them with 25mm (1in), 6 gauge, countersunk screws. Remember to leave enough clearance at the top and front edge for the doors to operate.

**33** Fit the base to the lower cross-rail and screw into a corner batten fitted to the sides in a similar way to those fitted in the top storage area.

**34** Cut and fit the back over the base and side pieces with screws.

**35** Make and fit the two doors, using the same method as that used for the fall front. This time, however, cut two backboards. Cut the uprights to the same height as the backboards. Glue flush on each vertical edge. The upright on the hinge side is 25mm (1in) wide; that on the opening side is wider to match the curves. The curved ribs, which have already been cut, can be trimmed to fit between the uprights, maintaining the curve surfaces. Once dry, test fit the doors and plane where necessary to obtain a 3mm (⅛in) clearance. Cut in a pair of 50mm (2in) butt hinges on each door.

*Test the fit of the lower doors before fixing in place.*

**36** Remove the doors of the home office and then cramp the thin ply sheet to the curves, fixing it with adhesive onto all the curved ribs and the uprights.

### Final finishing

**37** Dismantle the whole office unit and sand all surfaces in order to remove any marks that may be left.

**38** Apply the finish of your choice to all the components of the home office.

**39** Reassemble the unit and check that all the doors and the fall function properly. Adjust the components as necessary to obtain a perfect fit. Finally, fit a pair of catches to the fall and one on each door in order to keep the unit secure when shut.

*Apply the required finish and reassemble the unit.*

*The doors close to hide away office equipment when not in use.*

# USEFUL
# INFORMATION

# Glossary

## A

**abrasive paper**

A paper backing sheet with particles of abrasive material glued to one surface, used for smoothing and rounding wood.

**air drying**

A method of seasoning timber by stacking it so that the circulation of dry air slowly dries the wood.

**aluminium oxide paper**

A very hard abrasive paper, used mainly for sanding hardwoods and in power sanders as a sheet or belt.

**animal glue**

Adhesive made from the skin and bones of animals, often available as powder or small dry globules or pearls; largely superseded by PVA and UF adhesives.

**arc**

Any part of an unbroken curved line.

**arris**

A sharp edge produced where two surfaces meet at an angle.

**axis**

An imaginary straight line around which a solid piece of material or object appears to be symmetrical.

## B

**backing-grade veneer**

Inexpensive, lower-grade veneers that are glued to the back of a piece of wood, in contrast to the best-grade ones that are glued to the face edge or front; *see also* face quality.

**backsaw**

A small saw with a strip of brass or steel set over the top of the blade, both to keep it straight and inflexible and to add weight when cutting.

**barefaced joint**

A joint that has one shoulder.

**batten**

A strip of wood; often used as an unseen support to hold workpieces to walls, etc.

**baulk**

A groove or ridge in timber.

**bead**

A narrow strip of semicircular moulding used for decoration; or a convex, rounded shape produced by woodturning.

**belt sander**

A power sander where a continuous belt of abrasive paper is rotated around rollers to remove the finish from large areas of wood; sometimes cramped to a bench.

**bench dog**

Removable wooden or metal stop that is placed into pre-made holes in a bench and acts as a stop for a workpiece.

**bench hook**

A square or rectangular piece of wood with a batten attached to the top at one end and to the bottom at another; used for holding wood when cutting with a backsaw.

**bending**

Three methods are generally used to bend wood: steam-bending, applying pressure to steamed wood around a form; kerfing, using equally spaced saw cuts; and laminating, building up layers of wood around a shaped form.

**bevel**

An angle that slopes at more than 90 degrees; to cut such an angle.

**biscuit jointer**

A power tool that cuts matching shaped grooves in two pieces of timber, into which an oval wooden shape or biscuit is glued, like a dowel.

**bit**

The end of a tool used for cutting, biting or boring; bits used in drills are removable and interchangeable.

**blank**

A plain piece of wood that is cut to an approximate size for mounting in a lathe and turning.

**blister**

An area or patch of veneer that has come away from its mounting surface, usually because the glue has failed.

**blockboard**

A strong, rigid laminate board made from strips of solid wood laid edge to edge and sandwiched between two sheets of plywood; *see also* laminboard.

**book-matched veneer**

Leaves of off-centred veneer laid out and glued in place to produce a symmetrical design.

**bore**

To cut, drill or pierce a hole in wood.

**bowed**

A term for a twisted length of wood; *see also* winding.

**bradawl**

A small pointed tool, used for making holes or pilot holes for nails or pins; also called awl.

**burl**

US term for burr.

**burr**

A growth on a tree trunk, cut off and sliced to produce burr or speckled veneer; or the thin, rough edge of metal left after sharpening or honing.

# C

**cabinet scraper**

A thin piece of steel, either rectangular, convex at one end or goose-neck shape, used for a final smoothing of wood before applying finish.

**calibrated**

A tool marked with at least one scale of measurement, such as a ruler.

**carborundum**

A powder made from silicon carbide, mixed with water as a paste for extremely fine sharpening, and removal of rust spots on metal tools.

**caul**

Flat or curved stiff board, used to press and shape groundwork and veneer sheets.

**chamfer**

A flat surface planed on the edge of a piece of timber, usually at 45 degrees, either to soften a sharp edge or for decoration; to plane such a surface.

**checks**

Cracks, splits or flaws in timber, brought about by uneven seasoning; in veneer sheets, knife checks are splits made by badly adjusted blades.

**chipboard**

A man-made board manufactured by compressing small chips of wood and glue; difficult to screw and not very strong, but used for inexpensive furniture and units.

**chisel, bevel-edged**

A chisel with a tapered-profile blade; used for cleaning up the corners of joints or recesses, either by hand pressure or with a mallet.

**chisel, firmer**

A chisel with a rectangular-profile blade; used with a mallet to chop out large mortises and lock recesses.

**chisel, mortise**

A small chisel similar to a firmer chisel, used for the same tasks in smaller section.

**chuck**

In a drill, the part that holds a bit, adjusted either by a chuck key or opposing rotation; in a lathe, a piece of wood attached to the faceplate and used to hold a blank or workpiece.

**coarse-textured**

Used to describe the surface quality of open grain timber.

**collet**

A slit sleeve with an external taper, made in two or more segments, which tightens to hold a bit or cutter when it is pushed into an internally tapered socket.

**combination or universal machine**

A machine that combines a number of different operations into one unit, such as table saw, planer-thicknesser, slot mortiser, spindle router, etc.

**compound mitre**

A mitre angled in more than one plane.

**fretsaw**

A thin, narrow blade stretched vertically in a frame, used for cutting thin wood to ornamental, often scrolled, designs and patterns.

**frog**

The support, usually made of steel, for a blade in a hand plane.

**front elevation**

The front view of a workpiece in a scale or working drawing.

# G

**g-cramp**

An open cramp with one fixed and one screw-adjustable head, used for holding workpieces in position on benches, etc.; available in a variety of sizes.

**garnet paper**

A good general-purpose abrasive paper, suitable for use on both hardwoods and softwoods.

**gauge**

Also called a marking gauge, a length of half-curved-profile hardwood with a steel pin protruding from one end and a movable stock or fence that is locked in place to scribe lines at a fixed distance along timber; *see also* mortise gauge.

**gents saw**

A small tenon saw, used for cutting small joints or delicate angles; *see also* backsaw.

**glasspaper**

Coarse abrasive paper with glass as the abrasive, mainly for rough-sanding softwoods.

**grain**

The arrangement, direction and size of the fibres and particles in a length of timber.

**grind**

To make smooth or sharpen a surface by friction.

**grit**

The minute particles used in making up abrasive paper; also various gradings of roughness and smoothness of the abrasive surface.

**groove**

A channel or trench cut along a piece of timber; to cut such a channel.

**groundwork**

The piece of timber to which a sheet of veneer is glued.

**guide hole**

Another name for pilot hole.

**gullet**

The spaces between the teeth of a saw; a smaller gullet makes a finer cut; *see also* kerf.

# H

**halving joint**

Joint where both halves of wood joined together are of equal thickness, used for framing.

**hand saw**

Any saw powered by hand.

**hardwood**

Wood that comes from deciduous or broad-leaved trees of the family Angiospermae; not always harder than softwoods.

**haunch**

On a tenon, the part nearest the corner of the full-width wood that prevents the tenon from twisting or snapping off; *see also* sloping haunch.

**headstock**

The part of a lathe that contains the motor and gearing.

**headstock spindle**

The rotating drive cylinder protruding from a lathe headstock; used to mount a faceplate or drive centre for turning.

**heartwood**

The hard, dense cells at the centre of a tree; the most stable timber; *see also* sapwood.

**hollow**

A concave shape produced in woodturning.

**hone**

To produce the final, sharpest edge on a blade by sharpening on a stone such as an oilstone or diamond stone.

**housing**

A flat groove, cut across the grain of one piece of wood, that holds the end of another piece.

**HSS**

High-speed steel, the standard material used for manufacturing bits and blades; see also TCT.

# I/J

**in wind**

*See* winding.

**infeed**

The part of the table of a cutting or shaping machine that holds the wood before and as it is cut.

**inlay**

A piece of wood, metal or other material glued into a precut groove or hollow and smoothed flush with the surrounding surface; to insert such a piece.

**jig**

A proprietary or home-made machine or device that holds a workpiece or tool so that identical operations can be repeated.

**jigsaw**

A portable power saw with a small, narrow blade, which is used to cut curves and intricate shapes.

# K

**kerf**

The groove or cut made by saw teeth in wood.

**kickback**

The jump back made by a power tool when its cutter or blade jams; or the jump back made by a workpiece when thrown by a machine cutter or blade.

**kiln drying**

A method of seasoning wood in a kiln, which speeds up the removal of moisture.

**knots or knotting**

Hard outgrowths of branches found in timber, sometimes kept for decoration, but usually regarded as flaws; resinous knots should be sealed with knot sealer before applying a finish.

# L

**laminate**

A board made from thin strips of wood glued together tightly; to make such a board.

**laminboard**

A board that is made by gluing together thin strips of wood and sandwiching them between two sheets of plywood; it is similar to blockboard.

**latewood**

The dense, often dark wood that develops as narrow tree rings in the later part of the growing season.

**lathe**

A machine consisting basically of a headstock containing a motor, tailstock, lathe bed and tool rest; used for all the processes of woodturning.

**lipping**

A strip of thin timber, used to protect the edges of man-made boards or table tops.

**long grain**

Grain that is in the same direction as the axis on a piece of timber; *see also* axis and short grain.

# M

**machine**

A power tool fixed in one place in a workshop.

**marking knife**

A sharp knife with its blade bevelled on one side, used to mark wood for cutting.

**marking out**

Used to describe the process of measuring, making pencil marks and scoring timber for cutting to length and cutting joints.

**marquetry**

The decorative art of cutting out and laying pieces of veneer to make pictures or patterns; *see also* parquetry.

**MDF**

Medium-density fibreboard, a close-textured, heavy man-made board manufactured by gluing fine wood particles together with resin; a substitute material for solid timber.

**mitre**

A corner joint where the meeting pieces of timber are cut to the same angle, usually 45 degrees though this need not always be the case.

**mitre square**

A marking tool similar to a try square, but with a 45-degree angle between the blade and the stock, used to check the accuracy of mitre joints; *see also* try square.

**mock-up**

A trial version of a construction piece, which is made from scrap materials and used to test the measurements and design before starting the piece itself.

**mortise**

A square or rectangular hole or recess cut into wood to accept a matching tenon.

**mortise gauge**

A marking gauge with two steel pins for marking the edges of a mortise.

# O

**offcut**

A piece of scrap wood, usually left over after a workpiece has been cut; often used to protect work held in vices, or as support.

**oil**

Transparent liquid finish for timber, sometimes tinted; usually made from natural ingredients, or blended with polyurethane for a tougher finish.

**oilstone**

A flat-surfaced man-made stone, which is lubricated with light oil and used to sharpen and hone the blades of chisels, planes, etc.

**open grain**

Wood with large pores, known as ring-porous.

**orbital sander**

A power sander where a pad of abrasive paper is clamped to a baseplate that rotates in small elliptical movements.

**outfeed**

The part of the table of a cutting or shaping machine that holds the wood after it has been cut.

# P

**panel saw**

Smaller than a ripsaw or crosscut saw, a general-purpose saw used for cutting man-made boards to length.

**pare**

To remove fine shavings with a chisel, using hand pressure only.

**parquetry**

The decorative art of cutting out and laying geometrical pieces of veneer to make patterns; *see also* marquetry.

**particle board**

A range of boards made by gluing together wood chips or particles; *see also* chipboard.

**pilaster**

A thin wooden column attached to the front of a cabinet or wardrobe for decoration.

**pilot hole**

A small hole drilled into timber that allows the threads of a larger screw to bite into the wood without splitting it.

**plain-sawn**

A way of cutting a log so that the growth rings meet the face of each board at an angle of less than 45 degrees.

**plan**

The top view of a workpiece, drawn to scale; also called plan elevation.

**plane blade**

The removable cutting part of a plane; sharpened on an oilstone.

**plane, block**

A small general-purpose plane, often used for planing end grain.

**plane, jack**

A medium-length general-purpose plane, used for most planing tasks.

**plane, jointer**

Also known as a try plane, a long plane used for smoothing long pieces of timber and planing for butt joints.

**plane, shoulder**

A thin plane used for planing rebates or trimming square shoulder on large joints.

**plane, smoothing**

A small plane with a fine blade, used to give a smooth finish to wood.

**PAR timber**

Planed all round timber – timber that has been planed on all sides and is thus likely to be smaller than its nominal size.

**planer, surface**

A machine that is used to plane smooth the face side and face edge of a workpiece.

**planer-thicknesser**

Used in conjunction with a surface planer, a machine used to plane smooth the two remaining faces of a workpiece.

**plywood**

A board made by gluing together wafers of wood in a sandwich; often faced with veneer.

**power tool**

Any portable powered tool.

**press**

*See* drill press.

**punch**

Also known as a nail or centre punch, a length of steel tapered to a thin end, used with a hammer to punch pin or small nail heads beneath a surface.

**push stick**

A stick cut with a notch in it, used to push timber into a machine cutter or blade.

**PVA glue**

A general-purpose woodworking adhesive, also known as white glue, made from an emulsion of polyvinyl-acetate in water which sets as the water evaporates; a water-resistant version is available.

# Q/R

**quarter-sawn**

A way of cutting a log so that the growth rings meet the face of each board at an angle of more than 45 degrees.

**rabbet**

US term for rebate.

**rail**

A horizontal member of a window or door frame; or a supporting member in a table or chair.

**rasp**

A carving tool used to rough out shapes; *see also* file and riffler.

**rebate**

A recess, step or groove, usually with a rectangular section, cut into timber to receive a slotted-in matching piece.

**relief carving**

A carving in which the subject or decorative motif is set proud of the background surface.

**riffler**

A small double-ended carving file, used for intricate smoothing; *see also* file.

**rift-sawn**

In the US, a way of cutting a log so that the growth rings meet the face of each board at an angle of between 30 degrees and 60 degrees.

**ripping**

Cutting timber with a ripsaw.

**ripsaw**

A large handsaw, used for cutting timber in the direction of the grain.

**rotary-cut**

A method of cutting veneer by slicing a continuous sheet from a log; used mainly to produce veneers for man-made boards.

**rotary sander**

A power sander where a disc of abrasive paper is clamped to a faceplate that rotates in circular movements.

**rottenstone**

A finely ground abrasive, which is used to rub down finishes between coats.

**router**

A versatile power tool, used for moulding timber, cutting grooves and rebates, cutting housings and shaping timber for joints or decoration; can also be used as a fixed tool.

**rubber**

A cloth pad used for applying finishes and stains to wood; in French polishing, a cloth folded around an inner pad of wadding.

**runner**

A strip of wood along which a drawer runs and which supports it.

# S

**sandpaper**

A collective name for all the varieties of abrasive paper.

**sapwood**

The light, soft cells furthest from the centre of a tree; the least stable timber; *see also* heartwood.

**sash cramp**

A straight length of metal with one screw-adjustable head and a movable head that can be positioned in different places; used to hold large or long pieces of wood together.

**scraper plane**

A small, two-handled metal body that holds a scraper blade; used for taking tiny shavings of timber.

**screwdriver, ratchet**

An elongated screwdriver fitted with a ratchet device

that drives the head in one direction only when the handle is pushed in.

**scribe**

To mark or score wood with a pointed marking tool, to indicate where it should be cut or shaped; or to shape the edge of a workpiece so that it fits the profile of another piece or of a shaped or uneven surface.

**seasoning**

The various methods used to reduce the moisture content of wood; *see also* air drying and kiln drying.

**section**

A representation of a workpiece as it would appear when cut across, along a vertical or horizontal plane.

**set**

To adjust the teeth of a saw alternately in opposite directions, thus regulating the width of the kerf; or to adjust a plane blade relative to the sole, thus regulating the depth of cut.

**shakes**

Splits in wood caused by shrinkage or defects in growth.

**shellac**

A natural product exuded by the lac insect, used in manufacturing French polish.

**short grain**

Grain that is in the opposing direction to the axis on a piece of timber; *see also* axis and long grain.

**shoulder**

A squared end on one or both sides of a tongue or tenon.

**side elevation**

On a scale drawing, the side view of a workpiece.

**silicon-carbide paper**

Used wet and dry with water, a fine abrasive for hardwoods; a dry, self-lubricating version is used for sanding between coats of French polish.

**skew**

Of a nail or screw, inserted at an angle other than a right angle; to insert a nail or screw at such an angle.

**sliding bevel**

A marking tool similar to a mitre square, but with an adjustable blade that can be placed and locked at any angle; *see also* mitre square.

**sloping haunch**

On a tenon, a haunch cut on a slope, invisible when the joint is assembled; *see also* haunch.

**softwood**

Wood that comes from coniferous trees of the family Gymnospermae; not always softer than hardwoods.

**sole**

A flat metal or wooden base of a tool such as a plane, that allows it to slide smoothly over wood surfaces.

**sole plate**

A smooth, flat-bottomed metal surface attached to the bottom

of a plane or power saw, with the blade protruding through and held at a constant angle and depth.

**splitting out**

The splits and hole created when a cutter or drill inadvertently breaks through a face of wood.

**springwood**

Another name for earlywood.

**square**

To use a try square to measure or set out a right angle; or, when checking a workpiece for accuracy, a precise right angle.

**stile**

A vertical member in a window or door frame.

**stop**

A piece of wood fixed to the frame of a door on which the door shuts.

**stopped housing**

A housing that does not run across the full width of a panel or workpiece; *see also* housing.

**stopped mortise**

A mortise that is not cut through the wood; *see also* mortise and through mortise.

**straight grain**

Another name for long grain.

**striker plate**

A metal plate that is fixed onto the recess, which accepts a lock or latch.

**stringing**

A thin inlaid line of wood, used in furniture decoration or veneer; also the supporting side timber in a staircase.

**strop**

A strip of leather on which a sharp edge can be given to a blade by rubbing back and forth; to produce such an edge.

**stub mortise**

*See* stopped mortise.

**stub tenon**

A tenon that does not fit through a workpiece.

**summerwood**

Another name for latewood.

# T

**tack rag**

A resin-impregnated cloth used to pick up dust from a surface before applying a finish.

**TCT**

Tungsten-carbide-tipped bits or blades that stay sharp longer than ordinary HSS ones; used for all applications, but especially good on chipboard and MDF; *see also* HSS.

**template**

A pattern or shape cut out of thin rigid material, used for marking wood and guiding tools, particularly when making more than one identical piece.

**tenon**

A square or rectangular tongue or projecting piece, cut on the end of a piece of timber to fit into a matching mortise.

**tenon saw**

A large backsaw used for cutting joints and battens; *see also* backsaw, gents saw.

**throat**

In a drill press, the distance from the centre of the worktable to the column.

**through and through**

A way of cutting a log using parallel cuts through its length; this produces various types of board; *see also* plain-sawn, quarter-sawn and rift-sawn.

**through mortise**

A mortise that is cut through a piece of wood; *see also* mortise and stopped mortise.

**tongue**

A narrow strip cut along the edge of a board or panel that fits into a groove cut into a matching piece of wood; used in tongue-and-groove joints.

**try square**

A marking tool with a parallel-sided blade fixed at right angles to a stock, used to check and mark the accuracy of right angles.

**twist drill**

A cylindrical drill bit with a pointed tip and spiral grooves or flutes, used to drill holes and clear waste from the holes; *see also* dowel bit.

# U/V

**UF adhesive**

Urea-formaldehyde adhesive, available in powder form and then mixed with water before application; some UF adhesives require a catalyst to be mixed in as well.

**veneer**

A thin sheet or layer of sliced wood, glued or bonded to a surface, usually wood or man-made board; or a layer used in manufacturing plywood; to apply such a sheet to a surface.

**veneer hammer**

A wooden or metal hammer with one thin flat face on its head, used to apply pressure to veneer and remove blisters and air pockets.

**vertical grain**

The quality of grain of timber produced by plain-sawing.

**viscosity**

The measurable glutinous or viscous nature of a fluid.

# W

**warping**

A twist or swelling in a piece of timber, caused by the wood absorbing moisture or drying out.

**wavy grain**

A regular, wave-like pattern in the same direction as straight grain in a piece of wood.

**wild grain**

An irregular, random pattern of grain; wild-grain wood is hard to work, and blunts tools quickly.

**winding**

Term for a warped or twisted piece of wood.

# Author's acknowledgements

*I have been involved with the woodworking and furniture trades for over 30 years, and have also been involved as a lecturer and course planner in many colleges and university departments of Design and Manufacture. I remember many colleagues and friends. The world of furniture designers and craftsmen is full of lively and interesting people, who gain pleasure from designing and making fine and individual pieces that in themselves give pleasure to recipients. I recognize and thank them for their advice and help.*

*I have lectured in many design education institutions and I wish to thank my many colleagues for their interest and support. I have also been fortunate to have known many students on these design and craftsmanship courses and have gained much enjoyment from seeing them develop and utilize their professional skills in their chosen careers, in particular those from Rycotewood College, the School of Architecture at Oxford Brookes University and The Furniture College at Letterfrack, Co. Galway.*

## Other contributors

**Michael Bradley** who made the plant stand (see pages 208–11) is a woodturner from Farringdon, Oxfordshire, where he lives with his wife and son. He started woodturning with a local furniture maker after leaving school in 1969. His continued love for his craft encouraged him to branch out on his own in 1981. He currently has a small workshop in Farringdon, specializing in commissioned pieces.

Having served a four-year apprenticeship in cabinet and chair making, **Roland Gadsdon** who made the circular dining table (see pages 218–22) and the single bed (see pages 239–43) then went into research and development before opening his own workshop making and repairing furniture. For the last eight years he has worked as a lecturer, from which he gains a great deal of satisfaction. Periodically he enjoys making one-off pieces of furniture.

**Ian Heseltine** originally studied at Parnham House in Dorset and then set up his partnership with Declan O'Donoghue. Their workshop and studios, SF Furniture in Acton Turville, Gloucestershire, have developed an enviable reputation in the field of furniture design and making with an impressive list of clients. Ian designed and made the glass topped feature table (see pages 196–9) and it is recognized that his making abilities are at the forefront of his profession.

**Andrew Humphries** was apprenticed to his father's furniture making and restoration company, and is now recognized as one of the foremost craftsmen in these trades, having a wide clientele and restoring valuable pieces for many influential owners and lovers of quality classic furniture. For many years he taught these skills at Rycotewood College, and contributed to the education of fine craftsmen and restorers when the college's reputation was at its height; a fact recognized by past students who have successfully developed their own businesses. He made the chessboard (see pages 165–7), the mirror/picture frame (see pages 170–1) and the breakfast tray (see pages 223–5).

After a grammar school education, **Jack Lazenby** D.L.C. (Hons) who designed and made the small box (see pages 182–5) and the all-purpose workbench (see pages 188–92) apprenticed as an Engineering Patternmaker from 1942–7, going on to train at Loughborough College (now University) where he developed a passionate interest in the Arts and Crafts Movement and was influenced, helped and encouraged by Edward Barnsley CBE. He first became a lecturer in Furniture Making and Design at Rycotewood College from 1950 and was Chief Examiner in Fine Craft and Design for GCSE and 'A' Level with the University of Oxford Delegate of Local Examinations. Jack rejoined Rycotewood in the mid-1970s, and was an inspiration to many students between then and his retirement in the late 1990s. His craftsmanship skills and teaching ability helped students to reach the highest standards, while assisting the college to attain and maintain its premier position as one of the country's leading institutions. Many past students recognize the contribution that he made to their personal and professional development. Now retired, he continues to pursue his love of furniture making.

**David Ramsey** who made the pergola (see pages 193–5) and the curved back garden bench (see pages 257–65) is a furniture and interior designer with 30 years experience in commercial and private work. He studied at the Royal College of Art to obtain a Master of Design. His work has included designing furniture and interiors for hotels, in particular for bedrooms and bathrooms, and he has undertaken the complete design of the structure and interior of a 4-star hotel in Saudi Arabia. He has also taught arts and crafts in a grammar school and in several colleges. New ventures include the restoration of antique furniture.

**Chris Smith** who made the modular storage cubes (see pages 228–33) trained at Rycotewood College, and then set up a workshop in his home village of Tackley in Oxfordshire. Working mainly by himself, at first making only small items on speculation or to order, he now works with a wide range of architects, interior designers, shops and furniture manufacturers.

One of the most original and capable furniture designers who graduated from the Royal College of Art in the late 1950's, **Alan Tilbury** has had an outstanding career as both a teacher and practitioner. He has lectured in the Furniture School at the RCA for over 30 years and has designed furniture for many top British and European companies, as well as making special pieces for individual and corporate clients. He contributed to the section on 'Design and construction' (see pages 38–51).

# Publisher's acknowledgements

The Publishers would like to thank the following for their help with this book:

Mrs K. Medlock, Chandlers Ford (for permission to photograph her workbench and in her home)

Mr Ian White, Princes Risborough (for permission to photograph in his workshop)

**For providing props for photography:**

Peacock Blue
201 King's Road
London SW6
Tel: + 44 (0)20 7384 3400
for Boston checked bedlinen
(single bed project)

Holding Company
243–245 King's Road
London SW3
Tel: + 44 (0)20 7352 1600
for six-drawer wicker chest
(home office project)

Isaac Lord (for address, see tools suppliers)

Marilyn Phipps
The Battery
Admiralty Walk
Seasalter
Kent CT5 4ET
Tel: + 44 (0)1227 277 994
for cut-out birds
(birdhouse project)

Metabo UK Ltd
25 Majestic Road
Nursling Industrial Estate
Southampton SO16 0YT
(for machinery)

Purves & Purves
80–81 Tottenham Court Road
London W1T 9QE
Tel: + 44 (0)20 7580 8223
for suede square
footstools (chessboard
project), ivory Phoenix
chairs (dining table
project) and Zen rug
(home office project)

Record Power Ltd
Parkway Works
Sheffield S9 3BL

Smee Timber Ltd
Smokehall Lane
Winsford
Cheshire
(for timber)

**For providing images
for us to use:**

Axminster Power Tools Centre,
for permission to use images
of machine tools (for address,
see tools suppliers)

Batheaston
20 Leafield Way
Leafield Industrial Estate
Corsham
Wiltshire SN13 9SW
Tel: + 44 (0)1225 811 295

Stewart Linford Furniture Maker
High Wycombe

**For allowing us permission
to photograph on site:**

The Antique Trader
at The Millinery Works
85/87 Southgate Road
Islington
London N1 3JS
Tel: + 44 (0)20 7359 2019
Fax. + 44 (0)20 7359 5792
www.millineryworks.co.uk

Didier Aaron
21 Ryder Street
St James'
London
Tel: + 44 (0)20 7839 4716
Fax: + 44 (0)20 7930 6699

Eltham Palace Court Yard
Eltham
London SE9 5QE
Tel: + 44 (0)20 8294 2548
Fax: + 44 (0)20 8294 2621

The Fine Art Society Plc
148 New Bond Street
London W1Y 0JT
Tel: + 44 (0)20 7629 5116
Fax: + 44 (0)20 7491 9454
www.the-fine-art-society.co.uk

Geffrye Museum
Kingsland Road
London E2 8EA
Tel: + 44 (0)20 7739 9893
Fax: + 44 (0)20 7729 5647

Indigo
275 New Kings Road
London SW6 4RD
Tel: + 44 (0)20 7384 3101
Fax: + 44 (0)20 7384 3102

Ki UK Ltd
Commonwealth House
148-153 High Holborn
London W61V 6PJ
Tel: + 44 (0)20 7404 7441
Fax: + 44 (0)20 7404 7442

Norman Adams
10 Hans Road
London SW3 1RX
Tel: + 44 (0)20 7589 5266
Fax: + 44 (0)20 7589 1968

Rupert Cavendish Antiques
610 King's Road
London SW6 2DX
Tel: + 44 (0)20 7731 7041
Fax: + 44 (0)20 7731 8302
www.rupertcavendish.co.uk

SCP Ltd
135–139 Curtain Road
London
Tel: + 44 (0)20 7739 1869
Fax: + 44 (0)20 7729 4224
www.scp.co.uk

Skandium
72 Wigmore Street
London W18 9DL
Tel: + 44 (0)20 7935 2088
Fax: + 44 (0)20 7224 2099
www.skandium.com

Shaker Ltd
72–3 Marylebone High Street
London W1M 3AR
Tel: + 44 (0)20 7935 9461
Fax: + 44 (0)20 7935 4157
www.shaker.co.uk

Twentytwentyone
Shop:
274 Upper Street
London N1 2UA
Tel/Fax: + 44 (0)20 7288 1996
Office/warehouse:
18c River Street
London EC1R 1XN
Tel: + 44 (0)20 7837 1900
Fax: + 44 (0)20 7837 1908
www.twentytwentyone.com

# Suppliers

## UNITED KINGDOM

### Timber
The following may supply
mail order, otherwise look
in local directories under
'Timber Merchants':

John Boddy Timber Ltd
Riverside Sawmills
Boroughbridge
North Yorkshire YO5 19LJ
Tel: + 44 (0)1423 322 370

Interesting Timbers
Hazel Farm
Compton Martin
Somerset BS18 6LH
Tel: + 44 (0)1761 463 356

North Heigham Sawmills Ltd
Paddock Street, off Barker Street
Norwich NR2 4TW
Tel: + 44 (0)1603 622 978

### Veneers
Capital Veneer Co. Ltd
Unit 12, Bow Industrial Estate
Carpenters Road
Stratford
London E15 2DZ
Tel: + 44 (0)208 525 0300

C.B. Veneer Ltd
Progress Road
Sands Industrial Estate
High Wycombe
Buckinghamshire HP12 4JD
Tel: + 44 (0)1494 471 959

J. Crispin & Sons
92–96 Curtain Road
London EC2A 3AA
Tel: + 44 (0)20 7739 4857
Fax: + 44 (0)20 7613 2047

### Tools
Axminster Power Tools Centre
Chard Street
Axminster
Devon EX13 5DZ
Tel: + 44 (0)1297 630 000

Isaac Lord
Desborough Road
High Wycombe
Buckinghamshire HP11 2QN
Tel: + 44 (0)1494 462 121
Fax: + 44 (0)1494 445 124

T. Brooker & Sons Ltd
39 Bucklersbury
Hitchin
Hertfordshire SG5 1BQ
Tel: + 44 (0)1462 434 501

Murray's Tool Store
83 Morrison Street
Edinburgh EH3 8BU
Tel: + 44 (0)131 229 1577

WJT Crafts and Woodturning Supplies
New Farm Road Industrial Estate
Prospect Road
New Alresford
Hampshire SO24 9QF
Tel: + 44 (0)1962 735 411

## AUSTRALIA

The following retailers will be able
to supply most of your timber and
building materials. There are stores
around the country – contact the head
offices below for your closest store:

**Hardwarehouse**
Building A
Cambridge Street
Cnr Chester Street
Epping 2121
New South Wales
Tel: +61 (0)2 9869 8888

**Bunnings**
Bourke Street
Melbourne 3000
Victoria
Tel: +61 (0)3 9607 0777

For specialist wood suppliers, look in
local directories.

311

# Index

Entries in italic refer to
photographs or illustrations.

# D

templates, 309
  routing, 93
tenon saws, 63, 82, *82*, 309
tenons, 309
  *see also* mortise and
    tenon joints
texture, timber, 22
texturing, 141
thicknessers, 79, 80–1
Thonet, Michael, 187, 245,
  266, 267, 274, 275
three-ply plywood, 27
throat, drill presses, 309
through and through sawing,
  20, *20*, 309
through dovetail joints, 112,
  *112*, 113–14, *113*
through housing joints,
  110, *110*
through mortise and tenon
  joints, 104, *104*, 106–8,
  *106–8*
through mortises, 309
tiles, 35
timber, 12–33
  buying and storing, 24–5,
    *24–5*, 58
  conversion, 20, 20
  finishes, 48, 130–5, *130–5*
  hardwood, 13, 14–18, *15–18*
  measuring and marking,
    64–7
  movement, 41, *41*
  preparation, 66
  properties and defects,
    22–3, *22–3*
  sawing, 69, *69–71*
  seasoning, 21, *21*, 308
  softwood, 13, 14, 18–19
  veneers, 30–3, *30–3*, 48–9
tongue, 309
tools, 62–100
  abrasives, 115–17, *115–17*
  assembling projects, 120–5
  carving tools, 140–1, *140*
  chisels, 86–7, *86–7*
  cutting tools, 63
  drawing tools, 52
  drills, 96–8, *96–8*
  measuring and marking,
    62–3, 64–6, *64–5*
  for metals and plastics,
    146–7, *146–7*
  planes, 74–7, *74–7*
  saws, 63, 68–71, *68*,
    82–3, *82–3*

scraping tools, 118–19,
  *118–19*
shaping tools, 94–5, *94–5*
sharpening, 72–3, *72–3*
surfacing tools, 63
turning tools, 142–3, *142–3*
veneering, 136–7, *136*
toothing planes, 137, *137*
trammels, 262, *262*
transparent polish, 132
tray, breakfast, 223–5, *223–5*
trestles, 60
trivet, triangular, 168–9, *168–9*
truing oilstones, 73
try planes, 74, *74*
try squares, 63, 64, *64*, 66,
  *66*, 309
tung oil, *132*, 133
Tupper Corporation, 282
turning, 142–5, *142–5*
twin mortise and tenon joints,
  105, *105*
twin-thread screws, 123
twist drills, 96, 98, 100, 309

## U

UF (urea-formaldehyde)
  adhesives, 128, *128*, 309
Umbertino style, 187
United States of America, 186,
  216–17, 282

## V

Vallin, 227
varnishes, 48
Velde, Henri van de, 226
veneer cutters, *137*
veneer hammers, 137, *137*,
  *138*, 309
veneer pins, 137, *137*
veneer punches, 137
veneer saws, 137, *137*
veneer tape, *137*
veneered chessboard, 165–7,
  *165–7*
veneering, 136–9, *136–9*
veneers, 30–3, *30–3*,
  48–9, 309
vernier gauges, 64, *64*
vices, 60

metalworking, 146, *146*
Vienna School, 227, 244
viscosity, 309

## W

waferboard, 27
Wagner, Otto, 227
walnut, 15, *15*
Wanscher, Ole, 245
warping, 23, *23*, 309
water-based stopper, *130*
waterstones, *141*
wavy grain, 22, 309
wax sticks, *130*, 131
waxes, 48, *132*, 133
WBF plywood, 27
web cramps, 121, *121*, 231
Webb, Philip Speakman, 134
wedged through mortise and
  tenon joints, 104, *104*, 108
Wegner, Hans, 245
wenge, 18, *18*
Werkstätten, 226
whetstones, motorized, 72, 73
white polish, 48, 132
wide mortise and tenon joints,
  105, *105*
Wiener Werkstätten, 227
wild grain, 309
William III, King of England,
  173
Williamson, Rupert, 178
winding, 309
Windsor chairs, 266
wine rack, 162–4, *162–4*
wire wool, 115
  applying waxes with, 133,
    *133*
wood *see* timber
wood filler, *130*, 131
wood putty, 131
workbenches, 60–1, *60–1*,
  188–92, *188–92*
working drawings, 52–3, *52*
workshops, 56–9, *56–9*
Wright, Frank Lloyd, 217

## Y/Z

yew, 19, *19*
zebrano, 18, *18*

First published in 2001 by Murdoch Books UK Ltd
Copyright© 2001 Murdoch Books UK Ltd

ISBN 1 85391 779 6
A catalogue record for this book is available from the British Library.

Senior Commissioning Editor: **Karen Hemingway**
Managing Editor: **Anna Osborn**
Design Manager: **Helen Taylor**
Editors: **Christine Eslick, Dawn Henderson, Alastair Laing, Ruth Matheson, Claire Musters, Angela Newton**
Designers: **Laura Cullen, Colin Goody, Cathy Layzell, Shahid Mahmood**
Consultants: **John Bowler, Greg Cheetham, Ian Kearey, Mark Ramuz**
Photo Librarian: **Bobbie Leah**
Picture Researcher: **Claire Gouldstone**
Styled and location photography: **David Brittain**
Studio and location photography: **Dominic Blackmore, Alan Holtham**
Photography art direction: **Marylouise Brammer**

CEO: **Robert Oerton**
Publisher: **Catie Ziller**
Production Manager: **Lucy Byrne**

Colour separation by Colourscan, Singapore
Printed by Tien Wah Press in Singapore

Murdoch Books UK Ltd
Ferry House, 51–57 Lacy Road
Putney, London SW15 1PR
United Kingdom
Tel: +44 (0)20 8355 1480
Fax: +44 (0)20 8355 1499
Murdoch Books UK Ltd is a subsidiary
of Murdoch Magazines Pty Ltd

Murdoch Books®
Pier 8/9 23 Hickson Road
Millers Point NSW 2000
Australia
Tel: +61 (0)2 8220 2000
Fax: +61 (0)2 8220 2020
Murdoch Books® is a trademark
of Murdoch Magazines Pty Ltd